Harry Pearson has produced five books, contributed to a dozen more, written a weekly sports column in the *Guardian* for ten years and helped make the football magazine *When Saturday Comes* half-decent for nearly two decades. When not painting toy soldiers, building a Wild West town in $^1/_{72}$ scale or feverishly trying to work out how many more Macedonian phalangites he needs to finish before he can restage the Battle of the Granicus, he spends his time staring wistfully into space wondering where the years have gone. He lives in Northumberland. Contrary to all previous assertions, he does not own a spinet.

ACHTUNG
SCHWEINEHUND!

A Boy's Own Story of
Imaginary Combat

Harry Pearson

Little, Brown

LITTLE, BROWN

First published in Great Britain in 2007 by Little, Brown

A CIP catalogue record for this book
is available from the British Library.

ISBN: 978-0-316-86136-6

Typeset in Baskerville by M Rules
Printed and bound in Great Britain by
Clays Ltd, St Ives plc

Little, Brown
An imprint of
Little, Brown Book Group
Brettenham House
Lancaster Place
London WC2E 7EN

A Member of the Hachette Livre Group of Companies

www.littlebrown.co.uk

For Maisie, one of the girls I leave behind

'He could have lived a risk-free, moneyed life, but he preferred to whittle away his fortune on warfare.'

Xenophon, *The Anabasis*

Preface

An Introduction to the Elementary Game

'The judge smiled. Men are born for games. Nothing else. Every child knows that play is nobler than work.'
Cormac McCarthy, *Blood Meridian*

My friend Mathias and I were sitting on a rock together in the Northumbrian woods watching his son and some of his friends playing amongst the trees. It had been raining for a week and a smell of damp leaves hung in the air. 'There's going to be a battle in five, no three minutes,' one of the boys shouted. 'It's the Lion, the Witch and the Wardrobe,' another said.

'I'm going to be Aslan,' the first kid yelped. Another bagged the role of King Peter. 'And I,' Mathias's son Kai said decisively, 'I am going to be . . . Queen Susan.' The other boys looked at him quizzically. 'She's got a bow and arrow,' Kai said in response.

Mathias chuckled merrily. 'What a boy,' he said. 'He'll even pretend to be a girl if it means better weaponry.'

Mathias is German and the same age as me, born in 1961. I asked him if he had liked weapons when he was a child. 'Oh, of course,' he said, 'who didn't? But these boys always play at war. We didn't play at war. The subject of war is . . . *problematic* in Germany,' he smiled ironically, pleased with his knack for English understatement, 'and so we played at cowboys. For us it was OK to pretend to shoot someone, so long as you were pretending to be an American when you pretended to shoot him.' He looked at me, grinning. 'And you? Did you and your pals machine-gun the *bloody Jerries?*'

'Oh yes,' I said. 'When we were eight I'd have blown your head off as soon as look at you.'

A few minutes later my eight-year-old daughter Maisie came and sat on the rock with us. She had no interest in joining in the boys' game, which had gradually taken on a form not envisaged by C. S. Lewis, one in which Queen Susan's bow was making a noise suspiciously like an automatic rifle and Aslan had abandoned the old magic in favour of a surface-to-air missile. 'Kaboom!' Reepicheep chirruped as a rocket burst above the White Witch's head.

The week before Maisie had come home from school and said, 'Dad, did you know Britain once fought a war with Germany? We started a project about it. It's really cool. Britain won.'

I told her that it wasn't just Britain. That Britain had been helped by lots of other nations: the United States, Russia, Australia, Canada, India, New Zealand, the West Indies and so forth.

'All those countries ganging up against one,' Maisie said when I had finished my list, 'it's not very fair.' I smiled indulgently at the application of such a childish judgement to so great a conflict. 'Well,' I said, 'the Germans started it.'

Maisie was a bit disturbed by the idea of Britain fighting Germany because her best friend is Mathias's daughter Carla. The idea that sixty years ago the two of them would have been enemies was inconceivable to Maisie. Mind you, when I was her age the idea I would one day chat happily to a German would have seemed pretty far-fetched to me.

When I was Maisie's age they didn't need to teach you about the war. The war was all around you. Your body absorbed it like vitamin D. We watched it on TV and at the cinema; we read about it in comics and listened to the grown-ups talking about it. The names of planes and battles were part of our everyday vocabulary. To us, Cromwell was a tank not a Puritan regicide. When we saw a lemonade bottle floating in the river we yelled, 'Sink the *Bismarck*!' and threw stones at it until it smashed.

The sixties was an era of sweeping social change, but we spent our childhoods staring backwards. 'The swinging sixties?' my friend TK is fond of remarking. 'Not in Walsall they didn't, buddy.' TK is ten years older than me, but I feel the same way. To me, the Summer of Love was a six-week school holiday filled with Stukas, swastikas and bazookas.

'So,' Mathias said, 'what will we play at Games Club this time?'

'Princes of the Renaissance,' I said; 'it got good reviews. You can even buy the Pope in an auction.'

My friend Will and I formed the board-games group four years ago. The original idea for Games Club came from our partners, who had formed a book group. 'You should form a book group too,' they said. Personally, I didn't like the idea. I have always hated those people who pull rank in an argument. The type who say, 'Have you ever played international football/been a plumber/run a small African country? Well, I have, and I can tell you that what you are saying is total cobblers.' I have always hated people like that because, secretly, I fear I may be one of them. And a book group was a sure-fire way of having that fear confirmed.

So Will and I decided that we would do something antithetical to the book group. We would do something that was intellectually undemanding, trivial, pointless and involved limited commitment and minimum communication skills. In short, something truly masculine. Instead of making spectacular food like the women did we would buy snacks from the local garage; we would not discuss anything meaningful; we would not address the big themes; we would sit around drinking beer, eating bright orange cheese-flavoured corn-based snacks, rolling dice, moving hundreds of bits of plastic around big map-boards and yelling, 'And now all of Turkey falls to the mighty forces of the Yellow Emperor. Look on and despair you puny weaklings!' (Although clearly not every utterance would be quite as intellectual as that.)

At first we were a bit nervous about asking anyone else to join us. Even when a man reaches his forties the ridicule of other males is something he shies away from. We were cautious about whom to approach: 'What about this guy? Once when I was getting my coat I thought I saw a copy of Masterpiece in the cupboard.'

'Could be his wife's. He's pretty serious. He'd probably think it was stupid. I was wondering about Jonathan.'

'Are you sure? He's into compost and Mahler.'

We needn't have feared. Once Games Club was up and running we were fending people off. We had to limit places, putting a strict RSVP on invites with a serious warning that failure to attend could result in the privilege of playing Eagle Games' Blood Feud in New York being withdrawn for good. More or less total strangers would phone up or accost us in the street, begging to be allowed to come. More disturbingly still, several members of the book group openly talked of defecting, ditching the world of A. S. Byatt and Siri Husvedt for Waddington's Formula 1 or Buck Rogers – Battle for the 25th Century. We couldn't allow it, of course. The whole atmosphere would have gone to pieces if a woman had turned up. We needed to stay focused and competitive. And there's one thing guaranteed to disturb the focus and competitive edge of men and that's the arrival of the very thing they're supposed to be focused on competing for.

*

'And the objective of this game is?' Mathias asked.

'You're the head of one of the great *condottieri* families of the Renaissance – Malatesta, Baglioni, Gonzaga and so on – and you're trying to become the most influential nobleman in Italy.'

'And how do you achieve this?'

'Well, you can do it by building up trade, through investing money in great artworks and prestigious building projects, or—'

'Or you can fight with all the other players until you have utterly destroyed them,' Mathias laughed.

'That will, in all likelihood, be the most popular strategy.'

From the trees came a wild and gruesome cry. 'You're dead. I just cut off your head,' one of the boys shouted indignantly at Kai who, having emitted his death rattle, was now running around, apparently unharmed by his recent decapitation and wielding his bow like an axe.

'Yes,' the boy replied, 'but I've got the phial of magic potion from Queen Lucy that heals all wounds.'

'Pretending to fight a war again?' Mathias's wife Katarina said, coming up the path to join us. She was eight months pregnant, cradling her heavy belly in her arms as a gunner does a cannonball. 'I wonder when he will grow out of it.'

'I wouldn't hold your breath,' I said.

This is a book about men and battle. It is not about real battle (and since most of it is about me, it's not always about real men either), but about the make-believe battle that has filled my leisure time ever since I was given a Davy Crockett hat on my fourth birthday. It is about models and games, Action Man and cap guns, Rat Patrol, the *War Picture Library* and playing with toy soldiers. It is about growing up in the 1960s and not growing up thereafter. It is about how war is turned into a game (and how sometimes games are turned into war), the urge to play and the need to hide.

'A man,' Montaigne counselled, 'should keep for himself a little back shop, all his own, quite unadulterated, in which he established his true freedom and chief place of seclusion and solitude.'

What follows is a journey into what the French philosopher would have called a shop, but what most of us would recognise as a shed.

PART ONE

BASIC TRAINING

'The contemplation of ruins is a
masculine specialty.'

ERIK ERIKSON

1

Ratios and Scales

'You have only to play at Little Wars a few times to realize what a blundering thing Great Wars must be.'

H. G. Wells, *Little Wars*

It is Boxing Day. I am six years old. We are in the front room of my great-granny's house in a fishing village near Middlesbrough. The room is bakingly hot: my great-granny comes from a generation for whom heat equals luxury. A coal fire crackles in the grate, an electric radiator hums. The house is more thoroughly sealed than a Great Pharaoh's tomb. An ambient temperature sufficient to wilt a cactus is considered a bit parky by my great-grandmother. She is a lapsed Catholic. She gave up her religion to marry a Methodist miner. He fathered five children and then, with an inconsideration towards womenfolk for which northern husbands are noted, promptly and irrevocably died. Her departure from the Church of Rome has left her uncertain about what lies ahead. I am not sure if she believes she is destined for hell, but the warmth of her house suggests she is preparing for it.

There are fifteen of us crammed into this tiny room. Older women sit in armchairs, younger women in dining chairs, children on the arms of chairs or the laps of aunties. The men are arranged around the walls. My father has positioned himself near the front door, with its promise of fresh air and escape.

My granddad is tucked away between a low bookcase and a cabinet filled with souvenirs and knick-knacks. He always stands there. There is an oval stain where his Brylcreem has soaked into the wallpaper. It surrounds his head like a greasy halo.

I am sitting on the arm of my Uncle Alf's chair. Uncle Alf is the only man who is allowed to sit down. He cannot stand for long. His knee is dicky courtesy of some Jap shrapnel from the Battle of Kohima. Uncle Alf is a big man, with massive shoulders that threaten to engulf his head. He speaks in a guttural Teesside accent. His voice is so deep it sounds like it is playing at the wrong speed and so loud it makes the windows rattle and the tea tray shudder. Sometimes, by the time he has finished an anecdote the milk in the jug has turned to butter. He is frequently attacked in pubs and social clubs. The motivation for the assaults baffles him; it is less of a mystery to the rest of the family.

'Now here's a thing,' Uncle Alf says. 'I'm in the top house the other day, minding my own business, and I've just remarked to our lass what a bunch of work-shy shirkers these fellas at British Steel have become since nationalisation – fifteen of them to do one man's job, mind you – when, suddenly, this bar stool comes flying across the room and hits us on the shoulder.' He pulls a grim face. 'Luckily it had clipped our lass on the back of the head on the way through and that had taken some of the force out of it otherwise it might have done some real damage. Can you believe it?' Everybody shakes their head and mumbles astonishment.

'And what about your lass, is she all right?' somebody asks. Alf fixes the questioner with a look that suggests this is the stupidest thing he has ever heard in his life. 'All right? Of course she's all right. She's tough as teak, our lass.'

Uncle Alf looks around and sees me. He grins and holds up his right hand. Like the rest of him it is big and knobbly, like some kind of primitive tool or the weapon a caveman would have used when tackling a mammoth. 'See this, young Harry,' he rumbles, indicating his fist, and he waggles his right index finger under my nose, 'see this finger?' I nod. 'Well, this little finger has killed four men.' He demonstrates how he pulled the trigger on his Thompson SMG. 'Burmese jungle. Jap machine gun nest. Rat-a-tat-tat-tat!' The sound of his automatic fire ricochets around the room. No one except me pays much attention to it. They have heard it all before.

I have never actually lived through a war, though I sometimes feel as if I have. When I was a child and my family got together war stories inevitably broke out. Although I wasn't from what would be termed a military background, like most children born in the early 1960s I had many relatives with military experience. Grandfathers and great-uncles had gone through the First World War; fathers and uncles had fought in the Second World War or done National Service, often in places like Palestine, Korea, Aden and Malaya. Even those who had not fought in the wars had lived through them. They had heard air raid sirens, hidden in Anderson shelters, seen streets bombed to oblivion, been evacuated.

It was the same for every child I knew. This boy's uncle had been in a POW camp and when he came back had had to be weaned off his habit of hiding bread and soap; this lad's grandfather had served on the convoys that took relief supplies to Archangel and said it was so cold in Russia that when you spat it hit the deck as hail. If you mentioned Japan to that radgie old gadgie on the allotments he started swearing and he didn't care who heard; when a UXB had suddenly and unexpectedly turned EXB the blast had blown the lady from the chemist's across the kitchen and she'd burned her bum on the cooker. Ypres, the Somme, Tobruk, El Alamein and Monte Cassino were names so familiar to us they might have been nearby villages.

This made mine a singular generation in British history. Because, despite a national tendency to crow about our success on the battlefield, the fact is that Britain is not a land of soldiers and our experience of war is limited.

Until 1916 there had never been conscription in the United Kingdom; National Service – including the Second World War – had lasted for just twenty-five years. The British Army that fought at Minden, Quebec, Balaclava, Rorke's Drift and even at Mons in 1914 was small and professional. During the Napoleonic Wars, when every other nation in Europe introduced conscription, Britain resisted, filling ranks decimated by fifteen years of fighting by increasing the maximum age for volunteers from twenty-eight to thirty-three.

'Wanted,' the recruitment posters of 1809 read, 'Brisk lads, light and straight, and by no means gummy: not under 5 feet 5½ inches tall, or over 5 feet 9 inches in height. Liberal bounty; good uniforms; generous pay!' The British Army was made up – bar the odd press-ganging – entirely of blokes who'd answered the situations vacant ads.

This was not the case elsewhere. In France, Germany, Austria-Hungary and Russia conscription – usually by lottery – and later compulsory national service was the way the ranks of the armed forces were filled. By 1812 France, Russia and Austria were each conscripting one hundred thousand men per year, some of them boys as young as fifteen. 'I could lose the British Army in a single day,' the Duke of Wellington remarked sardonically, but accurately, as he marched about the Peninsula with his sixty thousand men. Meanwhile, in East Prussia Napoleon Bonaparte was preparing to cross the Russian frontier with six hundred thousand troops. Even a man as profligate with human life as the Little Corporal would have struggled to toss that lot away in twenty-four hours. (He whittled it down to around thirty thousand eventually, though it took him eight months.) At the start of the Great War

Britain's army was the same size as that of Belgium, and only half as big as that of Serbia. In 1914 the Germans had 1.75 million reservists. Britain had one hundred thousand.

Despite this compulsion (and the fact that the wealthy frequently dodged duties by paying others to do it for them), the Continentals tended to regard their vast amateur armies as exemplars of national pride and patriotism; proof that ordinary folk were prepared to fight to the death to preserve the regime and to shed their blood for the national interest. The Europeans looked down their noses at the British, wondering at the moral fibre of a country that paid men to make a career of fighting. The word mercenaries was often used. Though some of the most celebrated soldiers in history – Xenophon, Sir John Hawkswood and Count Wallenstein amongst them – were mercenaries, the term is generally pejorative. Fighting is like sex: doing it from desire or duty is one thing; doing it for money quite another.

In fairness to the Europeans it has to be said that the British tended to share this view. Although Cassell published an annual volume entitled *Celebrities of the Army* and men like Sir Garnet Wolsey and Lord Roberts of Kandahar were hailed as heroes, the public tended to regard the ordinary soldier as at best a nuisance and at worst a menace. 'I would rather my son went to prison than became a redcoat' wrote the mother of Field Marshal William Robertson. She was disappointed. He ended up not as a jailbird but a general.

In *The First World War* John Terraine asks why the conflict affected the British quite so dramatically. Other nations, he points out, suffered far worse casualties than Britain without convulsing quite so violently or becoming so, well, damnably emotional about it. Terraine is not terribly sympathetic. In fact, you sense the venerable military historian would like to give everybody he sees sniffling over 'Anthem for Doomed Youth' a good slap and the order to jolly well buck up. The traditional make up of the British Army is the answer to Terraine's question. The British had never fought in such large numbers before, and had never done so as naïve amateurs.

The experience of war was new to the British in a way it wasn't for the other nations. To the French, Germans, Belgians and Austrians, whose countryside had been regularly ravaged by hostile armies since the Reformation, war was an ever-present threat, a pestilence of steel and smoke that could sweep through at any time. Between 1859 and 1870 Prussia fought wars with Denmark, Austria-Hungary and France; France fought against Austria-Hungary and Prussia; and Austria-Hungary fought against France, Denmark, Piedmont-Sardinia and Prussia. Armies of three-quarters of a million conscripts rumbled across the countryside. Forty thousand dead and wounded were left on the field at Solferino; there were fifty-seven thousand casualties in the Seven Weeks' War, thirty thousand at Mars-la-Tour alone. During the same period the British Army mounted punitive expeditions in Bhutan and Abyssinia and joined France for an invasion of China. The French lost more men to enemy action in a single day at Magenta than Britain did in a decade.

In Europe war was one of life's hazards, a natural threat to be avoided like lightning or typhoid. To the British it was something that happened far away and was handled by rough men who were used to that sort of thing. The First and Second World Wars briefly changed all that. There are many reasons why the British are still so fixated on the events of 1939–45 and the sheer novelty is surely one of them.

I once met an old man who had been an officer in the First World War. Initially he'd been a volunteer in the Artists' Rifles, but later he'd transferred to the Essex Regiment. 'A very different attitude amongst the men,' the old man said. 'The Artists' Rifles was drawn from chaps who'd joined up as a matter of politics and patriotism. They saw the Kaiser as a brute, a terrible autocrat; a fellow who'd broken all civilised conventions by invading a neutral country, Belgium. They believed that what they were doing was right. But when they got out to Flanders and saw the fearful carnage they started to question that assumption, to wonder whether the ends justified the means. They were racked with doubt and guilt.

'The chaps from the Essex Regiment were rather different. Most came from the East End of London. Dockers, stevedores, foundrymen – tough fellows. They'd joined up out of patriotism too. But it was a different sort of patriotism, really, not what you'd call ideological. They'd grown up with one street scrapping against another, or Christians fighting Jews, or the English fighting Italian immigrants, or Aldgate fighting Shadwell, or whatever. They were fighters to a man; they didn't need a pretext. Somebody shouted "Fight!" and they all piled in, d'you see? To them the Great War was just a bigger version. It was the King's gang against the Kaiser's mob.'

Looking back on it now, the old man said with a rueful smile, the East Enders were right – there really was nothing more to the Great War than two big gangs fighting for nothing more than the sake of it.

I didn't know my grandfather's eldest brother Joe, but from what I'd heard of him and knew of my granddad I would judge that he was more Essex Regiment than Artists' Rifles. Joe had joined up at sixteen, lying about his age. He left behind a life of hard manual work in the inferno of Middlesbrough's Ironmasters' district where three dozen blast furnaces filled the sky with dark smoke and the streets with orange light.

The brothers left school at fourteen. They worked as laundry boys, but were fired after an incident in which Joe sneaked up behind a brewer's dray that was delivering to the next-door pub and shot a steam hose at the arses of the vast shire horses that pulled it. Alarmed, the horses set off at a gallop, sparks flying as their big hooves struck the cobbles, kegs of beer bouncing loose and smashing in the road. The street filled with yells and the smell of ale. 'You should have seen them buggers run!' my granddad said, still chortling fifty years later.

They moved on to work as sheet metal roofers on the big fabrication sheds for Teesside's burgeoning structural steel industry, carting buckets of iron rivets up long, long ladders. Once, when they were working on a roof in South Bank, my granddad said, a couple of older blokes had given them some lip about their hair (they were a family of redheads). Joe had walked over, picked up a three-pound hammer from one of the men's toolbags and casually dropped it over the parapet, watching as it fell to the ground a hundred feet below. 'Any more out of either of you,' he said, 'and you're following it.'

'Our Joe,' my granddad said with an approving chuckle, 'now, he *was* tough.'

Joe went off to fight and his family watched nervously whenever the telegram boy came down the street, fearful it was their door he would knock on. In the kitchen they had a map marked with flags to show the front line. After eighteen months Joe came back on leave. He brought with him a kitbag filled with cigarettes. Army rations, he said, but Joe didn't smoke. None of the brothers did. They spent their spare time in the boxing gym. They took their fighting seriously, and even in 1918 people knew that smoking made you short of breath. So he tipped the packets of cigarettes out onto the table in the scullery and told everybody in the street to pop in and help themselves to a packet when they needed one. 'It was about three foot high, that pile of cigarettes,' my granddad said, and by the end of the week it had gone. And so, by rights, was Joe, back to the Front. But while he was home news came that the armistice had been signed. 'Well,' Joe said, 'they won't be needing me any more now,' so he demobbed himself and never went back.

That wasn't, of course, the way the army did things. Joe was classified as a deserter. 'Once a week,' my granddad said, 'the military police would come to the door and our Joe would hide on the back slope of the coal shed 'til they'd gone.'

Eventually they gave up looking for him. They never caught my granddad's cousin Gilbert either. He'd taken early – and unofficial – retirement from the 17th Lancers at the beginning of 1918. He had a cavalryman's moustache and the family trait of whimsy. 'A strapping great fella,' my granddad said, 'he used to swim in the River Tees at Yarm with his bowler hat on.' 'Why'd he keep his bowler hat on?' we'd ask. 'So if ladies came by strolling along the bank he'd be able to tip it to them,' my granddad said. It was obvious, really.

My grandfather was too young for the Great War. When the Second World War started he volunteered for the navy but he was working in a chemical plant, a reserved occupation. He served in the Home Guard and cycled to work each day. Once when he was riding home along the coast road from the two-'til-ten shift the air raid warning sounded. He took shelter in the dunes and, tired, fell asleep. At dawn he woke up. 'There was a field of cows grazing on the other side of the road,' my granddad said, 'and they were just standing there normal, like. But when you took a closer look all their heads were gone.' A bomb had landed near by and the blast had decapitated the herd.

Eventually my grandfather got to sea. He was sent to work on the Persian oilfields in Abadan. The convoy of ships carrying Granddad and his workmates sailed through the Mediterranean menaced by German dive-bombers. Beneath the waves U-boats lurked like hungry sharks. The radar sonar bleeped rhythmically, the martial equivalent of life support machines.

*

My grandfather's brothers had served in the First World War, my father's in the Second. His eldest brother Randolph was in the Fleet Air Arm. Randolph was much older than my father and Dad's memories of him were blurred, like an out of focus photograph. Randolph was kind but a believer in discipline. Once, when my father and the other younger brother James had failed to lift their caps to the wife of the vicar, Randolph had punished them by making them march round and round the garden. He sat in a chair to make sure they did things properly and every time they came level with him he called out 'Eyes right!' And they turned their heads and saluted him. James later became an officer in the Green Howards, serving as a guard on the train that took Rudolf Hess to Nuremberg.

As a pilot of a Fairey Swordfish torpedo bomber (a biplane, all struts and wires, that rumbled like a bumble bee and flew at roughly the same speed) Randolph took part in the sinking of the Italian fleet at Taranto. He flew from HMS *Ark Royal* and soon became a Royal Navy test pilot. Navy test pilots are generally regarded as the best flyers of all: in the United States the very best were selected to be astronauts. By the time the war ended Randolph had flown and tested over 120 different types of plane and had been one of the two pilots who carried out the first landings by jets on an aircraft carrier. His survival in what was notorious as one of the world's most dangerous jobs was considered something of a miracle. A few months after the war finished he took an aeroplane up for a joyride, had an accident on landing and was killed. His first child was three months old.

The next brother, John, was a journalist on the *Middlesbrough Evening Gazette*. He was quick-witted and sarcastic, the bookshelves in his bedroom filled with the fashionable writers of the day: Ernest Hemingway, William Faulkner, Sherwood Anderson, Graham Greene. An improbably glamorous figure, grinning lopsidedly from beneath a flopping fringe of blond hair, John did not take kindly to the hurly-burly of family life. After one particularly grumpy display over Sunday lunch his mother said, 'I suppose you'd much rather have been an only child?'

'Yes,' he snapped back, 'and orphaned at fourteen.'

John learned to fly for a bit of fun in the 1930s and joined the RAF shortly after the war started. He flew fighters in the Western Desert and then in Europe. Randolph's pilot logbooks are understated, brief and to the point. John's are offhand, filled with the sort of slang you might imagine existed only in films such as *Mrs Miniver* or *Reach for the Sky*: 'Skipper winged by Jerry,' they say, 'and limped home under escort.' John was recorded missing, presumed dead, after he failed to return from a reconnaissance mission over Dunkirk shortly after D-Day.

One of the only photos I have ever seen of the two men not in uniform was taken in early 1939. They are standing with my father (still a chubby primary school boy in a cap and belted mac) and James (head cocked to one side, an adolescent boy who is just realising that he is actually rather handsome) on the headland overlooking the North Sea near Saltburn, smiling into the camera, their tweed sports jackets buttoned. Randolph is holding a pipe, John a rubber band-powered model aircraft.

Up in the attic of our house my father had set up a workroom where he made radio-controlled aircraft and pond yachts. Framed pictures of the brothers were dotted across the walls: Randolph after landing a Swordfish on a crowded beach in North Berwick one bank holiday Monday when the engine failed; John in Egypt, baggy shorts, a life jacket, eyes narrowed in the sun; Randolph waving from the cockpit of a flying Hurricane; John in a Spitfire; a flight of Swordfish above the Med.

I knew these men only from pictures and stories. For me, they inhabited a long-gone world of heroism and adventure not so very different from the one portrayed in the books of Arthurian, Celtic and Greek myths that were my favourite reading. Rosemary Sutcliffe's children's version of the great Anglo-Saxon epic *Beowulf* was the book I liked best. I studied the line drawings of Beowulf wrestling Grendel, ripping the monster's arm out of the shoulder socket, and I gazed at the photos on the wall. Like Beowulf they had pitched themselves against the forces of great darkness and won, but there was no happy ending.

When we finally leave my great-granny's house that Boxing Day night the chill of the December darkness briefly slaps us into silence. I am still thinking about Uncle Alf's index finger. 'Did you kill anyone when you were in the army?' I ask my dad when we get to our Riley. My dad was in Malaya with the 12th Royal Lancers (Prince of Wales's). He had a Dingo Scout Car, which was like an armoured car, only – and this is a major disappointment to me – without a cannon. I already know what the answer to my question is. I have asked my father this same question dozens of times, but there is always the possibility that he has overlooked something, that when I ask again this time he will say, 'Well, funnily enough, now you come to mention it there was that chap at Maxwell Hill . . .'

'No, I didn't,' my dad says.

'Uncle Alf did,' I say. 'When he was in the army he killed lots of people.'

'Only with his cooking,' my mum replies.

'What d'you mean?' I say. My dad laughs. He will tell me when I am older, he says.

2

Written Orders and Signals

'. . . war is hell; but peace, peace is fucking boring.'
Joaquin Phoenix, *Buffalo Soldiers*

I was off school for a fortnight with influenza. Day after day I lay in bed. Rest was what the doctor ordered, and since there was no daytime TV in those days there was really nothing to get up for anyway. My mother and father were at work. Neighbours and relations called in periodically to check I hadn't been kidnapped or set fire to anything. They brought Lucozade and bananas.

I filled the long hours of the day by picking the encrusted snot off my nostrils, trying to identify the bitter taste of the gunk I coughed up, turning my pillow over every half hour to feel the coolness of the cotton against my cheek and listening to Radio One on a tiny transistor radio a bloke from down the road who worked on the oil tankers had brought back from the Persian Gulf.

'What's the recipe today, Jim?' Uncle Raymondo asked Jimmy Young every morning; Leapy Lee sang 'Little Arrows', Val Doonican 'If I Knew Then What I Know Now'; and when the news rolled around every hour the Israelis were fighting the Arabs and the Vietnamese were battling the Americans in places I had never heard of.

For some reason the newsreaders never told you the

important things: who were the goodies, who were the baddies and who was winning. Besides, news of battles in other
countries made me feel jealous. Britain hadn't been involved
in a war for years. The Yanks and the Egyptians, Israel and
Syria, the Vietcong, Jordan and even the Aussies were driving
tanks, firing machine guns and launching rockets, and what
were the British doing? Arguing over whether we should have
decimal currency or not. It was so unfair.

I read all my books about Beowulf, Cuchulainn, Perseus
and the Medusa, Sir Gawain and the Green Knight, Robin
Hood. I read some old books of my dad's too – *With Wolfe in
Canada* and *The Lion of the North* by G. A. Henty and Andrew
Lang's *Red Book of Heroes*. Then I read them all again, pre-
tending I didn't know the endings.

One day my gran turned up with a big cardboard box
emblazoned with the legend 'Peak Freen Continental
Assortment'. Her next door neighbour, Mrs Garbutt, had
given it her, she said. It had belonged to the Garbutts' oldest
boy, Mickey. Mickey had just been taken on as an apprentice
at Haverton Hill shipyards and everyone was very pleased.
Mickey had been a troublesome youth, led astray by the
wrong sorts into various episodes of petty crime and fights in
car parks and on football trains, but now it seemed he had
settled down. 'You can't go far wrong if you've a job in a ship-
yard,' my gran said. Five years later my granddad would
advise me, 'You'll never be out of work if you can use a slide
rule.' The world was changing fast and lack of prescience ran
through Britain like some genetic disorder.

I opened the box. Inside, arranged in four neat stacks, were
over a hundred Pocket Library comics: *Commando, Combat
Picture Library, War Picture Library, Air Ace Picture Library* and
Conflict. I picked one up from the top of the stack. On the
cover was a colour illustration of a dogfight between a British
fighter and a German Me109, blasts of red and yellow flame

bursting from the wing-mounted cannons, the title of the story running diagonally across the top of the page: 'Ace in a Hole!' Inside, black and white drawings. A trio of Hawker Hurricanes swooped down on a German convoy in northern France. 'We've caught Jerry with his pants down, boys. Let's blast him!' Machine gun rounds ripped from the wings of the swooping planes, rat-a-tat-tat. '*Raus, raus!*' The drivers of the lorries sprang from the doors for safety as the petrol tanks detonated. '*Zum Teufel!*' – the cargo of munitions exploded. 'That's three truckloads of ammo our boys on the beachheads won't need to worry about.' The Hurricanes wheeled away. Behind them smoke rose from the burning lorries and the surviving squareheads mopped soot and cold sweat from their brows.

My gran is talking, something about making me a mixture of raw egg, milk and sherry that will build me up, but I'm not listening. I am entranced by the terse poetry of the prose. 'The planes tore across the moonlit sky, flak bursts blossoming around them.' One of the Hurricanes had been hit by enemy ack-ack. 'I've bought one!' Flames leap from the engine cowling. 'I'm going to have to bail out!' The hatch above his head is reluctant to open. 'Drat, it's jammed!' The Hurricane begins to spin earthwards. 'It's a gamble but it's my only chance!' The pilot twists his control lever, the plane tips upside down. Miraculously, the hatch flies off. 'Thank goodness for gravity!' The pilot, Ace Hart, falls earthwards. 'Sorry to lose the old crate, but . . .' He is upside down. 'Have . . . To . . . Right . . . Myself.' He somersaults in mid-air and pulls the ripcord. The parachute opens as the Hurricane crashes into the earth. 'Cripes!' The rest of the Hurricanes want to offer assistance but they are running low on fuel: 'If we don't turn back now we'll never get back to Blighty.' 'So long, Ace! And good luck!'

My gran returns with a glass that is engraved with advice

on how to tell if an egg is fresh by floating it in water. The
drink she has made is cold and custard coloured and smells of
the liqueur chocolates you are allowed to have at Christmas
because it's only once a year and one or two won't do him
any harm. I mean, when I was a bairn they used to give you
gin when you were teething. I drink it. It makes my throat and
chest feel warm. I eat a Wagon Wheel biscuit that is marginally bigger than my head and feel as if I am floating like the
pilot under his billowing parachute.

Down below, Jerry is waiting, rifles at the ready, as the
'chute catches in a tree.

'*Hande hoch, Englischer Schweinehund!*'

'Watch where you're pointing that thing, sausage
muncher.'

A German officer arrives in a Kübelwagen. 'For you, my
friend, the war is over,' he says. Our hero smiles, accepting
the proffered cigarette; a bubble hovers above his head:
'That's what you think, Fritz.'

Over the next week I read every comic in the box: *Hun
Bait, Typhoon Force, Seek and Strike, Tracy of Tobruk, Jungle Patrol,
Killer at Large.* In panel after illustrated panel tanks exploded
and bombers spiralled earthwards; '*Achtung!*' the stern-faced
stormtroopers yelled, while buck-toothed, myopic Japs died
with a cry of 'Aieeee!' (British troops faced the ultimate journey with a much manlier 'Aaargh!') and the plucky Brits
greeted explosions and bayonet charges with schoolboy cries
of 'Lumme!', 'Stripe me!' and 'Crikey!', dispatching enemies
with a snarled 'Tough luck, chum!'

The comics were filled with valour, patriotism and cowards
who met a sticky end. Gastronomy also featured heavily, perhaps reflecting the impact of food rationing on the British
psyche. The enemy was routinely identified by his diet. The
Germans were 'sausage munchers', the Japanese 'rice chom-
pers', the Italians 'ice cream wallahs'. Even the throwing of a

hand grenade was likely to be celebrated with a cry of 'Chew on this pineapple, squarehead!' Despite extreme provocation the forces of the Axis refused to hit back in kind, though the temptation to yell 'Stodge swallowers!' or 'Overcooked vegetable slurpers!' at the advancing Tommies must have been almost overwhelming.

The Second World War ended in 1945. It re-started in 1958. Or at least the children's version of it did. In the 1950s boys' comics did not concern themselves with the Second World War. In fact, they seem to have been trying to create the impression that it had never happened. As rationing and austerity measures bit chunks out of the British way of life the comics continued to publish pre-war series about the glorious Empire such as *The Wolf of Kabul*, in which a native bearer named Chung – who bore a strong resemblance to Johnny Weissmuller – roamed about the North-West Frontier slapping wily Pathans and mutinous Sepoys around the head with his favourite weapon, a cricket bat dubbed Clickabar, just to prove that, while brave and loyal, these native chappies really didn't have the mental capacity to get involved in running their own country.

It was only as the decade came to a close that strips about the Second World War started to appear. The *War Picture Library* series was launched in 1958. It was closely followed by the *Combat Picture Library* and, in 1961 – the year of my birth – *Commando Comic*, with its classic dagger logo. On top of these there were other, more short-lived titles: the *Pocket War Library*, *War at Sea*, *Conflict*, *Sabre Picture Library* and *Air Ace Picture Library*. And as if this were not enough to sate the public appetite, the traditional weekly comics such as *Hotspur* and *Albion* were abandoning Arthurian knights and Victorian heroes such as Chung and allowing themselves to be overrun by men in metal helmets yelling '*Feuer!*', '*Ja, Kapitän!*', 'In the name of the Emperor!' and '*Banzai!*'

Battle featured Sergeant 'D-Day' Dawson; *Lion* had ace pilot Paddy Payne; *Victor* offered the young cliff-climbing commando Joe Bones 'The Human Fly' and RAF icon Matt Braddock, VC; there was a spectral Spitfire pilot in *Spike*, while *Jet* had the Sergeant's Four and a comedy strip called the Kids of Stalag 41 which was basically the Bash Street Kids in a POW camp.

Men who'd actually fought in the war drew many of these strips, particularly in the early years. Denis McLoughlin, for example, who contributed to *Commando* for twenty years, had served in the Royal Artillery from 1940 until the end of the war. A graduate of Bolton School of Art, one of his first works had been a saucy mural painted on the wall of the RA depot in Woolwich. Much admired by his comrades, it was destroyed by a V1 rocket in 1945.

The character that particularly stays in my mind is Captain Hurricane from *Valiant*. In terms of tone, the adventures of the mountainous Royal Marine owed something to comedy war films such as *Hogan's Heroes*. The violence was played for laughs, slapstick Nazis reeling about cross-eyed with stars circling above their heads as the burly commando yelled about 'perishin' Kraut bilge rats' and tied a knot in the barrel of the nearest PAK 37mm.

The Captain was not much given to explanations, but that didn't matter since his scrawny cockney batman, Maggot Malone, provided a narrative of his adventures. This was hardly a difficult job, even for a man of Maggot's limited vocabulary, since just about the only thing Hurricane ever did was lose his temper with the forces of the Axis. 'Gor blimey, 'e's going into one of 'is ragin' furies!' Maggot would explain helpfully as the Captain – face sweating with effort and anger – battered a Panzer corps or a Japanese infantry battalion with whatever weapon came to hand (usually a German or a Jap soldier, gripped by the ankles in his powerful fist).

The Captain was a man so large he could have worn a wardrobe as an overcoat and he was stronger than French cheese. Which was lucky, since his parents had christened him Hercules, a name that would hardly have been appropriate for a seven stone weakling. Seven stone weaklings, or at least the only ones I had ever come across, were called Mitch. Mitch featured in the adverts for the Charles Atlas body building system that appeared alongside the deeds of Superman, Batman and the Green Lantern in *DC* and *Marvel* – American comics, as they were generically known.

Mitch was always getting sand kicked in his face by burly bullies (the bullies had got burly by humping sand around everywhere with them so they had some handy when they came across Mitch). In stepped Charles Atlas, a man with muscles of teak and the complexion to match. Charles was so manly that even the fact he was wearing leopard-skin trunks didn't deter him from posing on street corners, standing like he was holding an invisible firkin on each shoulder.

Mitch quickly discovered that, under instruction from Atlas, it was possible to scare off adversaries by tearing a telephone directory in half or blowing up a hot-water bottle until it was so full of air it burst. (How did someone discover you could do that, incidentally? Are there people who go round inflating things as a hobby? 'Hi honey. Sorry about the smell. Saw a pig on the way home and got thinking . . .')

The American comics generally seemed obsessed with muscles, also carrying adverts for chest expanders – a fearsome piece of equipment that had clearly been developed by a sadist who liked to imagine the look on men's faces when they caught their chest hair in a coiled steel spring. When it came to bullies, the chest expander was even more effective than Charles Atlas as, with minimum fuss, it could be turned into a catapult capable of propelling a pineapple several hundred yards.

American comics entered my life around the same time as the *War Picture Library*. I read the Fantastic Four, Hulk and Thor in between 'The Fight Against Fear', 'Check Mate!' and 'Commandos Die Hard!' It says something about the difference between the two nations that the American comics were in colour while ours were in black and white. More than that, though, the nature of the heroes differed wildly. The American kids had Spiderman, Daredevil, Batman and Thor. British kids had the Second World War. Burma and the Western Desert were our Gotham City and Megalopolis. The men who saved our world didn't have extraordinary powers, fancy gadgets or bizarre costumes (though Keith's granddad sometimes wore his old jungle hat when he pruned the roses and Mr Maynard from down the road who'd helped sink the *Tirpitz* owned a colour telly). Our superheroes were our dads, uncles and grandfathers, and there is something rather touching in that.

Not that everyone thought so. My mother was far from impressed by the contents of the box from my gran. Mum thought that reading war comics would retard my educational development. 'You need to read proper books,' she said. The problem with that was that the war hardly featured at all in 'proper' books. The only children's book I can think of from the period in which the war played a central part was Ian Seraillier's novel *The Silver Sword*, about the partisans in Poland. The war, it seemed, was lowbrow, proletarian. Brainy or respectable people preferred to ignore it as they might a street corner pub, a boxing match or union jack Y-fronts. If you wanted the war it was the comics or nothing. And for me it turned out to be nothing: as soon as I was feeling better Mum took Mickey Garbutt's box of pocket picture books down the garden and burned them in the incinerator.

If I wanted war comics in future I would have to make my

own. Luckily that was far easier than it sounded, thanks to Patterson Blick Instant Picture Books (with drawings by Dennis Knight). These were a kind of illustrative karaoke. The books told the story of some particular conflict – the Battle of Waterloo, the Charge of the Light Brigade, the War in the Desert – and provided a few large scenic backgrounds along with a sheet of rub-down transfers of soldiers, ordnance and other materiel that the enthusiast could arrange as he saw fit. You selected the figure or AFV you wanted to apply – taking into account perspective and dramatic effect – cut out the transfer, placed it in the correct spot and then vigorously scribbled over the back of it with a ball-point pen to get it to stick on the page. Inevitably in the excitement the pen scribbles tended to go over the edge of the transfer, so that the soldiers and tanks in your scene were surrounded by an electrical storm of ink.

There were dozens of different transfer books from Patterson Blick and rivals such as Panorama and Letraset, but the one that sticks out in my mind was *D-Day*, which came out when I was nine. *D-Day*'s main scene featured a particularly fine Sherman M35 with a flail on the front. The flail was a drum with lengths of chain attached that whirled round and round. It was designed to detonate landmines (though it would undoubtedly have done a good job of beating the dust out of carpets too). The Sherman was rumbling up Sword Beach, a mine exploding right in front of it in a vivid flash of orange, yellow and black. Clearly there was only one thing to do in this situation. I found the transfer of German stormtrooper falling wounded and laid it flat over the top of the explosion so that it appeared as if he was being thrown into the air by the blast. Then, for a finishing touch, I added the dying man's traditional cry 'Aaaagheee!' in a speech bubble. Looking back now, I'm not proud of it. But I ask you, what red-blooded English lad could have resisted?

By the time I had my first Patterson Blick I was over the worst of my flu and was convalescing at my grandparents' house. They lived at Marske-by-the-Sea and the sea air was good for me; not having a child lying on the sofa calling piti-fully for more cocoa was good for my mum and dad. At night, my granddad would go out with a shrimping net and torch. Later, my grandmother would boil his catch, drain it and tip it out on a newspaper on the kitchen table, and we'd sit, picking off the crispy shells, dipping the meat in lemon juice. My granddad's dog, Rebel, hovered by the gas fire. A border collie, Reb was so full of noxious wind that allowing him near a naked flame was tantamount to throwing bricks at a floating mine. There were lots of floating mines along the North Sea coast in those days. Every so often a live one would get caught up in a fisherman's net, or be spotted drifting off shore. If one was coming towards your ship you had to fend it off using a boat hook. Most of the mines, though, were no longer floating but set in concrete and used as collecting boxes for the British Legion. Spherical, painted red and with dozens of protruding detonators, they looked like gigantic angry conkers.

On Sunday mornings my grandmother got up early to put the cabbage on for Sunday lunch. By midday it had been simmering gently for three hours and was almost done, the house was filled with its pungent odour and condensation was running down the walls. After lunch the entire family settled on the sofa for *All Our Yesterdays*, presented by a balding Irish journalist named Brian Inglis. It featured a signature tune – maudlin brass above a trudging, footsore rhythm – so redo-lent of the miseries of childhood that just remembering it makes me feel like I am wearing an itchy shirt and being forced to eat malt extract.

Each episode of *All Our Yesterdays* concentrated on events from the same week twenty-five years before, which meant that from the mid-sixties onwards it was war, war and more war. It proved so popular with the public that in 1965 it featured in the TV top twenty for forty-nine consecutive weeks.

Strangely, for a child so obsessed with the war, I found the programme hugely depressing. Partly this was because it was broadcast just before the football highlights and seemed to drag on endlessly as I sat, eagerly anticipating the festival of mud, brutality and facial hair that constituted the English game in the 1960s. Mainly it was because quite a lot of *All Our Yesterdays* focused on life on the home front and was therefore accompanied not only by depressing music but also by any adult who happened to be in the house chirruping, 'Our Eileen had a dress just like that one!' or 'Eee God, d'you remember those powdered eggs?' or 'We were up to our ankles in that air raid shelter and you never knew where it had come from' – any of which was bound to be followed by a reminder that I didn't know I was born, young fella-me-lad.

Adults always told you how lucky you were not to have lived through the war, even when they had spent the whole previous hour boasting about how they had done exactly that. *All Our Yesterdays* reinforced that view. As far as I could make out, life in Britain during the war seemed to have been one marathon sing-song interrupted only by the occasional burst of jitterbugging and the odd bout of digging up football pitches so that cabbages could be planted. The latter was such a hideously unpleasant endeavour that, as far as I was concerned, it must have done more to damage national morale than the Luftwaffe. Imagine sacrificing soccer for brassicas. If I'd been around at the time I'd have volunteered for a suicide mission.

Admittedly, every so often *All Our Yesterdays* would be brightened up by film of a Stuka dive-bombing a radar station or a burning battleship, but there was far too little of that for me. When I watched something about war I didn't want to see misery, crap food and people warbling 'Roll Out the Barrel'. I could get all that now. I wanted to see explosions and tanks.

Luckily there was no shortage of that. Admittedly, what had seemed like the most exciting TV series ever, the American-produced *Rat Patrol*, had been removed from the BBC after just a few episodes following hundreds of complaints from Second World War veterans (the series was all about a group of Americans fighting in the Long Range Desert Group – a unit that was, in reality, exclusively British), but more accurate British-made war films were a staple of Saturday night and Sunday afternoon television. Generally they featured the patrician Sir Michael Redgrave as a senior RAF commander; Kenneth More and John Mills as gallant but distinctly lower middle class junior officers (grammar school boys who might, in other circumstances, have run a provincial hardware store); and Harry Andrews or Jack Hawkins as a crusty but benign senior officer whose barking toughness only partially concealed his big and tender heart. *The Cockleshell Heroes*, *Reach for the Sky*, *The Dam Busters*, *Dunkirk*, *The Desert Fox* (James Mason – a keen toy soldier collector, incidentally – brilliantly cast as everybody's favourite Second World War German, Erwin Rommel), *The Desert Rats* (James Mason as Rommel again – in fact, I think it was against the law not to have James Mason as Rommel, as it would later become compulsory to cast Donald Pleasance as Heinrich Himmler), *Ice Cold in Alex*, *Sink the Bismarck!*, *Battle of the River Plate*, on and on they went. Between 1942 and 1972 Britain and America made well over five hundred Second World War movies. Watched end-to-end they would have lasted longer than the conflict itself.

If there was no war film on telly you could always go to the cinema. *The Guns of Navarone* came out the year that I was born and was still touring the market-town cinemas of North Yorkshire a decade later. *Where Eagles Dare, 633 Squadron* (featuring George Chakiris as a very unlikely Norwegian resistance officer), *Mosquito Squadron, The Battle of Britain*, I saw them all at the Empire Cinema in Guisborough. My favourite war film at the time, though, was Michael Winner's *Hannibal Brooks*, which I saw at the Odeon in Stockton-on-Tees. I was ten. In *Hannibal Brooks*, by a series of bizarre circumstances Oliver Reed ends up leading a group of escaped POWs and partisans in a guerrilla campaign against the Germans while mounted on an elephant named Lucy. Basically, Olly spends the entire film riding an elephant and blowing things up. It seemed like the perfect life to me.

I usually went to see these films with my dad, or a friend and his dad. Women – mysterious and contrary creatures – didn't seem to get as excited about war as men did. Women preferred films in which people kissed or danced, or preferably did both at the same time. Women didn't need war because they had love. These are usually portrayed as polar opposites, but I am not so sure: the two most romanticised aspects of life are combat and sex, and there has to be a reason for that. Combat and sex may seem to have little in common, but both are, or at least were, highly dangerous. (Coarser readers may wish to insert their own 'but only if you're doing it right' joke here.) 'I would rather stand in the line of battle three times than give birth to a single child,' Medea told the Athenian patriarchs, and if you examine the evidence you can see why.

Medical experts estimate that in the early years of the nineteenth century 6–7 per cent of British women died in childbirth. Many historians dispute this figure, however: factor in deaths resulting from later complications and sexually transmitted diseases such as syphilis, and I think we would not be exaggerating too wildly if we said that in

Georgian England sexual intercourse killed 10 per cent of all British women who engaged in it. At the Battle of Waterloo, meanwhile, we find that of 23,991 British soldiers who took part in the fighting 1916 are recorded dead or missing – slightly under 8 per cent. During the Napoleonic Wars, sleeping with a man was more hazardous for British women than fighting the French was for British men. If Jane Austen and Mary Shelley had taken to the streets waving placards bearing the slogan 'Make War not Love!' they'd have been well within their rights. In 1815 the most lethal weapon any soldier carried on the battlefield was his dick.

The Second World War films were more sophisticated than *Commando* comics, but only just. When *The Dam Busters* was shown at the Guisborough Carlton the poster in the foyer carried the strapline 'The story of "the bombs that had to bounce" – and the air-devils who had to drop 'em', a proclamation to which any passing Wehrmacht officer would surely have responded with a cry of '*Donner und Blitzen!*'

The Dam Busters starred Richard Todd, a mainstay of British war films. He had also been a mainstay of the British war. The Dublin-born actor had served in the 7th Battalion of the Parachute Regiment, taken part in the Normandy Landings and had been a member of the Allied spearhead that cut through German lines to join the airborne troops, commanded by Major Howard, who had captured the Pegasus Bridge. In the film *D-Day the Sixth of June* Todd played his own commanding officer, while in Darryl F. Zanuck's epic *The Longest Day* he played the part of Major Howard, with a younger actor taking the role of Richard Todd. In the 1958 film *I Was Monty's Double*, meanwhile, M. E. Clifton-James, who had indeed been Monty's double, took the parts both of Monty and his double, thus playing himself being himself as well as playing the man he had been playing at being. The war had already gone postmodern. Little wonder that a primary school boy could get confused between fact and fiction.

The great outpouring of Second World War films had slowed to a trickle by the mid-seventies. *War Picture Library* folded in 1984 after 2103 issues, *Combat Picture Library* in 1985 after 1212. But *Commando* comic continues, publishing eight titles a year and selling over a million copies. It is bizarrely popular in Finland and Sweden, where it still appears in translation with titles such as *Slaget vid Midway*, *Den Beste Av Dem* and *Fruktans Minut*.

British television, meanwhile, continued to show an appetite for 1939–45 that grew keener by the year. A letter in the *Guardian* reported that in 2005 the five UK terrestrial channels had broadcast 180 films or programmes devoted to the Second World War, with BBC2 alone offering twenty-six films and forty-eight documentaries on the topic. 'For you, my friend, the war is over,' the cartoon Germans in the comics kept telling the British. But they were wrong. It is still going on, just not quite as fiercely.

3

Ranged Combat – Small Arms

'Never insult seven people when all you're carrying is a six-shooter.'

Colonel Potter, *M*A*S*H*

The year before I started school our family went on a canal holiday. There was me, my mum and dad and my maternal grandparents. We sailed peacefully along, the calm of the day broken only by various minor incidents, most of them perpetrated by my grandfather.

As I said, my grandfather was brought up in Middlesbrough, a place so rugged that the populace regarded a full set of teeth as a sign of affectation. As they grew up, my grandfather and his brothers, Joe and George, gained a degree of local fame. They achieved this by having fights with everybody and anybody. They were banned from pubs and dance halls throughout Teesside. When my father started work in the Middlesbrough steel industry he mentioned to one of the older men in the drawing office that his wife's family were called Fixter. He said the man turned white at the mention of the name. 'Which one is he?' he asked. My father told him. 'Hell's teeth,' the draughtsman said. 'Still, I expect he's calmed down a bit by now, eh?'

Up to a point, was the answer to that. My grandfather was worked by some mysterious inner mechanism that was a puzzle to us all, and probably not entirely explicable to himself, either. Whimsical and uncompromising by turns, he was given to strange pronouncements and actions – washing the dog's face with a dishcloth, or taking a sandwich and pretending to play it like a mouth organ. Summing up a man he felt had delusions of grandeur he said, 'He carries a briefcase, but there's nowt in it but a mallet and a copy of the *Daily Mirror.*' And even though he was sixty he still regarded a few well-aimed punches as a legitimate way of resolving an argument. To paraphrase von Clausewitz, to my grandfather fisticuffs was debate by other means.

During the first week of the canal holiday Granddad was on top form. He rammed some lock gates and almost provoked a fight in a crowded lunchtime pub by declaiming, in a voice so loud it rattled the windows, 'This beer's as flat as my cap. What's the landlord doing, filling the kegs from the bloody canal?'

Like many men from tough working class backgrounds my granddad had a paradoxical attitude to money: he was happy to give it away, but he didn't like spending it. When he found out that we had to pay to have the barge toilet emptied he was incensed. It seemed to him a means invented by the barge rental people to chisel more cash out of their customers. My granddad decided that he wasn't going to pay to have a toilet emptied. He would do it himself. He hit on the following scheme. He would wait until nightfall, sail into the Skipton basin, remove the toilet, tie a rope around it and drop it over the side. He would then circle the barge round the basin dragging the toilet behind the boat so as to flush it out. He would then haul the fresh, clean toilet back aboard, saving us thirty shillings.

This was indeed quite a plan. Unfortunately, my grandfather had failed to take into account the strain placed on a length of rope by a fully laden toilet when a moving vessel is dragging it through water. In the middle of the Skipton basin the rope snapped and the lavatory sank. Luckily the water was clear and my grandfather was able to locate it quickly, submerged just below the surface. He got a torch and a thicker length of rope. He weighted the rope with a spanner and fashioned it into a lasso before attempting to recover the lavatory by throwing the rope over the top of it.

This was not as easy as it might sound. After about an hour we heard men approaching along the towpath. Torches swung across the water. Eventually they alighted on our barge. A deep voice boomed out across the water. 'This is the police,' it said. 'We have had reports of suspicious activities in this vicinity.'

By now my granddad was starting to get a bit fed up. 'Oh,' he said, his gravelly voice dropping into the true Teessider's preferred tone of disgusted amazement, 'have you now? Well, I'll be buggered.'

'Are you poaching?' the policeman asked.

'No, I'm not,' my grandfather replied, 'I'm trying to lasso a bloody toilet.'

Unhappily for my grandfather, the police officer took this not for the surreal, but undoubtedly true, statement it was, but as an outrageous piece of irony. It is never wise to be sarcastic to a British policeman. Sarcasm is their exclusive preserve. 'Well, then, Hopalong Cassidy,' the policeman replied, 'perhaps you'd like to hitch up your horse, come down to the station and try practising your roping technique on the slop bucket in one of our cells.'

It was in the wake of this incident that my granny decided to take me into Skipton to go shopping. She said she wanted to buy me a treat. 'What would you like?' she said. 'I'll get you it.' There was only one thing that I wanted. Something I had coveted feverishly for months. 'I'd like a trifle, please,' I said.

'A trifle?' my granny said. She was clearly a bit taken aback by my request. 'Are you sure?'

'Yes,' I assured her, 'a trifle.'

My granny located a cake shop, went in and came out with a small box. 'One trifle,' she said happily. She opened the box lid to show it to me. I had already sensed it wasn't what I wanted, because what I wanted wouldn't fit in such a small box. Hopeful that I might be wrong, I looked in. Inside was a small circular waxed paper pot filled with bright red jelly and gelatinous custard, topped with whipped cream and a sprinkling of hazelnuts dyed livid green to give the vague impression of pistachios. I looked at it in disgust. Why had she bought me this when I had clearly and specifically asked for a trifle? Perhaps it was preparation for the real treat to come.

'Can we get my trifle now?' I asked.

My granny chuckled. 'That is your trifle,' she said.

'No, it isn't,' I said.

'Yes, it is.'

'I don't want it.'

'It's what you asked for.'

'No it is not!' I shouted. I started to cry. I flailed my arms. I slapped the box and knocked it to the ground. The contents splodged onto the pavement.

As a child, a recurring nightmare was that I was trying to explain something to an adult, something amazingly important like a volcano was about to erupt, a tidal wave was coming, or *Captain Pugwash* was about to start and the telly wasn't plugged in, and however hard I tried I couldn't make them understand a word I was saying. I explained and explained, but they just stared at me as if what I was saying was totally incomprehensible.

'A trifle, a trifle,' I raged. I felt as if I was stuck in my own worst dream. 'I wanted a trifle.'

Granny decided to take me back to the barge. By the time

we got there I was red-faced with anger and breathless with weeping. 'I wanted a trifle,' I roared at my father when he asked me what the matter was.

'I bought him a trifle,' Granny said, 'but he got in a paddy when I gave it to him and threw it on the floor.'

'She did not,' I wailed, 'she did not give me a trifle.'

'When you say a trifle,' my dad said, showing immense patience in the circumstances, 'what do you mean? A cake?'

'No!' I ranted. 'Not a cake! A trifle! Like in the films.'

My dad looked perplexed. 'He kept saying that,' my granny chipped in helpfully, 'like in the films. I couldn't think of any films with trifles in. Laurel and Hardy is the nearest, but that's custard pies.'

What was it with the grown-ups? I felt as if I was being driven insane by their mad obsession with confectionery. It was all cakes, pies and cream slices. What was the matter with them? 'A trifle!' I howled again.

'Show me,' Dad said. 'Show me what you do with a trifle.'

I turned sideways, brought my right hand up so it was a few inches below my chin and then stretched my left arm out in front of me. I squinted down the length of it at Granny and twitched my right index finger. 'Bang!' I said. 'Bang! Bang!'

My dad let out a sigh, half amusement, half exasperation. 'Not a trifle,' he said, 'a *rifle*.'

They had given me a pudding when I wanted a gun.

There was a time during the 1960s when every weekend seemed to bring a new gun. I had dozens of them, but I always wanted more. My bedroom looked like an international arms fair. Apart from numerous water pistols, half a dozen sparking ray guns and a couple of spud-guns (one made of blue metal that propelled its slug using pressurised air and the other a neat black revolver with a pearl handle that utilised the blasting power of caps) that were non-conflict specific, my armament came from two narrow historical zones – the Wild West and the Second World War. That was it. There were no Brown Bess muskets, flintlock duelling pistols or single-shot breech-loading Martini-Henry rifles like the ones they used in Cy Endfield's film *Zulu*, which my dad and I had seen five times at the little cinema in Guisborough, watching from the royal circle while down below the rough boys stamped and pounded the seats in time with the rhythmic shield banging of Prince Dabulamanzi's warriors until the usherettes' torches swung across the darkness like searchlights and they fell silent.

The Second World War clearly offered a much wider choice for the fighting boy. I had two very nice sub-machine guns, a Thompson with a barrel magazine and a throaty chortling noise when you pulled the trigger and a Colt SMG like the ones used by the US Marine Corps that made a clattering rat-a-tat-tat using a spring mechanism which you locked and loaded by pulling back a metal lever with a red plastic cap. For side arms I had a Luger Parabellum, a broom-handled Mauser, a Webley revolver and – best of all – a Colt .45 automatic just like the one carried by my first real screen hero, the actor David Hedison from the American TV series *Voyage to the Bottom of the Sea*.

If I needed to tackle a bunker I had a bazooka that fired ping-pong balls and a couple of plastic hand grenades with removable pins. 'Don't throw them, lob them – like bowling a cricket ball!' passers-by would exclaim helpfully as my friends and I flushed Japs out of the reed beds across the road from the ice cream shop. The advice was well meaning, but ill advised. I had handled dozens of different weapons but I had never even seen a cricket ball.

My Old West arsenal was equally extensive. I had a single-shot derringer and numerous Colt Peacemakers, all of which fired caps. Caps came in a roll. They were made of off-white paper with little blue-black blobs of cordite in the centre. They looked like flattened frogspawn and, like real black powder, they were useless in the wet.

My Wild West rifle was a source of some contention. I had wanted one like Marshal Matt Dillon used in *Gunsmoke*, but the one my father bought for me didn't look anything like it. The reason for this was simple. Showing a taste for the obscure that he would again demonstrate when it came to model kits, my father had bought a Colt revolving rifle instead of a Winchester magazine carbine. He explained that the revolver action was less likely to jam than the lever action of the Winchester and that the Colt's rifled barrel increased its range and precision, making it far more efficient in dealing out lead death to rustlers, redskins and general no good ornery varmints. To my way of thinking, though, reliability and accuracy came a poor second to being able to fire one-handed from the hip while dangling from a rope swing, and I threw another paddy.

When I left the house to meet my friends in the back garden I had guns in my hands, a choice of camo-pattern anorak or fringed jacket of buckskin (actually corduroy) on my back, a US Cavalry trooper's kepi on my head and, on my feet, what can only be described as paramilitary shoes. These were Clarks Commandos or Tuff Wayfarers. Both had a compass concealed in the heel of the right shoe and animal tracks on the sole. In addition, Clarks Commandos had a coloured chevron on the bottom, the colour of which cor-responded to the width fitting of your shoe – though, suspiciously, the chevron on every pair I ever saw was blue, which suggested that either my friends all had feet of uniform width, or Clarks were cutting corners on rubber dye. The prints on the soles of the Wayfarers featured hippo, wolf, buffalo, zebra, rhino and tiger along with less exotic beasts such as badgers. I was never sure what the point of this was. The obvious reason was to confuse anybody who was pursuing you, but the prints were tiny and there was only one of each, so the only way it would have worked is if it succeeded in convincing the tracker that a miniature menagerie had recently passed that way, hopping. The Clarks Commandos had just one big animal print on each shoe. This was marginally better but it still conjured up the image of a tracker – in all probability Magua the Huron (played by Welsh actor Philip Madoc) from the BBC Sunday afternoon serial dramatisation of *The Last of the Mohicans* – studying the path in the forest and saying, 'One wolf. Him travel south. On hindlegs only.'

Out round the back of the houses we play Japs and Commandos. The commandos have a strong point between a coalbunker and the brick sentry boxes of the outside lavs. The Japs come from the east, bursting out from behind Mr Pixton's woodshed. They are armed with an assortment of weapons: Colt Peacemakers, water pistols and walking sticks. We let them have it. Na-na-na-na-na-na ... Ptchang, ptchang ... Kaaaaaboom. Some of the enemy cling desperately to life ('You're hit!' 'Am not!' 'Are too.' 'Yeah, but it was in the arm. It's only a wound. It's not fatal.'); others seize the opportunity to play out a dramatic death scene. My friend Deano – widely regarded as the best dier in the village – takes the first hit, cries out, 'Aaaaargh, they got me!' and then staggers around for two minutes, knocking into dustbins, bouncing off fences and overturning watering cans until he finally falls in a twisting heap next to a plank-and-wire compost bin and expires with a violent shudder, his tongue protruding from the side of his mouth. 'Shoot him again,' someone says. 'He's not dead.' 'Am so,' the corpse snaps back.

'If you're dead how come your eyes are open, then?'

'When you die you have your eyes open.'

'Says who?'

'My Uncle Stan, and he saw hundreds of dead Chinkies in Korea.'

'The Chinkies aren't in Korea.'

'Are so,' Deano says.

'Ah so!' another boy, Stewpot, yells in what we all take for an oriental accent. He narrows his eyes and sticks his front teeth out over his top lip like the Japanese soldiers in the comics. 'Ah so, white dog! Ah so, white dog!'

'Arsehole, white dog!' Deano says. 'White dog's arsehole.' We all laugh. And we keep on laughing until the soldiers of both armies are lying on the ground together, clutching their stomachs. And every time the laughter stops somebody yells 'Arsehole, white dog!' and it starts all over again.

And the guns kept on coming. It was like that Emo Philips joke: 'In our school, you were searched for guns and knives on the way in, and if you didn't have any they gave you some.'

When an adult gave you a gun one thing was guaranteed. Whether it was a Buntline Special, a P38 Walther 9mm, a Johnny Seven light machine gun with bi-pod and telescopic sight or a sparking Dan Dare space pistol, they always said the same thing: 'You must never point a gun at anyone.'

Adults were full of this sort of stuff. When you were recreating the heroics of Richard the Lionheart using walking sticks and dustbin lids for swords and shields, and bows made from string and willow branches that fired bamboo arrows, they came stomping out of the kitchen to remonstrate about the noise and ended up delivering their other favourite weapon-related catchphrase: 'Oh yes, it's all fun and games until someone loses an eye.'

You couldn't lose an eye from cap gun fire, but still they said you weren't to point it at anyone. Along with their proclivity for kissing, this seemed to me conclusive proof that grown-ups were totally insane. 'You must never point a gun at anyone!' Honestly. If you couldn't point it at someone, what exactly was the use of a gun? If you didn't point it at anyone how would you shoot them?

Besides, the rule flew in the face of all evidence. If adults didn't point guns at people how come so many people got killed and wounded in war films? It couldn't all be ricochets. And in the Saturday night western even the goodies could clearly be seen pointing guns at people. Regularly. If they hadn't they'd never have been able to run them out of town, or arrest them. Because it was plain that the sort of evil-hearted, sneering varmints typified by Jack Palance in *Shane* would not be impressed if you told them to reach for the sky while safely training your Colt six-shooter on the nearest patch of dirt. 'One false move and the turf gets it.' Would Jack have dropped his weapon and come quietly if Alan Ladd had put it to him that way? I didn't think so.

It wasn't until thirty years later that I learned that when adults told you not to point a gun at anyone it was not the safety of the person you pointed the gun at they were really concerned about.

Notions about the possible malign influence of war toys were not new, it should be said. In Edwardian times French sociologists blamed German militarism on the preponder-ance of tin soldiers in Teutonic toyshops. In England, at around the same time, the National Peace Council organised an exhibit of 'peace toys' which they hoped would one day replace soldiers, guns and battleships in the affections of boys.

The exhibition was satirised by the writer Saki in his short story *The Toys of Peace*, in which a well-meaning uncle presents two young brothers with a gift of lead figures representing, amongst others, John Stuart Mill, Robert Raikes ('the founder of Sunday schools'), a sanitary inspector, a district councillor, Rowland Hill ('who introduced the system of the penny

postage') and Mrs Hemans, a poetess, along with models of
the Manchester branch of the Young Women's Christian
Association and a public library. The boys, Eric and Bertie,
are unimpressed.

'Are we to play with these civilian figures?' asked Eric.
'Of course,' said Harvey, 'these are toys; they are meant
to be played with.'
'But how?'
It was rather a poser. 'You might make two of them
contest a seat in Parliament,' said Harvey, 'and have an
election—'

Later, the brothers transform the library into a fort and
John Stuart Mill into Marshal Saxe and fight out a bloody
skirmish leaving the uncle to lament that the experiment 'has
failed. We have begun too late.' When I was a teenager Saki
was one of my favourite writers. He died in the First World
War, killed by a sniper while serving as an infantryman in
France.

In the 1970s the move against war toys was widespread.
Peace protesters even staged a rally outside one of Britain's
major wargame shows. As one of the blokes who organised it
later admitted, the fact that it was called Armageddon probably didn't help. In Sweden, toy guns were banned, but it was
noticeable, or so it seemed to me, that toy-shops in Stockholm
carried a far wider range of toy swords, axes, clubs and bows
and arrows than did their counterparts in the UK.

I once brought back a toy mace from a trip to Stockholm.
It consisted of a spiked ball of black plush suspended from a
wooden handle by a thick length of rope, and I gave it to the
four-year-old son of a friend. He quickly realised that the soft,
spiky ball was useless as a weapon and took to swinging the
handle instead. This made a noise that was very pleasing to

him. Especially when it struck the head of his two-year-old brother. A gun would have been safer physically, if not psychologically.

While most parents I knew had initially tried to ban war toys, fearing the effect they would have on their children, this ban had ultimately proved ineffective. There's no point outlawing toy guns when an inventive lad can make a very passable one out of Lego in the time it takes to say 'phallocentric aggression'.

I was once talking to a friend, the mother of a little boy. Suddenly her son was standing in front of me. 'How are you?' I said, but the boy didn't say anything. I was talking to his mother and he was jealous. He stared at me for a moment, then he pulled a revolver from the holster he was wearing, raised it until the muzzle was about three inches from my face, squinted down the sight and pulled the trigger, once, twice, three times, holstered the gun again and ran off. 'Oh, ho, ho,' I said, 'kids, eh?' But I didn't feel quite so jovial. Because, as I looked down the barrel of the gun, I had been overwhelmed by a powerful and violent rage, an urge to snatch the gun out of the boy's chubby little mitt and bash him over the head with it until he howled.

And I remembered something from my own childhood. How one day I'd built a bunker under the table in my grandmother's scullery using pillows and cushions as sandbags and spent all day defending it against the furious assaults by the combined forces of the Axis, pausing only for toasted teacakes and slugs of radioactive green American cream soda which Granny kindly decanted into my water bottle. In mid-afternoon Uncle Alf entered the scullery. By now I was so wired on a combination of sugar, adrenalin and my fantasy war that, instead of saying 'Hello' and accepting one of the Murray mints he invariably carried round in the pocket of his cardigan, I charged out of my bunker screaming like a banshee, and jabbed the barrel of my Lee Enfield rifle in his groin as if I was bayoneting a Nazi stormtrooper.

Uncle Alf did not bite his lip or chuckle. He did not say, 'Boys will be boys.' He grabbed the gun off me with one mighty hand, spun me round with the other and smacked my backside with the rifle so hard he broke the plastic trigger guard. I shot back into my bunker and spent the rest of the afternoon weeping, afraid to come out until he had gone.

I don't think Uncle Alf's action was clever, just or fair. I wouldn't behave that way and I wouldn't applaud anyone who did. Yet the incident taught me something. It taught me that if you point a weapon at someone you are likely to end up getting hurt. And, all in all, I think that is an important lesson to have learned.

Not that I did learn it, obviously.

4

Some Thoughts on Light Troops

'Children worship their toys. They ask of them what men have always asked of the Gods: joy and forgetfulness.'

Anatole France, *On Life and Letters*

One of my earliest memories is of being underwater. There is sunlight shining through the glassy surface above my head, but the weight of my wellingtons is dragging me further into the darkness. I kick frantically and one boot comes off, but still the sunlight recedes from view. Then suddenly a pair of sand-coloured desert boots breaks the surface. They are followed by trousers, hands, a cable-knit jumper and then, finally, my dad's face. He reaches across the soundless gap between us, his eyes narrowed, bubbles escaping from the corners of his mouth, grabs my waist and pushes me upwards.

I had been walking around the edge of Scarborough Mere with some older children. At one point on the path water was lapping over the edge of the bank. 'It's not deep,' I told them, 'look, you can see the bottom.'

'If it's not deep why don't you paddle in it? You've got wellies.' It was a girl. I cannot remember her name, but she had blonde hair and a pale blue dress like the Virgin Mary's. I felt the need to impress her, and a devil-may-care attitude seemed the best method. I had got into trouble this way before. Earlier in the summer another blonde girl had dared me to walk under the big piebald horse that pulled the fish-monger's cart. I had done it without a moment's hesitation, bending over slightly and scuttling beneath its heaving ribs. I emerged on the other side expecting a hero's welcome, but instead of applause every grown-up within fifty yards ran over and bawled at me not to be so damned stupid you bloody little idiot, one kick from that thing would knock your brains all over the high street.

It should have taught me a lesson, but it didn't. I absorbed lessons about as well as a stone absorbs jam. Eager to show how brave I was, I stepped into the lake. As soon as my foot hit the surface I realised that what I thought was moss on the bottom of the lake was actually the reflection of the over-hanging bushes. My booted leg sank further and further until I overbalanced and toppled in after it. I surfaced to see the children shouting for help. When I came up again there were people running along the bank, then I went under for the third time and my dad jumped in and saved my life.

The fact that I was wandering round Scarborough Mere in the first place was down to my dad. He was sailing his model racing yacht in a competition. My dad had made the yacht himself. It was what is called a Ten Rater, a model with sails that are set and reset using clockwork motors. Ten Raters were built to a simple formula related to sail area and water-line hull length that had been laid down by the Pond Yachting Association back in 1887. They were considered by aficionados to be the quickest but most difficult to handle of all scale sailing vessels. Magazines devoted to model boats described Ten Rater racing as 'the Formula One of pond yachting'.

My dad loved making models. He made me balsa wood aero-planes, a Wild West fort and a medieval castle. For himself he made huge radio-controlled gliders, high-grade American slot cars to race on a vast eight-lane wooden track above a pub in Yarm, remote-control tanks and motorised armoured cars. He also made plastic aeroplanes.

During the day Dad worked as an engineer for one of the world's biggest structural steel companies. He built, amongst other things, the Dartford Bridge, Britain's longest suspension bridge, and the Canary Wharf Tower, Britain's tallest building at the time. My dad liked making things. He didn't care whether it was a greenhouse, an oil rig or a $\frac{1}{32}$ scale Fokker Dr I triplane. A lot of the men my father worked with were the same; he knows men who make scale model railways and men who make their own steam-powered cars.

Once I appeared on a BBC radio arts programme reviewing an exhibition of Meccano bridges that had been held at the Baltic gallery in Gateshead. 'It's funny isn't it,' the presenter, an erudite and well-respected critic, said when we had finished recording. 'If a suburban bank manager had built a Meccano model of the Golden Gate Bridge in his garage at weekends we'd sneer at him as a sad bastard, but if an artist does it we hail him as a genius.' This seemed to sum things up very neatly, though I noticed he'd waited until the tape machines were switched off before he dared say it. By and large, I'd have to say, those who mock the model-makers are quite often the sort of people who'd struggle to make a structurally sound sandwich never mind a 350-foot-high office block.

My father approached tasks in a meticulous manner. He never committed himself to action until he had considered the job at hand from all angles. This is because he is an engineer. You don't turn up at a river bank, start knocking together a bridge, get halfway across and say, 'Hang about a bit, fellas, this isn't going to work. Let's pull it down and start again.' When you build a bridge you have to have a very precise idea of what you are going to do before you start.

My own approach to everything is, by contrast, completely haphazard. This suits my profession, writing, which is largely about making something then ripping it to pieces, chopping a bit off here, stuffing a bit in there and then botching it all back together again and again until you have either got it how you want it or, more likely, you simply can't be bothered any more. Writing is trial and error, with error predominating. This is not a good approach when you are building a skyscraper. Or a plastic model of a Bristol Bulldog Mk IIA.

I was very happy with Airfix (the dogfight doubles series held particular allure) but my father ignored them in favour of more exotic foreign makes such as Revell and Tamiya. You could not buy these in the village newsagent's; you had to make visits to specialist shops that smelled of cellulose thinners and sanding sealer and had massive radio-controlled Piper Cherokees suspended from the ceiling on sea-fishing line. *These* kits, my father indicated, were the genuine article. I would later recognise this same wilful obscurantism in my attitude to music. Airfix, my dad seems to have been saying, were OK. They were well-crafted, decent little pop kits, the polystyrene equivalent of Westlife or S Club. But they were essentially kids' stuff, whereas Williams Brothers or Historex, well, they were the genuine article, they were Otis Redding or Nirvana.

The bagged Airfix kits were hung on a special display rack in the local newsagent's, just along from the bookshelves of Mills and Boon romances and Westerns and before the greetings cards. The bigger boxed kits, like the one of the Apollo rocket, were on a shelf above the Dinky toys.

I was promiscuous in my choice of subjects, though any plane with unusually shaped wings or an exciting name generally caught my attention. The Grumman F6F Hellcat fitted into the latter category and the Vought F4V-1A Corsair (with its inverted gull wing) and the Westland Lysander IIIA (odd lozenge-shaped wings) into the former. The Hawker Typhoon IB, meanwhile, covered both bases. (The Typhoon also fired wing-mounted rockets and – and this was a clincher – had been piloted by *Battle Picture Library* air ace Wing Commander Robert 'Battler' Britton.) There was a gigantic Sunderland flying boat too, its vast body like the bill of some African wading bird; an equally mighty Flying Fortress (a particular favourite of mine thanks to its name and huge selection of revolving turrets and machine guns); a Mitsubishi A6M Zero; a North American Mustang P-51K; a Gloster Gladiator MkII, three of which, *Faith*, *Hope* and *Charity*, had defended Malta, the only land-mass ever to win a VC – and that's official.

As well as military aircraft I also built a De Havilland DH88 Comet. I was attracted to this plane because, alone among Airfix kits, it was made of bright red plastic. The Comet was one of the first kits Airfix had issued, appearing in 1957. The real Comet had been built in 1934. Aeroplanes had filled the public with excitement back in the 1930s. That was why my father's brothers had learned to fly – for the glamour of it. The Comet owed its celebrity status to a single event: victory in the Victorian Centenary Air Race from Mildenhall to Melbourne. Another kit I built, the Supermarine S6 seaplane, was arguably even more famous than the Comet. The S6 had won the Schneider Trophy, the aviation equivalent of the Americas Cup. Aircraft from Britain, the United States and Italy competed for the Schneider Trophy annually from 1913 to 1931. Tens of thousands of people turned up to watch the race in glamorous locations such as Monaco, Naples, Venice and, well, Bournemouth.

I bought my kits with my pocket money on Saturday morning and spent the rest of the day sitting in my bedroom, doors and windows firmly shut, fan heater turned up to the max, glueing bits of plastic together with polystyrene cement.

The fumes swirled about the room until they were so thick they were practically congealing on the walls. No wonder my head was filled with strange and wondrous visions. Nowadays you can buy glue that is solvent and odour free, of course. But where's the fun in that?

Whatever I built, whether it was Monty's Humber staff car (with female driver) or a Sopwith F1 Camel, two things were guaranteed: none of the joints would be quite flush and there would be clouds of fluff stuck all over it. I don't know where the fluff came from, presumably from the same mysterious source as the stuff that gathers in your navel, though as far as I recall it wasn't blue. However it got there, the result was always the same – my Messerschmitt Bf109 looked more like an Afghan hound than a fighter plane.

The plastic aeroplane kit was a British invention. The world's first, a Blackburn B-6 Shark torpedo bomber, was issued by FROG in 1936. FROG was based in Merton, south-west London, and founded by the Wilmot brothers, Charles and John, along with Joe Mansour. Mansour was a professional model-maker. He had been one of the craftsmen employed on what may well be the most prestigious scale-building project in history – the doll's house, designed by Sir Edwin Lutyens, that was made for Queen Mary in 1924 and, to this day, still fills up an entire episode of *Blue Peter* at least once every eighteen months. Mansour had already patented a system of making lightweight papier mâché fuselages for model aircraft when the Wilmot brothers joined him. Together they formed FROG and began their model-making empire with a range of ready-to-fly stick and tissue paper rubber band-powered aircraft. Later, to distinguish the new plastic models from the flying planes they called them Penguin because penguins are flightless. You may well be thinking that frogs are pretty much flightless as well, but in the case of the kit-manufacturing company FROG was an acronym for First to Rise Off Ground and, later, Flies Right Off Ground.

FROG went on making kits until the early 1940s, when more pressing needs for materials stopped production. The Wilmots and Mansour spent the war designing gliders and pilotless drone aircraft for the RAF under the guidance of the novelist Nevil Shute. When the fighting stopped they went back to working in small scale again, inventing the Jetex motor, an ingenious miniature jet engine powered by pellets of gas-releasing nitrates. Jetex motors were used for the vehicles in the Gerry Anderson puppet shows. When Captain Scarlet's Spectrum Pursuit Vehicle speeds along the road the thing that is propelling it and blowing up those dust clouds is a Jetex motor. Joe Mansour had built the world's most famous doll's house, invented the plastic kit, helped win the war *and* made the engines that powered *Thunderbirds*. The fact that he never received a knighthood is a national disgrace.

FROG's first plastic kit had been made from cellulose acetate. Later plastic kits would be made using polystyrene, a lightweight plastic polymer made from vinyl benzene. Polystyrene was accidentally discovered by a German apothecary named Eduard Simon back in 1839, but since there was limited demand for disposable coffee cups and ceiling tiles in those days it wasn't until 1922 that another German scientist, Hermann Staudinger, really investigated the material fully. Staudinger spent the next thirty years studying polymers, and by the 1930s polystyrene was being produced all over the world. Staudinger's work earned him the Nobel prize for chemistry in 1953.

The Airfix company was founded in 1939 by an Hungarian Jew named Nicholas Kove, who chose the name for no other reason than that it would come first in any alphabetical list of British toy manufacturers. Airfix initially made air-filled rubber toys then, after the war, Kove introduced the first

injection-moulding machines into Britain and switched the
company's entire production over to making hair combs. He
was so successful that within a couple of years Airfix was
Britain's number one comb maker. In 1948 the company was
commissioned to make a limited edition promotional plastic
model of the American Ferguson tractor that was just beginning to appear in Britain. Fifty models were produced in kit
form. A year later, John Gray joined the company as general
manager. It was Gray who pioneered the wholesale move into
models. In 1954 Airfix issued its first real construction kit, a
model of Sir Francis Drake's ship, the *Golden Hind*. The kit
was sold exclusively through Woolworth's, who baulked at the
original recommended retail price of four shillings and got
Airfix to halve it. The model, launched to tie in with the
dawning of what was ambitiously dubbed the New Eliza-
bethan Era was a massive success. Kove was nonetheless
unsure about the viability of the plastic kits. Actually, that's
not true. He was convinced they would fail. When his designers produced the prototype of the Supermarine Spitfire MkV
kit in 1955 he was so cross he threatened to dock the costs of
making it from their wages. It ended up the biggest selling
model kit in history.

Airfix were the vanguard. By 1970 there were dozens of
companies all across the globe making plastic kits. Riko,
Tamiya, Hasegawa, Italaerei, Esci, Heller, Historex, Revell,
Lindberg, Nichimo, Bandai, Imai, Aosina, Protar, Eidai, Cox,
Rovex Tri-Ang, Otaki, Warbirds, Airframe, Neptune, Gekko,
Mania, Matchbox, Delta, Monogram, MPC and the Czech
firm Kovozavody Prostejov all churned out planes, tanks, cars
and figures. Other makers had more specialist lines. AMT
made kits of construction equipment and a range of
Leonardo Da Vinci inventions; Addar made plastic ship in a
bottle kits; William Brothers of California had a range of $\frac{1}{6}$
scale historic nine-cylinder aviation engines (the celebrated 80

h.p. Le Rhône Rotary was a top seller); Palmer Plastics made life-sized gun kits which came complete with fixings so you could mount your plastic seventeenth-century Dutch wheel-lock pistol or Caribbean pirate blunderbuss on the wall of your sitting room, just between the flying ducks and the horse brasses; Pyro made a dozen dinosaurs, at least one of which has since been declared non-existent by palaeontologists; while Aurora of Long Island, New York, produced a splendid array of ¹/₁₂ scale glow-in-the-dark horror movie creatures including a werewolf, a mummy and the Hunchback of Notre Dame. The same firm also made a range of Camelot knights, Mr Spock, a Klingon warship and a series of figures from the hit TV series *Land of the Giants*. Not to be outdone for novelty, Airfix launched a 1:1 scale range of British garden birds.

Like the real military, these plastic forces create a whole network of spin-off industries. There was enamel paint, paint brushes, air-brushes, glue, cutting tools, files, thousands of information booklets and a whole range of decals and decal-related products. Micro Sol was a liquid you painted onto the transfers on the curved fuselages of aircraft so that they didn't lift or crack when they dried, Floquil weathering sets were pots of paints designed to make your AFVs look genuinely dirty, Liquaplate gave a realistic silver finish, Rub 'n Buff did the same job for steel and the Les Rationelles Super-30 (imported from France) was the world's best and most versa-tile electric-powered mini-drill.

Scale Models, *Military Modelling* and *Modelworld* magazines were full of descriptions of how to convert plastic kits. The idea was that you bought a standard kit, then you trimmed some bits off it with your X-acto modelling knife, stuck on some extra bits you had fashioned from chunks of sprue or sheets of Plastruct plasticard, or bought from the exciting Armtec range of battlefield accessories (three nationalities of jerrycan as well as pioneer tools and tow chains from around the globe) and filled and packed any gaps with an evil-smelling filler – known as 'soup' – which was made by mixing polystyrene shavings with polystyrene cement and produced such a foul stink that, had it been done on an industrial scale, it would have resulted in the United Nations imposing sanctions. A different paint job and sheet of rubdown transfers from the Letraset or Modelmark range of international decal sets completed the change.

Using these methods you could convert an Airfix $^1/_{72}$ 1912 Model T Ford into a First World War lorry, a Monogram $^1/_{48}$ Curtis P-40B into a Curtis P-36A, a Tamiya $^1/_{35}$ British Matilda into an Australian Matilda Frog with flame-thrower, an Ensign $^1/_{1200}$ Narvik class German destroyer into the earlier Leberecht Maass class German destroyer, and so on and so on.

Outsiders may wonder why you would bother buying a kit if it wasn't the one you actually wanted. The answer to this is simple: the kit you actually wanted did not exist. Despite the combined efforts of the plastic kit-making factories of Britain, Europe, the United States and Japan, the fact was that whole armies of obscure AFVs, planes, ships, ordnance and troops remained totally unavailable. And those, of course, were just the ones that had caught your eye while flicking through Macksey and Batchelor's *Tank: A History of the Armoured Fighting Vehicle*, Blandford's *Bombers, Patrol and Transport Aircraft 1914–1919* or Niels M. Saxtorph's *Warriors and Weapons 3000 BC to AD 1700 in Colour*.

That, at least, is the practical explanation of the conversion obsession. There is a psychological reason behind it too. By doing a conversion you took a mass-produced item and made it into something personal and unique. You took the kit out of the hands of the man who had designed it and made it your own. It was like a dog cocking its leg on a lamppost, though not that much like it, admittedly. The thing about this mania for the different was that it created a paradox. Because if you followed the steps outlined in the conversion articles in the hobby magazines you were not making anything personal and unique at all. You were simply replacing the plans of the original designer at Airfix or Hasegawa with the plans of some bloke with acne and sideburns and a semi-detached executive home in Hitchin. The conversion articles were therefore entirely purposeless, save in one respect – they told you what someone else had already done, so you knew there was absolutely no point in doing that yourself.

Despite the fact that my ability to make the model in the box was questionable I quickly embraced the idea of conversions. To some, this may seem to have been unwise. After all, if I couldn't make an adequate job of the basic kit what were the chances of mastering this more advanced skill? My attitude was different. To my mind, it was not the difficulty of the basic kits that had defeated me, but their simplicity. I was like Einstein trying to open a tin of sardines, a genius flummoxed by the everyday. And, leaving aside the genius business, in some ways I was right. The more complicated something is the more opportunities it offers to disguise your mistakes. Every chef knows that an elaborate dish offers ample opportunity to recover, whereas if you bollocks up an omelette there is nowhere to hide it but in the dustbin. Having said that, I am forced to admit that my conversions were just as crap and fluffy as my original efforts. Luckily I was soon to discover another, more lasting interest.

I first discovered Airfix H0/00 soldiers on holiday in Ireland. My dad and I were supposed to be fishing, but it rained almost constantly and when the rain stopped the midges bit like hell and the trout didn't. After a week we abandoned angling altogether. There were some Irish boys my age in the

caravan next to ours, but they refused to play football with me
because they said it was 'a garrison sport'. (To Irish national-
ists soccer was a game brought in by the British military –
they played the indigenous Celtic games of hurling and
Gaelic football.) I was forlorn. Then, one day, in the newspaper shop in the cattle-market town of Ballinrobe I
discovered a huge cache of boxes of Airfix soldiers. Possibly
in tacit acknowledgement of the Republic of Ireland's less
than glorious role in the conflict, there were none of the usual
Second World War figures. Instead, there was box upon box
of figures from the Great War – British infantry and horse
artillery, Germans in pickelhaubes, French *poilu* in greatcoats
and American doughboys in Smokey the Bear hats. I bought
a box of each and played with them for hours on the fold-
down dining table in our caravan, using cushions and a mint
green tablecloth to form a rolling landscape.

I had recently become obsessed with stories and films
about miniature people. I read all the *Borrowers* books and *The
Little Grey Men.* My favourite TV cartoon was the *Micro
Ventures* series in which Professor Carter and his family were
shrunk down to the size of a beetle and went exploring in a
car the size of a matchbox; my favourite TV programme was
Land of the Giants, in which human space explorers crashed on
a planet where everything was twelve times normal size. Now,
as the rain drummed on the roof and the chemical toilet
belched acrid fumes, I crouched low over the table and
viewed the scene with the eyes of a 20mm tall Tommy. The
Yanks had a Lewis machine gun and the French had bicy-
clists. *Plus ça change.*

A friend who is keen on Airfix told me that when she and
fellow fanatics got together of an evening they often played
Airfix charades. In Airfix charades, she explained, a person
strikes a pose and the others have to guess which figure it is.
She said her favourite was the German infantry officer. I

could picture him instantly. He was wearing jackboots, jodhpurs and a cap, aiming a Luger, his spare hand poised delicately over his hip. If you'd removed the pistol his position was pretty much the same as the infamous pouting point that had served Victoria Beckham so well during her days in the Spice Girls. I imagine that when the soldiers were alone in the box the officer would say, 'Tell me what you want, what you really, really want.' And the Panzerfaust crew would chirrup back, 'We'll tell you what we want, what we really, really want – a thousand-year Reich!'

If I had to choose a pose I would call for a partner and do the American First World War infantrymen 'carrying ammunition box'. They were both running with right knee bent and left foot kicking out behind, each clutching one side-handle of the ammo case. Despite their uniforms the effect was distinctly non-martial. They looked like two thoroughly nice young men skipping across a meadow with a picnic hamper.

Plastic had been around for a very long time. Celluloid was invented in 1870 by John Wesley Hyatt who promptly put it to immediate and vital use in the manufacture of billiard balls. Alexander Parkes of Hackney Wick had patented Parkesine in 1862 and gone bankrupt two years later. Galalith, a substance made from milk protein, had been around since the 1890s. Oddly enough, even in France no one considered the economic benefits of fashioning toy soldiers from a by-product of the cheesemaking industry, though Coco Chanel used it to make jewellery. Bakelite was invented in 1907, and in Britain Beetle thiourea, introduced in 1928 as Beetleware, was used to make tea-sets, despite the obvious problems of persuading people to drink out of something developed by the British Cyanide Company. Surprisingly, then, the first plastic infantrymen did not appear until as late as 1952, brought to the world by the French company Société d'Édition Générale Objets Moules, or SEGOM as they are known to save ink. The first British plastic soldiers were produced a year later by a Pole, Meyer Zang, who later sold the company to Britain's who produced them under the Herald brand. (The British modelmaking industry had been greatly enriched by immigrants. The famous Britain's Agincourt knights were the creation of a German Jew, Otto Gottstein, who, like Philip Ullman and Arthur Katz, the founders of Mettoy (makers of Corgi cars), had escaped from Nazi Germany. Roy Belmont-Maitland, the founder of Tradition, had also evaded Hitler. Add to that Kove and Mansour and you can see that this miniature world was a distinctly international one.) The first Airfix polystyrene figures – the Guards Band – appeared in 1959; the German Second World War infantry combat group, complete with PAK anti-tank gun and two figures armed with flame-throwers, was delivered to the world a month before I was.

When I came back from Ireland I stopped buying plastic kits and started buying the soldiers: Ancient Britons and Romans; Eighth Army and Afrika Korps (the 'ps' traditionally sounded, giving the impression of a unit of dead bodies); Red Indians and US Cavalry; Confederate and Union infantry; Arabs and Foreign Legion. I added to the ranks with cheap 'Empire Made' pirate versions of the Airfix figures that came dozens to the bag and were invariably enmeshed in flash. Flash was the plastic that escaped from the mould during the casting process. Basically, the mould was in two halves and if these didn't fit together tightly when the mould went into the centrifuge polystyrene leaked out through the cracks, so that the figures emerged surrounded by a thin film of plastic, like the aura of a saint. After a while I started to paint them. I went to the newsagent and looked at the little screw-topped bottles of Airfix enamel paints. The range was divided into two types, gloss and matt. I bought gloss because I had no idea what matt meant.

Airfix's figure output was varied but haphazard. Artillery and cavalry were generally AWOL, the Germans in both major conflicts strangely – and perhaps deliberately – left chronically undermanned. As a result, conversion mania soon gripped me again. The military hobby press – *Military Modelling, Battle, Wargamer's Newsletter* and *Airfix Magazine* – were full of elaborate descriptions of how to turn a Red Indian brave into a Han Chinese cavalryman, or a Napoleonic cuirassier into one of Cromwell's Ironsides using tissue paper, plasticine, gardening wire and a heated knife blade. (Hot blades cut more cleanly through plastic. They also burn your mother's best tablecloth.) It was always recommended that, to avoid the cavalryman falling from his mount, you secure him in the saddle by heating a pin in a candle flame and then, when it was red hot, shoving it through the underbelly of the horse and up into the rider's arse. The accompanying diagram looked like something from a 'how to' manual for the Spanish Inquisition.

There was a whole lot of smells associated with polystyrene kits and figures: white spirit and lead-based enamel paints were harsh and chemical, turpentine warm and mellow, the brush-cleaning equivalent of cognac. Glues all had their own particular scent, from fruity UHU to fishy Evo-Stik. Undoubtedly the nicest smell, though, was banana oil which, contrary to what you might think, isn't actually made from bananas, it just smells of them. It's actually a type of amyl acetate and is also used as a flavouring in chewing gum and as a solvent in nail polish remover. I find these two facts somewhat disturbing.

A jar of banana oil was de rigueur for the figure converter. Aeromodellers used it to tauten and harden the tissue paper on the wings of balsa wood aircraft. In the 1960s, before the invention of self-hardening epoxy putties such as Green Stuff and Milliputt, wargamers used banana oil to form a tough, resilient coat round plasticine. I used it a lot in 1975 when I was converting a battalion of Airfix First World War Germans into British colonial infantry *c*.1879 by putting plasticine sun-helmets over their pickelhaubes. I spent an entire summer holiday doing that and listening to a cassette of Bob Dylan's *Blood on the Tracks*. To this day, I can't smell an over-ripe plantain without thinking of the Battle of Isandlwana and singing the opening verse of 'Tangled Up in Blue'.

As a boy I loved my Airfix figures. Why, then, did I grow to dislike plastic soldiers so much? Anatomically they were much better proportioned than lead figures, the detailing was clear and precise, the animation undoubtedly superior. And yet . . . The problem was they were, literally, lightweight. There was a sense of impermanence about anything made of plastic, of built-in obsolescence.

Nowadays, because of the fear that at some point we're going to end up buried under our own rubbish, we tend to think of plastic as indestructible; unfortunately for the plastic modeller that is very far from true. The problem with plastic is that it is naturally brittle. To make it more flexible you have to add a chemical agent – a 'plasticiser' – to it. Over time this evaporates and the plastic returns to its original state. Airfix kits and figures made in the 1960s are now as friable as old biscuits.

Luckily there was a way round this, if you got to the figures fast enough. You could soak them in a splendid American product called Dash Dandy. Dash Dandy was designed to stop the plastic dashboards of elderly motor cars snapping off whenever anyone slapped them in rage because they were stuck behind a caravan. If you dunked your figures in Dash Dandy you'd get years more life out of them before they turned to dust and got sucked up in the Hoover.

By the late 1970s the plastic kit industry had crashed. Oil prices had risen, forcing up prices, while modellers had realised that once you had made the kits there was little you could do with them except stick them on a shelf and watch them crumble away because you'd never even heard of Dash Dandy. In 1981 Airfix went bust. They were bought by Palitoy and so could justifiably claim to have been rescued by Action Man. By then, however, I too had moved on.

5

Movement – All Arms

'I am not putting the knock on dolls. It's just that they are something to have around only when they come in handy . . . like cough drops.'

Sky Masterson, *Guys and Dolls*

'Me and our kid had a tortoise called Bernard,' my friend TK said.

'Bernard?' I said.

'After Bernard Cribbins. He'd done those records, hadn't he?' TK started singing. 'Tried to shift it, Couldn't even lift it, We was getting nowhere—'

'Don't give up the day job.'

'It's mainly evenings, actually.'

TK's mobile rang. TK is a taxi-driver from Cannock in Staffordshire. He has a variety of ring tones on his mobile. He has different ones for different people so that when he's driving his cab he can tell who's calling without having to look at the display screen. One day when I was in his car with him, the phone rang with the *Mission: Impossible* theme. He said it was one of his regular clients, a woman from Shrewsbury. I asked why she had *Mission: Impossible*. He replied, 'Because she's this big fat lass and I always think it'll be impossible to get her in the car door.' When TK's wife calls the phone emits a Tarzan yell. This time it was Willie

Nelson singing 'Crazy'. 'My mate Rich,' TK said, 'he's a psychiatric nurse.'

When TK had finished on the phone – 'Rich's done some Mamelukes of the Imperial Guard for me. Lovely paint job. Ink washes and everything' – he said, 'We'd wanted a parrot, but our mum had a thing about birds' feet. Turned her stomach to look at them, she said. So we ended up with a tortoise instead.'

'Did you teach him to talk?' I said.

'You're a bit of a cheeky monkey, you, aren't you?' TK said. 'No, we didn't teach Bernard to talk. But we had brilliant fun with him, anyhow. We used to play this game, right.' TK started chuckling just at the thought of it. 'We had this 54mm plastic Britain's German artillery officer. Cap, Luger and binoculars. Came with the PAK 38 50mm anti-tank gun gift set.

'What we'd do is, we'd stick the officer onto Bernard's back with some plasticine and we'd pretend he was Rommel in his tank.'

I said that I could see that, though somewhat lacking in firepower, Bernard would have been a reasonable likeness for a panzer.

'Oh, he was,' TK said, 'especially after our kid painted the swastikas on his shell.

'Me and our kid,' TK continued, 'would stick Rommel on Bernard's back and put him in the middle of the lawn, then we'd take cover in the undergrowth and try and knock him off with rounds of mortar fire. Obviously it wasn't real mortar fire, it was just clods of soil, but they exploded when they hit the ground, like.

'The tactic was,' he continued, 'to try to disable Rommel's panzer by first giving Bernard a bit of a fright so he pulled his head and feet in. When that happened Jerry was a sitting duck to Captain Bulldog Brown and the men of 5 Commando.'

TK paused for a moment's thought. Then he said, 'Kids wouldn't get away with it nowadays, throwing clods at a pet. They'd call the psychiatrists in, wouldn't they?'

I said they would, but that even with recent advances in mental health care the psychiatrists would still probably struggle to help a traumatised tortoise.

'I don't think we realised it was cruel,' TK said. 'I mean, I really loved Bernard. I cried buckets when he had . . . The Accident.'

TK said that his family had been going away on their annual holiday. They usually left Bernard with TK's cousin, but this summer the cousin was away too so there was no one he could go to. 'Me and our kid wanted to take him to Blackpool with us,' TK said, 'take him on the beach. But Mum said they wouldn't let him in the boarding house. "It's strictly no pets," she said. We told her we'd smuggle him in and out wrapped in our swimming towels, but she wasn't having it. Truth is, she wasn't much more fond of tortoises than she was of parrots. She said seeing Bernard munching a lettuce leaf put her right off. Said it was like watching a little bald old man chewing a sandwich without his teeth in. Our granddad, in other words.'

So they had decided to leave Bernard in the garden where he would be able to help himself to the plants. 'There wasn't anything special,' TK said, 'because our dad didn't care for flowers. He thought they looked untidy. He turned the soil in the beds over twice a year and he weeded them, but he never planted anything. He'd been a sergeant in the Welsh Guards and he couldn't bear anything that wouldn't stand up straight.

'The only trouble was our mum was worried Bernard would escape from the garden,' TK said. I pictured a tortoise with swastikas painted all over it trundling round the streets of the West Midlands, and I saw her point.

'Well, our dad had an idea. He drilled a hole in Bernard's shell, threaded some string through it and tied it to a post he'd banged into the middle of the lawn. He figured that way Bernard would be able to roam around and get to food and water, but he wouldn't be able to tunnel out under the fence.'

It had seemed like an ideal solution. When they came back from Blackpool a fortnight later, however, a grisly sight greeted them. 'Instead of just roaming about at random,' TK said, 'Bernard must have walked round the lawn in a strictly clockwise direction. Every circuit he made wrapped the string round the post in the centre of the grass. And over those couple of weeks he'd gone round and round and round, and the string had gradually got shorter and shorter and shorter.

'When we found him he was tipped right up on his back end.' TK imitated a spread-eagled tortoise, tilting his head to one side and flopping out his tongue. 'Bernard was bound to that post like an Apache's captive,' he said, 'and dead as a door nail.'

He let the horror of the scene sink in. 'It was a dreadful pity,' he said later. 'Apart from anything else, me and our kid had bought these new Action Men from a shop off the Golden Mile and we'd been planning to use Bernard as an armoured personnel carrier.'

Action Man combat-rolled into the life of British boys in 1966. He was accompanied by a jaunty, deep-voiced advertising jingle in the style of Frankie Laine's theme for, well, just about anything Frankie Laine did a theme for, really. Palitoy of Coalville, Leicestershire, manufactured 'the movable fighting man' under licence from American toy giants Hasbro.

Action Man was a straight replica of Hasbro's GI Joe figures, which had premiered in toy stores in 1964. Maybe straight isn't quite the right word in this context, though. The original Action Man came in three guises – soldier, sailor and pilot. Arranged in a line they looked like the inspiration for the Village People, an impression the 1974 decision to add a Sioux brave to the line-up did little to alleviate.

It had been touch and go whether GI Joe made it to the shelves at all. The situation in Vietnam was escalating and Hasbro were well aware that sales of war toys tended to dip when there was a real war going on. Hasbro president Merrill Hassenfeld had been faced with a tough choice between putting his company's weight behind Joe (designed by Don Levine) and a miniature grocer's shop – the brainchild of Rube Klamer. After careful consideration the president decided to back the military and Joe went into development. This phase of operations was carried out with immense secrecy. Fittingly, the future Action Man even had a code-name: The Robot. His launch fully vindicated Hassenfeld's faith. GI Joe generated $17 million in sales in his first year of production.

GI Joe had been named in honour of a 1940s film about the American war correspondent Ernie Pyle. Pyle is perhaps best known in Britain as a pun in one of Ernest Hemingway's only recorded jokes – 'I am Ernie Haemorrhoid, the poor man's Pyle.' GI Joe caught on all over the world. In fascist Spain he was issued as Geyperman, while in France he appeared as Group Action Joe, just in time for the Paris student riots.

A British rival, Tommy Gun, was launched in a swift counter-offensive against the American invader. Tommy was smaller and weedier than Action Man. Perhaps this was the result of wartime food shortages. Rationing in the UK hadn't been abolished until 1955; to my generation the phrase 'When I was your age I'd never even seen a banana' was as familiar as birdsong. Despite coming armed with a rather tasty Sterling SMG, Tommy couldn't get the better of Action Man. He was a fake and an impostor. He was like those *Top of the Pops* albums that featured all the chart hits but not by the original artists. Besides, Action Man was a hardened combat veteran. In his native land he had already fought and defeated another rival, Mattel's Big Jim, despite the fact that Jim had biceps that actually bulged when you bent his arm.

The first thing that had to be established about Action Man was that he was *not* a doll, he was a 'poseable action figure'. Just because you were dressing and undressing something that was roughly the same size as Barbie and was made by the same company that produced Sindy, Tressy and Tiny Tears, didn't mean you were playing with dolls, no matter what your mum might occasionally say on the subject. This was very important. Because playing with dolls was the second most girly thing a boy could do (the first most girly thing a boy could do was, of course, to hang around with girls).

My first Action Man was, unsurprisingly, the soldier. Like all Action Men he came with a training manual that claimed 'You can move your Action Man into positions that a real life soldier can assume.' Beneath this headline was a series of line drawings apparently showing Action Man taking part in the local adult education yoga class. He also had a dog tag. 'Soldiers wear them so if they get killed people will still know who they are,' my friend Deano explained helpfully.

'But couldn't they tell by looking at his face?' I asked.

'Not if his head had been blown off with a bazooka,' Deano replied.

Action Man came in a box with bullet holes in it, had a fetching scar on his cheek that suggested he might have been a duelling student in Heidelberg and a cap of plastic hair (black, brown, blond or auburn) so hard it could deflect heavy artillery rounds with ease. No details are given as to who the life model was for GI Joe, but Action Man always put me in mind of Frank Sinatra. Sinatra's latest war movie, *Von Ryan's Express*, had come out around the time Action Man had appeared in the shops. In it Sinatra had played a Nazi general. But he was a good and noble Nazi general. Well, as good and noble as anybody could be when played by Frank Sinatra.

Future events add weight to this theory. In the 1970s Palitoy brought out an Action Man with hair that was described as 'realistic', though frankly it was only realistic if you happened to know somebody who had hair that resembled the stubble on a carpet tile. Surprisingly, the idea was considered so brilliant that in the States Hasbro copied it. Oddly enough, Frank Sinatra had a well-publicised and groundbreaking hair transplant at around the same time. Coincidence? I think not.

The scar on the cheek was all part of Hasbro's policy of making GI Joe so overtly masculine that he couldn't in any way be confused with a doll, even by your mother. It had a more prosaic value, too: the scar made his face unique and therefore patentable. It should be said that the scar had to work pretty hard to establish Action Man's manliness, because in other areas his masculinity was sadly lacking.

GI Joe's crotch and what to do with it had been the cause of much concern to Hasbro. On the one hand they wanted him to be a real man, on the other they didn't want to frighten the customers. They settled on a compromise. GI Joe would come in moulded-on blue trunks, with a significant bulge in the front of them. Unfortunately for Joe, when the moulds were being made in Japan a cost-conscious local production engineer pointed out that removing the pants and the bulge would save 1.5 cents per figure. And so Action Man was emasculated for the price of a fruit salad chew.

The Action Man soldier came in what were described as 'regulation cut' denim fatigues and a plastic cap. Just whose regulation the cut was based on I was never sure. At the age of seven the only uniform I had ever seen that looked like what my Action Man was wearing were the ones sported by the army of the Eastern European People's Republic in the TV series *Mission: Impossible*. This was hardly auspicious, since the soldiers of the Eastern European People's Republic were total morons. Every week Jim Phelps and his gang easily outwitted whole battalions of them, generally using an ingenious plan that involved the distracting powers of a woman with large pointy breasts, played by a blonde actress who had previously appeared in *A Man Called Ironside*.

Looking at the first Action Man uniform now, its origins remain a puzzle. In fact, the fatigues and the cap call to mind one of the enemies from whom GI Joe should have been keeping America safe. The only additions that early soldier figure needs are a bushy beard and a big cigar and he would be a dead ringer for Fidel Castro.

Clearly then, for any combat-fashion-conscious boy this generic army outfit simply would not do for dressing his poseable action figure. Luckily, Action Man had an extensive wardrobe of alternative clothing from which to choose. Argyll and Sutherland Highlander, 17th/21st Lancer, saboteur, frogman – you name it, Action Man had the outfit.

The only trouble was lack of funds. Action Man was expensive. He retailed at 32s 6d, the cost in those days of twenty pints of beer – nowadays the equivalent price would be around £45. Given that defence spending for most junior warlords amounted to a couple of shillings a week, hard choices had to be made. The commander of every Action Man platoon was forced to make agonising decisions. Did you buy the Bivouac machine gun set, or the medic set (with miniature bottle of blood for transfusions), or the Beachhead assault flame-thrower? Or did you save the money and put it towards the Australian jungle fighter uniform, which had the advantage of coming with a rather vicious-looking machete. ('It was for cutting through the undergrowth. They didn't use it as a weapon,' my dad informed me. Yeah, right, Dad.)

There was a way around this. You could collect tokens in the form of red stars from Action Man boxes and stick them onto a special card. When you had saved enough you could send off to Palitoy for a free Action Man. This was a system familiar to me from Green Shield stamps and from Embassy coupons. Embassy coupons were little blue dockets that came inside packs of Embassy cigarettes. Both my parents smoked Embassy Regals and my dad stored the coupons in a pewter beer mug on the mantelpiece. Every so often, he would get them down and we would all sit around and count them. We'd then scan the Embassy coupon catalogue to see what we could buy. You could buy everything from onyx orna-ments to hostess trolleys and patio furniture. Rumour has it that if you smoked hard enough for long enough you could accumulate enough coupons to buy yourself an oxygen tent.

Unfortunately, I was not much good at saving the Action Man tokens. I either threw the box away before I remem-bered to cut them off, or lost the card on which I'd stuck them. Besides, the word was that the Action Man they sent you was of an inferior type, weak jointed and feeble – the runt of the Action Man litter.

The Australian jungle fighter set was part of the Soldiers of the Century series which also included a Second World War Russian infantryman, an American Green Beret and a French Resistance fighter, who with his black sweater, beret and neckerchief looked like he might have spent his pre-war days hanging out on the Left Bank with Sartre and de Beauvoir.

The series also included a fantastic Nazi stormtrooper, who was more or less irresistible even though you knew he was the enemy. Not least, this was because the German uniform was so much smarter and, well, more military-looking than that of his British counterpart. The Tommy's helmet was shaped like a soup plate and covered with what appeared to be one of your mum's old hairnets; he tucked his trousers into something resembling spats; his blouson never quite met the tops of his pants; and his kitbag looked like the sort of khaki rucksack in which fishermen carried their sandwiches, thermos and pots of maggots. The German, meanwhile, had jackboots, a helmet that was all sharp angles and a shiny silver SMG. The only downside for the Jerry was that his hand grenades came with a wooden stick attached, which gave them the look of a lollipop. 'Lick on this, English pig dog!' Nazi Action Man would probably cry as he hurled his high explosive bomb at the Allied troops charging up the beach.

Action Man wasn't totally obsessed with combat, however. When not dealing out lead death to enemies of a variety of ethnic and political persuasions, he liked to relax by doing judo, mountaineering, playing football, going scuba diving, indulging in a spot of space or polar exploration, or racing a go-kart. He also had a rather splendid deep sea diving suit complete with metal boots, a big round brass-coloured helmet and a diver's knife with the sort of evil serrated edge which is vital when fighting a giant octopus.

In 1968 Talking Commander Action Man hit the shelves. In adverts, this looked like the answer to our prayers. Deano's birthday was superbly timed to coincide with the release date. The Talking Commander had a string and tag at the bottom of his throat. You pulled it out and he barked commands in clipped yet plummy tones very similar to those of Colonel White in *Captain Scarlet*. There were eight commands in all. The trouble was, they were all more or less totally unrelated and came babbling out, one after the other. You pulled the string and he snapped, 'This is your commander speaking . . . Enemy aircraft! Action stations! . . . Volunteer needed for a special mission . . . Mortar attack! Dig in! . . . Action Man

patrol, fall in!' The ordinary Action Men didn't know
whether they were coming or going.

Worst of all, TC instructed his men to 'Hold your fire until
I give the order', but never gave the order. With TC in
charge, your platoon would be overrun without discharging a
single bullet. As if that wasn't bad enough, the location of the
string meant that if you weren't careful the tag slipped down
into TC's jacket. When this happened, TC had to take his top
off before he could issue any orders. Naked from the waist up
and spouting a stream of consciousness, this clearly was not
the behaviour of an officer, unless the officer was Allen
Ginsberg. 'I should've got the jeep,' Deano said bitterly, 'or
the space capsule.' It was an incredible disappointment to us.

As, it has to be admitted, was Action Man himself.
Because, despite the promise of hours of militaristic, or just
plain manly, pleasure, Action Man struggled to deliver. He
was sold on his realism, but the only area in which he truly
replicated the world of the modern soldier was that his life
was in thrall to the machinations of the oil industry. Action
Man was made of plastic. When the price of oil went up, so
did he. In the mid-1970s, with OPEC apparently intent on
bankrupting the west, Palitoy started making Action Man's
body shell thinner and harder. He looked even more muscle-
bound than before, but he was far more likely to crack in
combat than his predecessors.

The first problem with Action Man was the cost. You
could buy dozens of Britain's $1/32$ scale figures or hundreds of
Airfix H0/00 troops for the cost of one bog standard Action
Man. Action Man was so expensive that the chances of
assembling enough figures for even a minor skirmish were
negligible. Most of us had only one Action Man to fight both
sides of any engagement. We were compelled to do a sort of
fast-change duel in which British Commando Action Man
tossed a grenade into an enemy machine gun nest then swiftly

sloughed his togs and slipped into his Wehrmacht get-up in order to yell '*Gott in Himmel! Aaaargh!*' and fly into the air. Of course, if the situation was reversed things got even more complicated. The German threw his hand grenade, dived behind a bush and re-emerged as a British infantryman just in time to cry out, 'Lumme, ol' squarehead has launched one of his "ice-cream cornets". I'd better grab it and—' A quick snap of poppers and he was a passing French maquis fighter offering a typical comic strip commentary on events: '*Sacre bleu!* It looks like Tommy iz going to give ze Bosh a taste of 'iz own medicine.' Then a jiggling on of jackboots and '*Achtung! The Britisher dog has thrown back my grenade. Aaargh!*' All of which was an awful lot of effort for limited dramatic reward.

Mainly, though, it was the figure itself that was the problem. It was very hard to get him to stand up, for one thing. This was because Action Man – with his impressive pecs, bulging shoulders and pert bottom – was very top heavy, a trait he shares with Barbie, though for different reasons. On parade, he regularly fell flat on his face like a fainting recruit. The snowshoes that came with the mountain troop set were a big help in keeping him upright, but you can't really wear them when you're on patrol with the Anzacs in the jungles of Borneo. Getting him to kneel was equally difficult, and could only successfully be resolved by bending his feet outwards so that he looked like the victim of some hideous limb malformation.

Then there were Action Man's hands. These were apparently designed to grip things, but what – a cocktail glass, a meerschaum pipe, a clarinet? Certainly they didn't seem to grip weapons. The knife dropped feebly from his hands. To get a Sten gun into Action Man's mitts and aimed at the enemy you had to twist the arms into such weird angles it looked like he was doing an impression of Jerry Lewis in *The*

Nutty Professor. If you put a pistol in his right hand he pointed it at his own left arm – as if he was seeking to buy a trip back to Blighty with a self-inflicted wound.

His musculature was grotesque as well. When you twisted his arms his bulging biceps divided in half, giving him the look of a Picasso abstract. If you took his boots off in a hurry his feet would come off too. To get them back on you'd spend ages fiddling about trying to grab the clear plastic joint and yank it out, while in the background Talking Commander Action Man – who had made the mistake of diving into the kitchen sink in the scuba diving outfit – drawled incomprehensibly, 'Thiiiiiis faaaaall arse air maaaaan!'

Even the splendid deep sea diving set had its limitations. Action Man was simply too tall to go deep sea diving in the bath. Even when he was lowered to the bottom, borne down by the weight of those enormous metal boots, the top nuts of his helmet still protruded above the surface of the water. The only place Deano and I could find that was the requisite depth was an old wooden rain butt near his granddad's greenhouse. Lowered over the side of this using the exciting winch that came with the set, Action Man disappeared into the murky depths, and for a happy few moments Deano and I imagined he was down at the bottom of the barrel prising open a treasure chest or battling for his life against a man-eating tadpole. Unfortunately, possibly due to the excitement created by our hero's imaginary actions, or because he had been distracted by the urge to pick the top off a particularly choice scab on his knee, Deano momentarily lost control of the winding gear and it toppled into the rain butt with a splash and sank.

Action Man was stranded at the bottom of the seabed. By my calculations, based on the scientific application of maths and having seen the John Wayne film *Donovan's Reef* on several occasions, he only had enough oxygen to keep him going for three minutes. In a bid to get him out I balanced on a stone, leaned over and plunged my arms into the butt with my face half an inch above the water. At this point Deano's grand-mother appeared from behind some vast rhubarb plants. She was a small but ferocious woman who wore a belted gabar-dine mackintosh twenty-four hours a day, but only put her false teeth in on special occasions such as VE Night and the Coronation. Gums gnashing, she came scuttling over and pulled me away from the rain butt, snarling, 'What if you'd fallen in head first and drowned, eh? You'll be the bloody death of me you dozy little buggers.' She then cuffed us both around our heads to show her concern for our safety and sent us on our way. Deano's dad later rescued Action Man from the murky depths using a garden fork. Unfortunately, one of the prongs punctured his dry suit and he was never able to submerge successfully again.

The go-kart looked like it would be fun, but it wasn't. It was remote control. This meant you could stop it and start it using a handset that was attached to the kart by a wire. The wire was really, really short. You couldn't operate it when standing upright, you had to crouch. This meant that when Action Man set off you had to run after him with your knees bent, dodging around tables and dogs like Groucho Marx chasing an heiress. The alternative was to turn the steering wheel so that the kart went in a circle. That meant that either you spun around and around until you were dizzy or Action Man went round and round you until he was as tightly bound to your legs as Bernard the Tortoise had been to that lawn post.

The whole thing was summed up by the Action Man foot-baller. He came with a frame that allowed him to 'really kick' the ball. You had to clamp him into it using a series of braces that closed around his waist and legs like something from Frankenstein's laboratory. When he was finally secure you could pull a lever and get him to weakly toe-poke the ball. If you timed it perfectly it travelled about fifteen inches. And that was Action Man in a nutshell. He was a useless muscle-bound lunk.

His total hopelessness was pointed up every week in the *Beano* by the actions of General Jumbo. This was the comic strip to inspire any model-obsessed child. Jumbo's real name was Alfie Johnson, but he was nicknamed Jumbo either because he had big ears or was grossly overweight – accounts vary – but suffice to say there wasn't much in the way of an anti-bullying initiative in the town of Dinchester in those days. Jumbo had saved the brilliant inventor Professor Carter from being killed by a car – the Prof, typically for a man of science, was short-sighted and totally clueless when it came to self-preservation – and as a reward the inventor had given him his own radio-controlled NATO defence force made up of what pretty much amounted to robot Action Men. At the press of a button on his special wrist-mounted control panel, Alfie could summon up an air strike, a broadside from a bat-tleship or an infantry and armoured assault force with artillery support. For some reason the Prof stopped short of giving Jumbo a nuclear capability, or you can bet the bullies and burglars of Dinchester would have finished each week's strip with a mushroom cloud where their heads ought to have been. The real Action Man simply couldn't compete.

Others felt differently, of course. Over the past decade Action Man has become a very popular collectable toy, with prices for the ludicrous Talking Commander rising to £400 depending on his condition (always rubbish, as far as I was concerned). According to a report in the *Daily Mirror*, one chap with an Action Man obsession had been abandoned by his wife and children after reducing the family to penury. Mark Woodcock, thirty-one, told the paper that his habit was 'part of my nostalgia for childhood. That's when I was happiest and carefree.' Woodcock owned 150 Action Men, enough for a fair old skirmish, though like most Action Man collectors he vigorously denied actually playing with them. Because, let's face it, that would be infantile.

I wasn't totally down on action figures per se. Once, when I went to the big auction house in Teesside with my father to spend a happy day bidding on, and failing to get anywhere close to winning, some 54mm Napoleonic figures by the 1950s French designer Roger Berdou, I noticed on the tables for the following day's sale a whole box of Evel Knievel action toys.

Evel Knievel was the American stuntman who had thrilled a generation of boys during the early 1970s by leaping over double-decker buses on his motorbike while dressed in a costume apparently borrowed from the Las Vegas-period Elvis Presley. Knievel had finally come to grief – psychologically, if not physically – when he had made an unsuccessful attempt at jumping across the Snake River Canyon on a rocket bike. After that he had retired, and now made a living painting oils of western and wildlife scenes. Real men don't do watercolours.

The Evel Knievel poseable action figures were really great. They came with a friction drive motorbike that actually did what it showed it doing in the TV adverts – wheelies and death-defying leaps from a plastic ramp (you had to supply your own double-decker buses). I have far happier memories of the figures of the white cape-wearing stuntman than I have of Action Man. But maybe that is not so surprising. After all, as the Old Testament makes plain, the Evel Knievel men do lives after them.

My fascination with Evel Knievel and disillusion with Action Man marked a gradual move away from military hobbies towards the world of fast cars and spectacular crashes.

Grand Prix racing, rally-cross and speedway began to fill my dreams; Hot Wheels Sizzlers, Corgi Rockets and slot car sets (my dad, true to his nature, opted for a Revell $\frac{1}{32}$ scale rather than Scalextric) my bedroom floor. The soldiers, tanks and aircraft were stored away in boxes in the attic. It was only a phase. Not the beginning of the end but the end of the beginning. They would be back, in ever increasing numbers. I had not yet begun to fight.

6

Artillery Fire, Ball and Canister

Post: 'I am always fearful that when I put this game down on the table and people see the box-art they will think I am some kind of neo-Nazi.'
Reply: 'They already know you're a gamer. What other shame could possibly compare?'

Exchange on www.boardgamegeek.com

I went to a Quaker School. It was the early 1970s; hippies were everywhere, militarism in all its forms was frowned upon. I blamed the Americans for that. The war they'd embarked on in South-East Asia had turned out not to be quite so thrilling as it first appeared. In fact, all in all, it had proved to be rather unsavoury. It had ground on for ten years and still not come close to a resolution. Anyone who had watched as many war films as I had knew that you had to have an ending. Yet, despite all their experience of making movies, the Americans didn't seem to be able to come up with one.

Vietnam hung over everything like the scent of a damp bonfire. 'Violence is never the solution,' the older boys said sententiously as the common room TV screen filled with images of bombs falling from B-52s and blossoming in flashes of orange and red amidst the foliage below. And if you quibbled with their pacifist beliefs they'd bend your arm up behind your back until you begged for mercy.

It was some time around third year that the books started to appear. The older boys had them. They had graphic covers plastered with Nazi insignia and the pages gave off the whiff of something illicit, something skewed and perverse. Sometimes fourth years would turn up in our form room and, when they'd taken care of their main task of the moment (usually kicking the door of one of the metal lockers repeatedly with their cherry red Dr Marten boots – an act which would have seemed like mere mindless vandalism had they not had the presence of mind to stuff a small boy in there first), read out a passage or two to whet our appetites. One that particularly stuck in my mind featured a soldier on the Russian Front whose penis froze and dropped off.

This scene was from a novel called *Blitzfreeze*, latest in the Wehrmacht canon – and never has the word canon been more relevant to works of fiction – of a writer named Sven Hassel. The older boys were very keen on Hassel. He formed a cornerstone of their cultural life, alongside *Slade Alive!*, the *Skinhead* books of Richard Allen, Consulate Menthols and random, sadistic cruelty. Hassel was the real thing, they assured us as they spat in our hair; *Commando* comics were for kids.

You listened to older boys when they told you this stuff. If they said that T Rex were teenyboppers and you should listen to Diamond Dogs that's what you did. Well, you had to. If you said, 'Actually, I find Bowie's lyrics affected, while his much-trumpeted bisexuality is, in my view, nothing more than puerile attention seeking,' they'd have dangled you out of the first floor library window by your ankles, which was a fairly convincing argument to a coward like me.

At the prompting of the older boys, the war library of us child veterans changed rapidly and inexorably. Out went the adventures of Battler Briton and Sergeant Hurricane and in came *The Bloody Road to Death* and *The Beast Regiment*.

It was easy to see the appeal of Hassel's world to the teenage male. It was one of camaraderie, hunger, cold, loathsome authority figures and the constant threat of sudden and extreme violence. It seemed that serving in a penal battalion of a Panzer Division was not at all unlike being at boarding school, though the food was probably better.

In Hassel's books violence rumbled on as remorselessly as in a shoot 'em up computer game. It was broken only by long, rambling tales related by a character named Tiny, in a cocker-nee style not dissimilar to that of Maggot Malone. Later, I would realise that these shaggy dog stories were inspired by the ones in *The Good Soldier Švejk*. In fact, they resembled Hasek's in every particular save one – they weren't funny.

Hassel's novels were phenomenally successful. They sold fifteen million copies in Britain alone. As a result, his influence reverberated through the world of war fiction. *Battle* comic followed the Hassel template, offering a junior, illustrated version. *Rat Pack* saw a group of convicts released from prison to undertake suicide missions. *Darkie's Mob* followed the adventures of Captain Joe Darkie as he led a group of lost soldiers on a vengeance campaign against the Japanese in Burma. In *Commando* and *Valiant* the soldiers were fighting to win a war or to overthrow the Nazis – here they were just killing people for the hell of it.

Other purveyors of Nazi pulp to adolescent boys and still-adolescent men quickly emerged: H. H. Kirst, author of *The Night of the Generals* (billed as 'a spellbinding novel of murder, evil and perversity'); W. A. Ballinger (the pseudonym of Scots pulp writer Wilfred McNeilly, the man behind numerous Sexton Blake adventures), who gave us *Women's Battalion*, a thrilling Third Reich lesbian sex and violence yarn; and, the most prolific of them all, Leo Kessler, the pen name of Charles Whiting who, amongst other things, had written a well-received account of Ernest Hemingway's career as a war correspondent. Leo Kessler churned out a whole shelf full of novels with titles like *Claws of Steel*, *Death's Head* and *SS Panzer Battalion*. Importantly, Kessler's adopted surname featured the same attractive double S as that of Hassel, allowing the publisher to render it as the twin lightning strike symbol of the Schutzstaffel and build sales on what would nowadays undoubtedly be referred to as the strong public brand awareness of the SS corporate logo.

Hassel and Kessler were the type of authors whose books were sold in newsagents. In the days before chain bookstores, that was often the only place the provincial reader could buy a novel. The selection was not particularly edifying. Alongside Sven's splatter and the Mills & Boon romances, you'd find the bloody Nick Carter spy novels, Dennis Wheatley's Satanist horrors and dozens of westerns by J. T. Edson.

Edson was the biggest-selling western author in the world, quite an achievement considering he came from the East Midlands and had never even sat on a horse. When asked how he researched the background for his books he replied matter of factly that he didn't need to because in the 1960s he had watched hundreds of episodes of *Wagon Train*, *Have Gun Will Travel* and *Bonanza* while he was running his fish and chip shop in Melton Mowbray.

J. T. was joined on the shelves by dozens of other cowboy writers. It was plain by looking at them that when it came to westerns having a brusque and manly set of initials was almost as essential as having a double S in your surname was for a writer of Wehrmacht pulp. Alongside the man from Leicestershire you'd find T. V. Olsen, D. C. Benson and the somewhat less macho sounding W. C. Tuttle.

Years later, when I thought of Hassel I imagined he was some sort of pulp writing hack. The Second World War equivalent of Richard Allen, author of the *Skinhead* novels, who turned out not to be a sharp, young East End geezer but a chubby middle-aged Scots-Canadian named James Moffat who lived in Somerset. I imagined that Hassel's story would be similar. I envisaged a man from Peterborough named Chris who had never been nearer the Eastern Front than Cleethorpes.

I decided this would make a funny article for the features pages of the newspapers – 'We all thought he was a Nazi stormtrooper, but actually he was a chartered accountant from Cheam!' – so I did some research. What I found out was hugely disappointing. It turned out Hassel really had fought on the Russian Front, as a tank driver in the 27th Panzer Division. And where was the fun in that? Thwarted in my pursuit of a tongue-in-cheek tale of a man who wrote hospital romances under the name Daphne Fothergill one week and blood and guts stuff entitled *The Legion of the Damned* the next, I gave up and forgot all about Sven Hassel until I started to write this book.

Looking into it again, I found out Hassel was a Dane who had served in the German army throughout the war. In interviews he claimed that his novels carried a strong anti-war message. This seems to have slipped past the publishers who, on the covers of his books, stressed the SS in his surname. The titles didn't help, either. *Wheels of Terror* doesn't really sound like the outpourings of Mahatma Gandhi. In the 1990s Hassel told interviewers that he was unhappy about the covers of his books and had instructed his agents that, from now on, they were to be more sober and not emphasise the gore so much. Yet when a selection were re-issued as part of the Cassell Military Classics series in 2004 the twin S-es were still rendered as the lightning strikes and printed twice as large as the rest of the letters in his name. The message clearly wasn't getting through. And, from an advertising point of view, why should it?

Despite apparent public revulsion, Nazis remain very important in terms of sales. A classic example of this was the controversial cover of Avalon Hill's 1980s Second World War card game Up Front. Rodger MacGowan, a veteran graphic artist, did the box art. Since the title of the game came from a cartoon, drawn by Bill Maudlin, about the exploits of a group of GIs, MacGowan's original box art featured American combat troops. He sent it in to Avalon Hill in Baltimore. They rejected it. They wanted Germans on the box, they said. MacGowan had already had a minor run-in with the suits at Avalon Hill over his designs for the boxes of some other Second World War games. He had tried to put troops from different nations – Britain, Russia, Japan, France – on the covers only to be constantly queried over why there were no Germans. Fed up, he designed a new cover for Up Front. It featured an SS officer so angelic he made John Boy Walton look like, well, Josef Goebbels. MacGowan's view was that Avalon Hill would be so disgusted with this Aryan recruiting poster that they would return to his original design. His plan backfired: Avalon Hill accepted the new box art without a moment's hesitation. The game came out with the comely, apple-cheeked Nazi on the cover and quickly became a bestseller.

Hassel's biography was a matter of fevered Internet speculation. Hassel himself claimed to have been born Sven Pedersen and to have changed his name to Hassel, his mother's maiden name, when he joined the merchant marine aged fourteen. After military service, he said, he attempted to escape the ravages of the depression in Denmark by going to Germany and joining the Wehrmacht. He was assigned to the 7th Cavalry regiment, became a naturalised German and took part in the invasion of Poland as part of the 2nd Panzer Division. Then, exhausted by combat, he deserted, was captured and put in one of the Sonderabteilung penal battalions. Subsequently he served in the 2nd Cavalry and later the 11th and 27th Panzer regiments seeing service in every theatre except North Africa, reaching the rank of Lieutenant and winning the Iron Cross 1st and 2nd class. In 1945 he surrendered to the Russians in Berlin, was interned and then returned to Germany in 1949. An attempt to join the Foreign Legion was abandoned when he married Dorthe Jensen and went to work in a car plant instead. With his wife's encouragement, he wrote and published his first novel, *Legion of the Damned*, before collapsing with a crippling illness. In 1964 he moved to Franco's Spain for the good of his health and to write full-time. And he remains there to this day.

However, a Danish journalist named Erik Haaest was not convinced. Haaest has dedicated his life to exposing Hassel as a liar and fantasist. He said Hassel was born Børge Villy Redsted Pedersen and was actually a Danish Nazi and minor criminal who avoided military service, instead spending most of the war informing on his fellow Danes to the Gestapo. According to Haaest, the move to fascist Spain had less to do with his health than the safe haven El Caudillo offered.

If Haaest had left it there I might have believed him. Instead, he went on to allege that Hassel had been jailed by the Nazis for a litany of crimes including bicycle theft and impersonating Himmler, and that after the war he worked as a conman, passing himself off as a Viennese baron. Haaest was equally scornful of Hassel's literary output, claiming that the biggest-selling Danish author since Hans Christian Andersen is a subliterate who had a ghost writer for his first book and got his wife to write the rest, Dorthe apparently having gained a broad knowledge of the German military during her days working as a prostitute in Copenhagen. By and large, it has to be said that Haaest's account of Hassel's life is substantially less plausible than Hassel's own.

And yet there were inconsistencies in Hassel's official biography. Originally, for example, he'd claimed to have fought for Finland in the Winter War against the Soviet Union and to have been awarded the Mannerheim Cross for gallantry. When it was revealed that the Finnish military archives had no record of his service or the award Hassel quietly dropped that part of his life story and never mentioned it again. He had also told some early interviewers that he was an Austrian whose family had been liquidated by the Nazis and that he had only come to Denmark in his late teens, something which again soon disappeared.

Perhaps Haaest had a point. Maybe Hassel was an unsavoury figure. Or perhaps it was Haaest who was deluded and Hassel merely confused, thrown by the traumas of the war. As the Union General George Meade remarked: 'I don't believe the truth will ever be known, and I have great contempt for history.'

Hassel had hoped that by showing the full horror of war he would put people off it, but the massive sales of his books tend to suggest that by the 1970s it was full horror that people wanted. The same was true of war films – the further away from the actual experience of the Second World War we got the more violent they became. *Saving Private Ryan* made *The Longest Day* look like the proverbial Boy Scouts' picnic. Steven Spielberg's film is often billed as the most realistic war movie ever made. Certainly most people would think it is closer to the truth than Zanuck's film. Yet who knew more about the reality of war, Richard Todd or Tom Hanks?

PART TWO

ON CAMPAIGN

'The die is cast.'

JULIUS CAESAR

7

Rules for Advanced Players

'He's a tin soldier man living in a little tin wonderland.'
The Kinks

One Monday night TK phones. He is very excited. 'You got time to talk, buddy?' He has just come back from visiting a friend of ours, Manfred Siedlitz, who lives near Kulmbach in the wild forests of north-east Bavaria. While TK was there Manfred took him across the border to Austria to see his chum Klaus Immelmann. Recollections of the experience render TK virtually incoherent with emotion. 'This guy Klaus's house. Harry. Pal. Hey. Wow. Incredible!' TK says. His Black Country accent extends and flattens some vowels and sharpens others. It's like a free jazz musician fiddling about with the mute on his trumpet. 'From the outside, mate, it just looks like a normal, everyday, boring semi-detached house, but you go inside and . . . It is absowlooootely moind-blouwing.'

You go in through the front door of Klaus Immelmann's house, TK says, and in the hall are purpose-built floor-to-ceiling glass cabinets that fill both walls. In them are a series of $^1/_{16}$ scale soldiers painted in the uniforms of the minor German states at the time of Napoleon. There's Reuss, Waldeck, Lippe, Saxe-Weimar, Würzburg, Oldenburg, you name it, TK says, pre-1812 uniforms and post-1812, the lot, maybe four hundred of them. You go into the lounge and it's the same story. This time it's 54mm figures of the armies of Bavaria, Baden, the Rhinebund and Württemberg; beautifully detailed little dioramas using 30mm flat (two-dimensional) *Kieler Zinnfiguren* of incidents from the Battle of Eylau (1807) and the Retreat from Moscow, the last desperate charge of the Berg Lancers at the Berezina in 1812.

The basement is where Klaus prepares and paints his figures. He's got a long workbench; lamps with daylight bulbs; rows of paint pots, varnish tins and bottles of acrylic inks; magnifying glasses on stands; clamps and vices; knives and files all neatly laid out like a surgeon's tools; thousands of uniform books; signed prints by the leading authority on Napoleon's Imperial Guard, Colonel John Elting. He has cabinets here too, full of figures at various stages of preparation. Upstairs in the two bedrooms, TK continues, are more figures, 54mm, 75mm, 30mm, 1/72 scale; mainly Napoleonic, some Seven Years War, a cabinet filled with Bavarian Imperial troops from the Age of Marlborough. TK's not sure how many there are in total, but he thinks we're talking somewhere in the region of five or six thousand.

'I've got to tell you this, pal,' TK says, talking so fast now it's practically Morse code, 'even in the kitchen there's a high shelf that runs right round the room and on it there's these beautiful, immaculate 300mm resin models of Napoleon and his marshals.'

'And what does Frau Immelmann make of it?' I ask.

'Oh, Klaus's not married.'

A friend of mine who's a recovering alcoholic told me that the key thing about the descent into alcoholism is that the sort of people you drink with gradually changes. As your drinking hardens so do the drinkers you associate with. 'The way it works is you can always go on kidding yourself. You can always point to somebody sitting at the table and say, "Hey, but look, I don't drink as much as *this guy*." Then, one day, you realise – you are *this guy*.'

TK was my *this guy*. Whenever I looked around my office at the stacks of Bisley filing cabinets and the floor-to-ceiling shelf units that held A4 box files containing the fruits of an obsession that began when I bought eight 25mm Miniature Figurines 'S' range Napoleonic Grenadiers of the Imperial Guard (Kneeling at the present, Code FN12s) from a shop in Middlesbrough aged twelve on the way to watch Boro play Oxford United (1–0, Armstrong 73), and wondered if, maybe, it was time to call a halt, I thought of TK.

I don't know how many model soldiers I have. I'm frightened to count them. I can give you an idea, though: last year, when my Greek, Persian and Early Imperial Roman armies were finally complete I decided to sell the leftover figures on eBay. I rounded them all up from various boxes, box files and drawers and counted them. There were 723. This was the spare stuff, the lead equivalent of my loose change. Most of them went to a bloke called Simon in Knutsford. The parcel weighed 3.2 kilograms.

I do know what I have: Ancient Assyrians, New Kingdom Egyptians, Achmaenid Persians, Early Imperial Romans, Classical Greeks, Seleucid Persians, Carthaginians, Dacians, Sarmatians, Goths, Royalists, Roundheads, Zulus, Afghans, British and Indians and twenty-four files of Napoleonic troops containing at least 2500 infantrymen, including those of the minor German states. I don't know how many there are, but one thing I do know is that *there are nowhere near as many as TK has*.

TK, by his own estimate, has thirty-five thousand figures. Though it has to be said that at least half of them are plastic and made in the former Soviet Union, so in my book they don't count. It's plain to me that lead or white metal figures have a weight that is both literal and moral. Lead is for grown ups; plastic is what kids have. But for some reason TK just cannot be made to see sense on the issue. So we have agreed never to speak on the topic.

I wasn't sure if TK really needed a *this guy* but if he did there was Big Bill, a retired Fleet Air Arm flight sergeant. His figure collection filled up practically the whole of the ground floor of his house, most of the garage and several sheds in the garden. He walked me round it one summer afternoon, pointing at shelves, opening cabinet drawers, lifting up boxes and exclaiming, 'Ha, look at that! A brigade of Cossacks! Now, where they hell did they come from?'

Big Bill is a stocky man with white hair and a bushy white beard. He reminded me of Raymond Briggs' Father Christmas. He is merry, loud and garrulous, but with a reputation for falling out with people. One figure trader had upset him by continually calling him 'my son'. 'In the end I'd had enough,' Big Bill growled. 'I said, "Listen, you pipsqueak, I flew the Shackleton bomber that delivered the British A-bomb to Bikini Atoll, so you can stop calling me 'son' and start showing a bit of respect." He didn't like that one little bit,' Big Bill said with a triumphant chuckle. They hadn't talked since.

A few years ago, Big Bill grew disillusioned with model soldiers and began selling his collection and putting the money into Meccano and 00 railways. 'I'm building the Canadian-Pacific,' he bellowed at me down the phone. You might assume he meant a section of it, though I wouldn't rule out him doing the whole thing. He said he had sold nearly one hundred thousand figures. 'Still got about twenty-five thousand to get shot of,' he barked, 'so if you know anybody who wants one hundred and seventy-five Hittite chariots, send them in my direction.' I promised him I would.

I asked TK if Klaus Immelmann was a wargamer. 'Oh no,' said he, and I detected a slight note of superiority in his voice, 'he just has the figures. He doesn't actually *do* anything with them.'

TK and I are both wargamers. So was Big Bill. We didn't just collect model soldiers for the sake of it, we did it for a purpose. Compared to the collector's life – buy the figures, paint the figures, put them on a shelf and dust them occasionally with one of those photographer's puffer brushes – that of the wargamer was tough, both physically and mentally.

TK and I had fought against the odds on the battlefields of six continents. We had waged war with flint-tipped arrows, bronze swords, Brown Bess muskets and flame-throwers. We had lugged box files of lead weighing as much as a Scorpion tank from one end of the country to the other, on public transport. We had tasted the sweet joy of victory and watched in horror as guards divisions we had spent months assembling and painting ran screaming from the scene at the first sound of the enemy rifles. We had heard first-hand the unmistakable rat-a-tat-tat of mugfuls of twenty-sided gem dice rattling across tetrion-coated extruded polystyrene terrain boards; stood for ten, twelve, fourteen hours at a stretch at the edge of a twenty-foot by six-foot table, beneath the buzzing fluorescent tubes of an ice cold sports hall, calculating howitzer fire by adding and subtracting dozens of pertinent attack and defence factors, multiplying by the number of artillerymen in the battery, multiplying by thirty-three and then looking up the result in tables so complex they would have made a non-combatant's brain melt like toasted cheese. We had survived a three-day re-fight of the Battle of Leipzig, living only on combat rations of instant coffee, cheesy wotsits and munchmallows, sleeping on the floor beneath the battlefield at night and waking up as stiff, chilly and encrusted in crumbs as a bag of frozen chicken Kievs. The collectors were chocolate soldiers. We were combat veterans.

Despite that, I was very reluctant to tell anybody – any out-sider, I mean – about the wargaming aspect of my life. Hobbies have become a bit of a dirty word these days. In the 1960s you'd often hear friends of my granny remark approv-ingly that so and so's daughter's husband had got himself a nice little hobby. A hobby – marquetry, stamp collecting, whatever – was considered a bit of a step up from what men normally did when left to their own devices: getting drunk, betting on greyhounds and chasing hairdressers. Not any more, though. Nowadays, hobby is a word people tip-toe around. They have euphemisms for it – leisure interest, dis-placement activity. Once, I heard a woman discussing her husband's 'niche interest' and it took quite a long time before I realised she meant his passion for racing radio-controlled stock-cars.

Even amongst the inadequate milieu of hobbies, wargam-ing ranked very low. The non-believer regarded it, at best, as the province of socially inadequate geeks, at worst of gun-fetishising belligerents. In my experience, the latter is totally unfounded. Blaise Pascal said that all of man's troubles stem from his inability to sit quietly in a room alone. Most wargamers I knew would happily sit quietly in a room for hours, days, weeks – usually with a Rowney Series 34 sable paintbrush in one hand and a toy soldier in the other. If all the men on this planet spent their time colouring the brass czapka plaques on their 1810 Duchy of Warsaw voltigeurs the world would be an altogether safer place, believe me. The charge about dorks was, as you may have guessed by now, harder to refute. And so I hid this aspect of my life tightly away in the closet. I often felt it would have been easier if I 'd chosen a more socially acceptable niche interest such as fox-hunting or sadomasochism.

I told myself that fighting battles with toy soldiers at least had creative associations. 'Number 999 in the vast library catalogue of books I have never written is the story of a successful city man who seemed to have a dark secret in his life; and who was eventually discovered playing with tin soldiers or some undignified antic of infancy. I may say that I am that man in everything except his successful business career,' G. K. Chesterton, a toy soldier enthusiast, had written unashamedly in his autobiography. H. G. Wells had penned the first book on wargaming, *Little Wars*, and fought on his living room floor against armies commanded by Jerome K. Jerome and the publisher Frank Palmer. Robert Louis Stevenson wrote articles on the subject. G. M. Trevelyan and his brothers had thousands of German-made Allgeyer semi-round soldiers, bought from a shop in the Burlington Arcade, and manoeuvred them across a drawing room carpet at Wallington that had been trodden a decade before by Algernon Swinburne and John Ruskin. The Brontës had been wargamers, so had Dennis Wheatley, A. J. A. Symons (author of that extraordinary experiment in biography, *The Quest for Corvo*), Winston Churchill and Gavin Lyall. Norman Bel Geddes, visionary futurist designer and architect and father of the actor Barbara Bel Geddes, who played Miss Ellie in *Dallas*, hosted wargame parties of such lavishness they merited a photo-feature in *Life* magazine.

In recent times, it has to be admitted, things have gone a bit downmarket. I blame Games Workshop for that. Games Workshop is the biggest manufacturer of wargaming figures on the planet. They have 319 shops in seventeen different countries and 4000 licensed distributors worldwide. The company has a turnover of over £140 million a year and pretax profits of £14 million. Games Workshop does fantasy figures. *Lord of the Rings* and Warhammer 40K are the cornerstones of its dark empire. Their shops are black T-shirt and metal-studded belt central. The customers admire *Lord of the Rings* director Peter Jackson so much they mistake him for a fashion icon. I don't want anything to do with it. The whole fantasy thing turns my stomach.

To my mind, three men are responsible more than any others for the creation of this abhorrent perversion of the hobby: J. R. R. Tolkien, creator of Middle Earth, Robert E. Howard, creator of Hyboria (which was kind of Middle Earth with breasts), and E. Gary Gygax, the mild-mannered Canadian inventor of Dungeons and Dragons. 'All three of them should be put up against a wall and shot,' I said to TK one day when I was feeling particularly aggrieved at World of Warcraft's continued encroachment into our territory. He raised an eyebrow. 'I think you're getting a bit carried away there, mate,' he said.

'Are you sure?' I said.

'Oh yes,' TK said. 'I mean, two of them are already dead. It would be a waste of bullets.'

But if you mentioned wargaming to non-wargamers, Games Workshop was what they thought of because that was where their kids went. 'Do you have Orcs?' the parents of eleven-year-old boys inevitably asked.

'No, I do not have Orcs, Riders of Rohan, Dark Elves, Skaven, Kroot Mercenaries BattleTech, HeroClix, Gangs of Mega-City One or many-horned fucking genetic-mechanoid arse-faced pigmen from the Purple Pustule of Tharg T bloody M either,' I wanted to yell. 'The worlds of Mordheim, Aarklash, Rag'Narok and Cadwallon remain as deep a mystery to me as shampoo and soap and the tender breath of a woman are to the men who invented them.' But it is hard to take the moral high ground when you have just bought three hundred Garrison 20mm Macedonian phalangites from a man called Alistair in Auckland, New Zealand.

In an attempt to counterbalance things, I made notes on anybody vaguely cool who was involved in the hobby. Alex Harvey of the Sensational Alex Harvey Band, Mike Myers, the champion racehorse trainer Henry Cecil and sci-fi writer Michael Moorcock, who managed the considerable feat of juggling a large collection of toy soldiers with a warm and lasting friendship with the hardline feminist Andrea Dworkin. Even the news that Lord Black of Crossharbour, discredited former owner of the *Daily Telegraph*, had once been a keen Napoleonic gamer was a source of pride. The Canadian entrepreneur might have been an unscrupulous financial bandit, but hey, the guy was no dweeb.

In Peter Biskind's book on Hollywood in the 1970s, *Easy Riders, Raging Bulls*, I came across the following passage: 'Martin [Scorsese] was sharing a house with Robbie Robertson of The Band at that time. "They didn't go out much," Margot Kidder said. "They just hung around at home, took cocaine and played with Marty's collection of toy soldiers."' Sadly Margot made no mention of scale, period or what rules Marty and Robbie used.

A few years ago I met up with a wargamer called Dave (50 per cent of all wargamers are called Dave – it's the law) who was buying some figures from me. I arranged to meet him in a branch of Caffè Nero which, as he pointed out, had lettering on the fascia that made it look like Caffè Nerd and was therefore very suitable. Dave said he had been accumulating figures for years without any specific purpose. Box files of them were currently providing extra insulation in his loft. Like me, he never took stock of what figures he had. I said, maybe if he did he'd realise he had too many figures. He replied that he felt that was impossible because 'you can never have too much of something you didn't need in the first place'. I realised at once that this was a life-changing aphorism. Though whether it changed my life for good or ill I was no longer sure.

Most of the time the little men brought a ray of happiness into my life. Often, when I was working and struggling for an idea or the final paragraph of a newspaper column, I'd get up from my desk, pull open a drawer at random and inspect the contents. It didn't matter what was in it, though I knew before I opened them because all the drawers were labelled. I know, I know, but when you've accumulated ten thousand toy soldiers it's a bit late to start worrying about being anal. Whether it was lowly French line infantry or mighty Carthaginian elephants, the sight of the glittering, brightly coloured figures always cheered me up.

At other moments, though, the little men oppressed me. A friend who was reading *Plan of Attack*, Bob Woodward's book about the launching of the Second Gulf War, said, 'The logistics of it are mind-boggling. Before they could ship out all the food they'd need in the desert they had to sink reinforced concrete piles to support the platforms they store it on because it was so heavy; if they'd just put it down on the ground it would have sunk into the sand and disappeared. Can you imagine having to think of all that?' Well, actually, I could.

My figures needed organising into regiments, painting, varnishing, glueing on to bases; officers and missing figures needed to be found; they had to have terrain to manoeuvre over, hills to march up, woods to hide in, rivers to ford, houses to shelter behind; they had to have somewhere to be safely stored away so they wouldn't get caked with dust or attacked by the moisture that could start oxidation. They needed rules and regulations for how fast they could move, how far they could fire, how well they could fight and how much of a buffeting they'd put up with before they turned and ran back to the safety of their box files. They needed generals. They needed flags. They needed two more chariots to complete the Pharaoh's royal squadron. They craved attention like a phalanx of toddlers.

I lay in bed at night fretting about how I would ever finish them, where I would keep them and how I would find the money to pay for everything. War, as Woodward makes plain, is an expensive business. Little wars were a little expensive too. In the mid-1990s I sold off all the wargame armies I had spent the previous decade accumulating in favour of collecting figures that had been designed before 1972 and were now out of production. There were a number of reasons for this. I liked the early wargame figures more than the ones that came later. The later figures had hands and heads that were disproportionately large, modern figure designers, like modern artists, having tired of mere figurative realism. The old figures were smaller and better proportioned. They had charm, they had nostalgia and, like all toy soldiers, they would accumulate value.

The rarity of these veteran figures would, I stupidly imagined, limit my spending and simultaneously nurture a nest egg for my retirement. The trouble was that whereas before I could put off buying figures that I saw for sale, safe in the knowledge that they would still be available next week, next month or next year, now I no longer could. Now every batch of 1968 Hinton Hunt 20mm Norman knights or 1963 Stadden $1/72$ Crimean War Russian Infantry (in greatcoats) advancing at high porte that came up on eBay, or appeared in the classified ads in *Wargames Illustrated*, *Miniature Wargames*, *Military Modelling* or *Military Modelcraft*, was a one-off, unrepeatable chance of a lifetime. When I got them I experienced a wild buzz, much as the gambler gets when he wins a big bet. And when I didn't I was seized with the collector's nightmare – a vision of the decades of regret and bitter recrimination that would follow as I slowly realised that such an opportunity would never, ever present itself again. A mania born of terror and desire gripped me.

Unlike governments, I couldn't raise taxes, so I made cuts. I'd already given up smoking to spend the money I saved on

figures. This was a fine idea. And frankly it was as well I stuck
to it. Because if I'd spent the same amount of cash on tobacco
I've since spent on little lead men I'd be talking through a hole
in my neck. Now I went into overdrive. I sold a collection of
1960s cycling books and bought French cuirassiers; two hundred vinyl LPs furnished a small English Civil War army; fifty
picture sleeve punk singles bolstered the exotic ranks of the
Great King of Persia; a Schuco clockwork Grand Prix racer
bought on my first trip to London when I was ten contributed
to raising a division of Bavarian infantry; four Revel $\frac{1}{32}$ scale
slot cars recruited a couple of boxes of Samurai. I felt as if all
the lead I had handled, carved and inhaled had given me lead
fever. Day after day the postman struggled up the drive, back
bowed and knees buckling under the weight of the parcels.
Ancient Indians came from Maine, North West Frontier
Tribesmen from Baden Württemberg, Carthaginians from
Ohio, Spartans from New Zealand. I sold and I bought. My
bank statements and my credit card bills suggested I had put
our domestic economy on a total war footing. Soon my
finances had begun to look like Brandenburg after the Thirty
Years War, broken, charred and apparently incapable of sus-
taining life now or in the future.

'Who buys a minute to wail a week? Or sells eternity to
buy a toy?' I knew the answer to Shakespeare's question. It
was staring back at me every time I looked in the bathroom
mirror. I felt as if I was caught in a miniaturised maelstrom,
spinning towards insanity and ruin.

My mind was filled with the incessant demands of my lead
armies. I began to wonder who was in charge: me, or them?
I owned them yet somehow I had become their captive.
Sometimes I wondered how it had got this way. And sometimes, like Burt Lancaster in *The Sweet Smell of Success*, I
wished I wore a hearing aid, so I could switch off the babble
of the little men.

8

Edged Weapons and Armour

The collection held him prisoner.
'And of course, it has ruined my life!'

Bruce Chatwin, *Utz*

In the early 1980s there weren't many old-style barbers left. Everything had gone unisex in the 1970s and as a result it was very difficult to find anybody who would cut your hair without washing and blow-drying it and giving you tea and a biscuit and a copy of *Arena* to flick through. Personally, I was suspicious of these types of outfits. My belief, based on considerable experience in places called Bonnie and Clyde, Cinderellas 'N' Rockin' Fellas and the like, was that they didn't actually cut your hair at all. They just folded the untidy bits away and fixed them there with the heat gun. It was the hairdressing equivalent of brushing dust under the rug. Everything looked fine until you washed it yourself. When you did all the messy bits came untucked again and you were back to square one. When I got my hair cut I liked physical evidence. If I left the hairdresser's without the feeling that somebody had scraped the back of my neck with a rusty hacksaw blade before tipping a packet of itching powder down my shirt collar I felt I'd been short-changed. I feel exactly the same way about male grooming products. If it says 'soothing' or 'balm' on the label I reject it out of hand. If it doesn't sting when you put it on, I'm not interested.

The barber in East Finchley was just about the only one within a thirty-minute bus ride of my flat. He had a little corner site with a red-and-white striped pole running along one side of the doorframe and a window display of Wilkinson Sword razorblades and line drawings of what looked like Warren Beatty modelling the latest range of feather cuts *c.* 1973. The shop itself was the size of a front room. There were two big barber's chairs from Chicago, but only one was ever used. The barber worked alone. The second chair was just there to create an impression.

No matter what day or what time you went in to the East Finchley barber's there was always a wait to get a haircut, and while you waited you sat with a line of other blokes on a bench along one wall. The barber provided no newspapers. There were no three-year-old copies of *Punch*, *Reader's Digest* or *What Caravan?* on offer. While you sat there you were expected to listen politely to the barber and the person who was sitting in the chair. That was an unspoken rule of the barber's shop: the barber and whoever was in the chair talked and everybody else paid attention. The barber would frequently look up, scissors and comb in hand, and address a remark to the shop, but it was a rhetorical flourish; the audience wasn't expected to respond. You didn't interject when you were on the bench. You got your turn to speak when you went in the chair.

The barber held forth on a whole range of topics. If an Italian café owner was in the chair they'd talk about Italy, if it was a barrister they'd talk about the law. On one memorable occasion there was an Italian barrister in the chair and the barber swiftly produced from his coat pocket a document that had been handed to him by a carabiniere during a holiday in Rimini the previous May. 'I couldn't speak Italian, he couldn't speak English,' the barber told us, snapping the scissors in the air to emphasise the jaw-jaw of mutual incomprehension. He gave the document to the Italian barrister, a debonair fellow with a pink scalp and round, wire-rimmed glasses who rather put me in mind of Marshal Louis Nicolas Davout, Duc d'Auerstaedt, Prince d'Eckmühl and so on and so forth.

The Italian barrister studied the piece of paper, his eyebrows rising and falling in a manner that suggested his brain was breathing deeply. 'It says you are in violation of traffic laws,' he said after a minute, 'because you did not pay at the tollbooth when you entered a stretch of the autostrada near San Marino. You must report to a police station within two weeks and pay a fine of sixty thousand liras. Unfortunately the deadline has passed by some . . . three months.'

'Blimey, do you think they'll have handed my name over to Interpol?' the barber asked.

The Italian barrister said he thought the barber would be safe for a while yet.

When I was in the chair the barber and I talked about toy soldiers. I had learned during the conversation with the old officer from the Artists' Rifles (for it was here, amongst the comb sterilisers, that I had encountered him) that the barber was a keen military modeller. He'd served in the 2nd Dragoons (Royal Scots Greys) and he painted only figures and vehicles representing that regiment. For as long as I had been going to the shop he had been engaged on a 120mm mounted figure of a Scots Grey (known in those days as the Royal North British Dragoons – a piece of information I feel compelled to blurt out against my better judgement by a force more powerful than myself) during the famous charge at Waterloo in 1815. 'You have to have a focus,' he said. 'When you go down to Tradition, or up to Michael's Models in Finchley, well, blimey, you'd go boss-eyed just looking at 'em all. It's like with stamps, isn't it? A philatelist doesn't go off harum scarum after any old stamps, he has a specialism – stamps of the Empire, stamps with birds on them, cricket stamps. If you're collecting you have to have a clearly defined area. Otherwise, well, you're talking about anarchy, aren't you?

'Now this chap here,' the barber continued, indicating me with his scissors and addressing the shop, 'is a specialist in the Battle of Quebec. He is a Wolfe man.' He gave a little howl and we all chuckled.

The barber was right about the anarchy of unfocused collecting. A bloke in Lincoln who said he had some figures he thought I might be interested in had phoned me up late one night. He was well spoken but you could practically smell the beer down the phone line. 'Plenty of spare Hintons, Higgins's, Jacklex,' the bloke slurred, 'Colonials. I'm still gaming myself, but there's too much stuff really. Kids keep breaking in the shed and nicking them. It's more trouble than it's worth. You can have what you want.' I asked him what there was. 'Oh tons of stuff, Pathans, Indians, British,' he said, 'Zulus, Dervishes, Hadendowah, Beja, Taishi camel riders. I can't be bothered with counting anything. I'm not packing anything to post. You'll just have to come round and have a look if you want it.'

I told him I'd try to get a mate of mine to come and have a look. Lincoln was a fair way from Cannock but TK said he would be practically halfway there on Saturday because he was giving a regular fare an early morning lift to East Midlands airport, three divorcees on a charter flight to Cephalonia. 'Hoping to find Captain Corelli and his mandolin,' TK said. 'Though to be honest with you, mate, I don't think even an Italian would want to hand his ukulele to these girls. Ferocious, they are. One of them's got Godzilla tattooed on her bum.'

'How come you've seen her bum?' I said.

'I didn't ask to,' TK said, 'but if this lass wants you to see her bum you've got very little choice in the matter, believe you me. Especially when you're doing eighty-five on the A38.'

TK arranged to go and see the bloke at lunchtime after he'd dropped off the divorcees. He phoned me up that night. 'Hey, bloody hell,' he said, 'you think you've seen everything, bud. I tell you. Blimey.' The man, TK said, lived in a rambling old house down a country lane. Garden out front all thistles and nettles, windows caked with grime, slates missing from the roof, pointing in a shocking state. Inside the house, TK says, there is just stuff everywhere. 'H, the guy is a *hoarder*. Compulsive. He's kept everything. And I mean *everything*.' There are piles of newspapers and magazines, massive piles: huge stacks of *National Geographic*, the *Daily Telegraph*, *Railway Modeller*, *Private Eye*, *Military Modelling*, the *Daily Express*, *Reader's Digest*. Great towerblocks of boxes, videos, unmade plastic kits, model railway scenery, engines and carriages, Airfix H0 plastic figures – 'The blue box figures, from the 1960s,' according to TK – dozens and dozens of them, still on the sprues, unopened, untouched. And then wargame figures. All scales from $^1/_{300}$ upwards. Thousands painted, tens of thousands, hundreds of thousands unpainted. Parcels of figures with the string and the brown paper still on them. 'Bought mail order and never even unpacked.'

Outside in the garden there's a big tongue-and-groove pitch pine shed stacked from floor to ceiling with box files filled with Jacklex 20mm artillery and transport sets that have been out of production since 1978. 'You know how we've been looking for years and years for that Boer Voortrekker ox-cart?' It's true. The big South African cart with its team of four oxen and family of Boer migrants has been our Holy Grail for at least a decade. 'Well,' TK said, 'this afternoon I counted over seventy of them still in their boxes. And that was from files you could get at just by opening the door. God knows how many more there are at the back. And you know what, the fella says he's got a lock-up a few miles away and that's got even more figures in it.'

The boxes and stacks of magazines take up all of the floor space in the living room and what must have been the dining room, TK said. There's just narrow corridors between them. One leads from the kitchen to the fella's chair and table, another from the chair to the TV set, a third from the chair to his painting table and a fourth from the chair to the foot of the stairs.

'What's it like upstairs?' I asked.

TK said he didn't go up there; he didn't like to. There was a bathroom up there but he didn't use it. 'Took a leak behind the car when I left.' The whole place was eerie. You didn't want to stop. 'Nothing against the fella himself,' said TK, who always sees the best in people, 'couldn't have been nicer. Good lad all round. But the whole set-up. Ooooh dear. He made me a cup of tea and when he opened the fridge to get the milk all that was in it were ten cans of Co-op lager and a few takeaway cartons.' TK forbids my asking about the state of the rest of the kitchen.

TK said he couldn't be certain, not being a builder, but he thought the number of figures this bloke had hoarded must constitute some sort of physical danger. It was all very well putting boxes of lead all over the house, but in the end lead was dense and boxes of figures were heavy. A bloke I knew in Stevenage, who'd been attracted to wargaming by watching Michael Bentine's *Potty Time* as a kid, had been buying Napoleonic figures and stuffing them in his attic for years when one windy night one of the ceiling joists cracked and a division of Duchy of Warsaw infantry fell through the bedroom ceiling, narrowly missing his wife.

TK reckoned that might be the case here, though there is

no woman in evidence. He found the whole experience deeply unsettling. I say I can understand why.

'I don't think you can, buddy,' TK said, 'because you see the thing is, H, mate, I was looking round this dirty old house, all these piles of stuff and the wallpaper peeling off and the smell of old newsprint and there, in the middle of all the squalor, is the bloke's painting table all neatly arranged with his brushes and paints tidy and clean and all lined up. You know what I realised, H, mate? I realised that if I hadn't met the wife, this, this would have been me. Jeeeesus.' TK let out a sigh, like a man who has walked away from a car smash unharmed and only just realised how lucky he is.

Homes like the one that horrified TK are likely to become more prevalent in Britain in the future. eBay is circulating junk like a tornado. According to Gary Ashburn, 'Collecting is one of the fastest growing and hottest hobbies in the world.' And Gary should know. He is the star presenter on Sky Digital's Authentic TV (channel 687) which is more or less totally devoted to people who feel their lives aren't complete unless every nook and cranny is filled with hand-painted, limited edition, lovingly crafted commemorative dinner plates adorned with the face of Marilyn Monroe. Or, as Gary put it, 'Authentic TV will capture the universe of collecting like no other show or channel anywhere. Each show is an adventure and a great deal of fun.' To which I felt moved to whoop and shout, 'Way to go, big guy!' Well, almost.

One of the most popular areas of model collecting is die-cast. The craze for collecting toy cars had really kicked off in the eighties with Mint and Boxed, a shop that seemed to be permanently filled by futures brokers in red braces buying original 1960s Corgi Batmobiles, or the Dinky models of Thunderbird 5. Original vintage cars are now pretty expensive so most collectors go after modern limited edition die-cast. Modelzone, the nationwide chain of shops, produces a top ten best-selling die-cast chart every month. In March 2005 the Efe AEC Regal Green Line bus was at number five, with the RC2 Knightrider car (complete with plastic David Hasselhoff) at number four with a bullet, and the Corgi special edition Spitfire holding firm at number one.

Personally, I wasn't sure whether buying something from a shop was really collecting at all. To me, collecting implied at least a little bit of a hunt, and maybe some cut and thrust at an auction rather than simply sending your credit card details to a retailer in Slough. They called it collecting, but to me it was just shopping.

It was through the East Finchley barber that I met Arthur. I'd walked into the shop one Wednesday morning and the barber had nodded in my direction and said, 'Now this boy'll be interested in this.' The man sitting in the chair getting what remained of his hair clipped was talking about his days serving in the first Chindits campaign under Orde Wingate. 'Now,' the barber said, pausing in his cutting and addressing the customer in the mirror, 'tell me, was this Wingate as eccentric as everybody says?'

The man let out a high-tar chuckle and in the barber's mirror you could see his eyes widening to indicate that this was an understatement. 'You could say,' he said. 'One morning we were out on inspection. Out comes Wingate onto the parade ground, stark bollock naked except for an alarm clock slung round his neck on a length of parcel string. He walks about a bit, then he stands in front of us, legs akimbo. "Now, men," he says, "you are probably wondering why I have appeared before you in this state," which, as you can imagine, was a question that had occurred to more than one of us. "Well, there is a very good reason, men. You see – I am . . . John the Baptist."'

Everybody in the shop cracked up. The customers sitting on the bench rocked back and forth; the barber had to sit down on the arm of the spare chair. When the noise had subsided and the barber had wiped the tears from his eyes and got back to business, he said, 'And did it ever bother you that you were about to be parachuted in behind Japanese lines and the man leading the expedition was several pence short of the full shilling?'

The man in the chair smiled. 'Mmm,' he said, 'not much, actually. And I'll tell you why. Do you know what King George II said about General James Wolfe?'

'I don't,' the barber said, 'but I know a man who will,' and in an unprecedented break with protocol he pointed a comb at me. General James Wolfe, victor of the Battle of Quebec, was the British Army's answer to John Keats: brilliant, sickly, romantic and destined to die young. He was a great lover of poetry, too. In the hours leading up to the Battle of the Plains of Abraham, on a still and moonless night, as the longboats carried the British infantry down the St Lawrence river, Wolfe recited Thomas Gray's 'Elegy Written in a Country Churchyard' to his officers. When he had finished he said quietly, 'Gentlemen, I would rather have written those lines than take Quebec.' Wolfe destroyed Montcalm's French army with a combination of surprise and a single, brutally accurate volley of musketry. But he was fatally wounded as the enemy fled the field, categorically proving Gray's assertion that 'The paths of glory lead only to the grave.' It was the death – heroic as that of Siegfried or Beowulf – Wolfe had dreamed of since boyhood.

Despite his aptitude as a commander, not all of Wolfe's fellow officers had appreciated him. There was a fear that the young general was insane, and this worry was voiced to the King. I quoted his famous response to all in the barber's shop: 'Then I wish he would bite some of my other generals.'

The man in the chair winked at me and chuckled. 'There

you are,' he said. 'As anyone who's been in a war will tell you, it is a crazy situation. And, sometimes, in a crazy situation a lunatic's the best person to be in charge. Montgomery was an oddball and General Patton was as mad as a sack of ferrets. Thought he was Hannibal reincarnated. Good God!' He turned to me. 'So you know a bit about Quebec, do you?'

Arthur lived in a mansion flat close by and he invited me to call in and have a cup of tea with him after my haircut. And I did. It turned out that we had more in common than just General Wolfe. After leaving the British Army, Arthur had joined the civil service, working in a government department so obscure and dull that whenever he told me the name I forgot it instantly. In his spare time he'd painted and designed military figures, modelled and wargamed. He'd founded one of the first wargame clubs in the country in the early sixties and there are still people around who recall how he would cunningly wait until his opponent was making some key tactical decision and then begin noisily and messily snorting snuff. He had also contributed to several books of nineteenth-century tactics and taken a leading role in an assortment of re-enactment societies. 'I have,' Arthur said, 'devoted all my leisure hours to violence.'

Arthur was a short, square man and just about the only person I have ever met who genuinely did have a twinkle in his eye. He spoke in a throaty whisper; you were never quite sure if he was addressing his remarks to you, or just himself. He took an Edwardian attitude to physical appearance, frequently dismissing people because their eyes were positioned in a manner he found suspect, or their hair was too coarse, or their fingers too stubby. If Arthur said he couldn't stand the sight of someone the chances were that he meant it quite literally. It didn't take much to upset him; a lower lip with an appearance of dampness was enough to see him swat aside the claims to pre-eminence of a leading historian of the

Great War. 'Has a mouth like a pound of raw liver,' Arthur declared. 'You can't expect any sense to come out of a great, drooling cakehole like that one.' Beards were a particular annoyance. He denounced them as unhygienic, which was a little rich for a perennial snorter of snuff. 'Imagine,' Arthur would say with an expression that simultaneously conveyed horror, disgust and glee, 'having to sit opposite that fellow watching him eat a plateful of scrambled eggs first thing in the morning. Gaargh! It would turn your stomach.'

Arthur had, by this time, sold all his wargame armies. It was not that he was fed up with wargaming or toy soldiers; he was just worried about what would happen to all his regiments if he died suddenly. 'Not sure if any of my relatives would be interested,' he said, 'or would know how to dispose of them to the proper people. I couldn't bear the thought of them ending up dumped.'

It was a genuine fear, one from which a lot of older wargamers suffered, and justifiably so. TK and I had once tracked down the widow of a man who had designed and cast a nice and now very rare range of 20mm figures back in the 1960s. He had lived in Wellingborough. It took us a while to find his wife because she was Italian and everyone we asked who had known her husband said she had gone back to Italy when he died. Eventually, after about six months, we discovered her new address. It turned out she hadn't gone back to Italy. She'd moved to Leicester.

We phoned her up and then TK went round to see her because she said there was still a big stack of boxes filled with toy soldiers in the garage that she had brought with her when she moved. She said TK could go through them and make her an offer for anything we wanted. We were both very excited about the prospect of this, because the figures were very good and the chances of ever getting any of them had previously seemed very remote. Sadly, when TK looked through the boxes he found that all the figures were 54mm. The only wargame figures he could find were half a dozen beautifully painted 20mm Roman legionaries that had been designed by John Braithwaite of Stockton-on-Tees around 1970.

When TK showed these to the Italian widow she said, 'Oh, you like these ones?' TK said he did. 'That is such a pity,' the woman said sadly. 'There were three or four boxes full of them, but I couldn't move everything. I thought the little ones would not be worth much money so I took them to the tip.'

'I felt a bit sorry for her, to be honest,' TK told me on the phone, 'so I didn't say anything at the time. But when I was driving back home along the A38 I pulled into a lay-by and bellowed for five minutes. You should see the paintwork. Lovely, it is.'

'Did you get the name of the dump?' I asked.

'I thought of it, buddy,' TK said, 'but she'd moved a year and a half ago. You can't go rooting round under eighteen months' worth of dirty nappies, fag ends and fifty-seven varieties of shite looking for a few shoeboxes filled with Imperial Romans. We have to draw a line somewhere, mate.'

Arthur's figures, a huge and lovely collection of 30mm Napoleonic soldiers, many of which he had had made especially for him, had been transported to America. 'A Yank bought them and utterly dunned the poor chap,' another veteran wargamer told me later. 'Spun him some yarn and got them for a fraction of their true value.' I wasn't sure I entirely believed that. Arthur didn't seem like the sort of person you could baffle with bullshit. And besides, the veteran was a man with an ill-concealed dislike of Arthur and an apparent predilection for mischief. The two men had been friends many years before but had fallen out over a matter so convoluted and fraught with symbolism, double meanings and significant undercurrents that listening to it was the equivalent of watching the director's cut of *Donnie Darko* in Serbo-Croat while hanging upside down in a centrifuge. All that emerged in the end was that Arthur had made a habit of getting into bitter disputes. He collected enemies with the same passion he had collected figures. 'A friend,' Arthur said, 'is a very fine thing. But an enemy, an enemy keeps you on your toes.'

9

The Charge!

'Why live in the world when you can live in your head?'
Pulp, 'Monday Morning'

TK said he had a new digital camera with a pixel count that was even higher than his cholesterol level. He said, 'I'll take some photos of my Spanish Napoleonics and email them to you. Beautiful, they are. Rubbish at fighting, like, but you can't hold it against them. You want to get a digital camera, H, mate. Brilliant things.'

I said I'd thought about it, but then considered how much they cost and the number of figures I could buy for the same money and dropped the idea.

TK said I needed taking in hand. 'You need a bit of advice from an older, wiser and, dare I say, craftier fella, buddy. You don't buy the digital camera for yourself, do you? You buy it as a gift for your missus. That way you've got the camera, you've made her happy and you haven't spent a penny on yourself, so your war chest's totally untouched.'

I had never fought a battle against TK, but I knew that if ever I did he'd rout me inside three moves.

TK collected the same old 20mm figures I did. That's how I'd met him. I'd placed a wants ad in *Military Modelling* and one Saturday afternoon the phone rang and it was TK. He said to give him my address and he'd send me a box of figures. I asked how much he wanted for them. 'You don't need to pay me,' TK said, 'just make a note and next time you've got anything interesting going spare give me a bell.'

There may seem something sweetly innocent about this willingness to give a total stranger what amounted to fifty quid and tell him to pay it back when he felt like it, and maybe there was, but in every other aspect of his life TK was a man of infinite guile. He had once organised a massive refight of Borodino – twenty-four foot by seven foot table, seven thousand $^1/_{72}$ scale figures – in a scout hut near Shrewsbury. There were a dozen participants taking command of various army corps. TK had cast himself in the role of the Russian C-in-C Prince Mikhail Ilarionovitch Kutuzov, wily, dogged, garrulous, fat and fond of strong drink (so no similarities there, then). A photocopier salesman from Leighton Buzzard was Napoleon.

TK ensured that he was the last to arrive at the hut. He brought in his box files of Russian troops from the boot of the car. Amongst them were four files clearly labelled 'Cossacks'. TK made some fuss about these, eventually placing them on a table behind the Russian battle lines.

'Inside every army,' Sir John Keegan noted, 'there is a crowd trying to get out.' The Battle of Borodino was marked by an episode that proves the Sandhurst historian's point. In the middle of the afternoon, as the French seemed on the verge of the decisive victory which would have brought an abrupt end to the Czar's resistance, word swept suddenly and swiftly through the ranks of *La Grande Armée* that a huge body of Cossacks and Bashkirs led by General Platov had swept around the flank and was about to attack the baggage train. The French feared these wild light cavalry more than any other troops, not because of their fighting qualities – which, in the open field, were negligible – but because of their brutality. The baggage train was the home of the army's camp

followers, the women who sewed and cooked for the soldiers
and generally ended up as their wives and mistresses too. The
thought that the baggage train was about to be ransacked by
these brutes of the steppes briefly halted the French attack on
the Russian positions. As it turned out, General Platov never
showed up, but the hesitation had allowed the Russians to
regroup. The battle ended in a stalemate. Kutuzov and the
remains of his army slipped away in the night, denying
Napoleon a decisive victory.

The refight in the scout hut produced much the same
result. At the end of the day, with his army still holding the
Russian redoubts, TK claimed victory. 'I'm just wondering,'
he said, 'why didn't you throw your reserve into the attack?'

'We were worried about those bloody Cossacks,' Napoleon
replied testily.

'What bloody Cossacks?'

'Those bloody Cossacks in the boxes behind you,' Joachim
Murat, a computer programmer from Ruislip, snapped back.

'Oh, you mean those,' TK said, and he picked up the box
files and brought them to the main table. He lined them up in
a row and then slowly he flipped open each lid in turn – flop,
flop, flop, flop. They were all completely and utterly empty.

'Marshal Ney went berserk,' TK says delightedly when he
recalls the incident. 'Came charging round the table and
jumped on us. It took Barclay de Tolly, General Bennigsen
and Louis Nicolas Davout to pull him off. Bit me on the
shoulder, the bugger. I had to have a tetanus jab, the works.'
TK says he still has the scar; he regards it as a badge of
honour. TK thinks it is a lasting tribute to his cunning and
brilliance. And I think he is right.

TK was introduced to wargaming back around 1963 when
the hobby had about two hundred adherents across the globe,
all known to one another through the subscription list of Jack
Scruby's magazine *War Game Digest*, which was published in

Visalia, California and shipped worldwide, but mainly to England and Wisconsin.

TK was in a pub in Selly Oak, in Birmingham, one evening when a bloke came and stood next to him at the bar. They began chatting. The bloke, who was Rich the psychiatric nurse with the beautiful Mamelukes, somehow brought up the subject of model soldiers. He said he'd been collecting 30mm metal figures of the American Civil War made by a firm called SAE, which stands for Swedish African Engineers. The figures were designed by a Swede, Holger Eriksson, for a firm in Cape Town.

He also said that he'd got a book written by a Yank on how to fight battles with them. The book was *How to Play War Games in Miniature* by Joseph P. Morschauser III, sometime editor of *Newsweek* magazine. Rich said he hadn't actually found anyone to try it with yet, but if TK was interested he could come round his house the following Friday and they'd give it a go. 'And as I walked home after, I got an odd feeling, H,' TK says with the solemnity of a man relating an epiphany. 'I felt this little chat had changed my world for ever.'

The following Friday TK went to Rich's house. Rich had a table, he had figures and he even had a manual. 'The two of us knew what we wanted to do,' TK says, 'but we had no idea how to start doing it. I got there about seven-thirty, and six hours later we were still trying to fathom it out. So we called it a draw and agreed to meet the following week. I was so excited when I got home I never got to sleep. I just lay in the dark with my eyes shut and my mind whirring until it was time to go to work.'

The same thing was happening all over the country. Donald Featherstone's book *War Games* had been published in 1962 and would be reprinted fourteen times over the remainder of the decade. Airfix had started to release their plastic figures, and for those with more cash there were the one-inch lead wargame soldiers that Charles Stadden and Russell Gammage had started producing in the mid-1950s.

Charles Stadden's military career had begun with a stint in the Royal Artillery that ended after forty days when his parents pointed out to the army that he was under age and dragged him home again. When the war broke out he was called up to the Cyprus Regiment. He was part of the BEF and was evacuated at Dunkirk. He went to the Middle East, fighting against the Italians in Eritrea and the Vichy French in Syria. After a spell as a horse-breaker for the Royal Army Service Corps he was posted to the 8th Army, and took part in the Invasion of Sicily and the battles at Sangro, Cassino, Arnezzo and the Gothic Line, rising to the rank of sergeant-major. He then moved on to wargames, his first commercially produced model soldiers appearing in 1951. Of Stadden's 54mm soldiers, an enthusiastic Austrian collector wrote in *Tradition* magazine: 'Marvellous figures, each as exciting as a beautiful woman and twice as expensive. But it is a dull lover who counts the cost!' By the late 1950s he was offering over five hundred different models for collectors to paint and Tradition, the main outlet for his work, had opened a large shop near Fortnum and Mason's in Piccadilly.

Gammage had been born in a workhouse in Ipswich. He served in the Royal Navy during the Second World War, then studied design in illustration at London College. While working as an art teacher he took night classes in gold and silver work at the Central School of Arts and Crafts in London and made his first figures, a set commemorating the Coronation, for the model railway firm Graham Farish in 1953. A year later he had his own company, Rose Miniatures, which he would run from his house in Plumstead for the next four decades. His main retail outlet was a shop called Regimental in Berkeley Square.

There were many reasons for the growth in hobbies in general and military hobbies in particular in the late 1950s; increased leisure time and larger disposable income both played a part. Another major contributory factor was the sheer dreariness of Britain in the post-war years. It is hard to imagine just how wearily boring life in the UK in the decade following the end of the Second World War actually was. You get a flavour of things by taking a look at the long-running magazine *Wide World*.

Wide World was launched in the last years of the reign of Queen Victoria. Originally it had billed itself as a factual magazine under the strap-line 'The truth is stranger than fiction'. Unfortunately, a series of well-publicised hoaxes suggested that in fact the truth, as published in *Wide World*, often was fiction. This was confirmed by the appearance of a tale by A. J. A. Symon's subject, the writer and con artist Baron Corvo, in which the phoney Italian nobleman claimed not only to have been buried alive but also, even more improbably, to be the godson of Kaiser Wilhelm.

Wide World survived these knocks and continued to thrive. In the September 1954 edition, set amongst adverts for pipe tobacco, rupture appliances and build your own canoe kits, is a letter singing the praises of extravagance: 'One must have a safety valve. In my own case, although by no means wealthy, I occasionally indulge in a good cigar or a bottle of wine. The fact that I can't afford them seems to make them all the more enjoyable – "forbidden fruit" so to speak!' The idea that buying a slim panatella every few months displayed a cavalier abandonment of caution shows how severely pinched life was. Another correspondent notes his special interest in cabbage seeds and wonders if any other readers would care to correspond with him on the topic. *Wide World's* masthead proclaimed it 'The True Adventure Magazine For Men'. No wonder battles with toy soldiers seemed so exciting.

My own introduction to wargames came ten years after TK's, but by the same chance and manner. Malcolm, an older boy at my senior school, sidled up to me in the junior cloak-room. I'd hardly exchanged a word with him prior to that moment and assumed he was just going to give me a dead leg, or empty a jar of ink into my blazer pocket, or make me stand at the door and keep nix while he smoked a Number Six. Instead, he asked would I like to come round for tea some time and try a battle game? I'm not sure how he knew I'd be interested. Perhaps he just sensed it, like Rich must have sensed something similar in TK. Maybe there is a wargaming equivalent of gaydar – a geekoscope, or something.

I went round to Malcolm's house in a suburb of Middlesbrough. It was one of those big pre-war detached houses with mature trees in the garden, an Aga in the kitchen and a smell of Labradors and beeswax. Upstairs in the loft Malcolm had a table tennis table and, on it, amongst hills made from mounds of sand and forests made of bits of old sponge painted green and stuck to twigs, were hundreds of 20mm figures representing – in a slightly wayward fashion – the armies of Napoleon and Wellington. I was stunned. It was like I had opened a door and seen a vision of the rest of my life.

'It's kind of a sand-table,' Malcolm said, undisguised pride mingling with a hint of condescension. It was indeed a kind of sand-table, in that it was a table with piles of sand on it. A real sand-table was something else entirely. Sand-tables were a military and TV staple. They were what Sir Brian Horrocks had used on the television programme about the great com-manders, moving hordes of miniature tanks around to show how Monty had bested Rommel at El Alamein in 1942; what army planners used to work out tactical problems; and what later the BBC newsreader Peter Snow would employ to explain exactly where the Paras were on the Falkland Islands.

The sand-table was a substantial piece of hardware. Measuring roughly eight feet by six feet it had plank edges that housed a nine-inch-deep bed of sand. This was coloured using powder paint, dampened and then sculpted into shape. The effect was very realistic. Unfortunately there were downsides, the biggest of which was that nearly forty cubic feet of wet sand weighed so much that if you had built one in the loft without strengthening the joists first you'd have found that over the next few seconds you were fighting your battle in the first floor bedroom, the sitting room and finally the cellar.

Malcolm had a set of rules, which had been written by a pair of brothers who lived near Worthing, at that time the centre of the wargames world (now, of course, it's Newark in Nottinghamshire). They ran to over twenty pages. This was daunting in some ways, but comforting in others. The big fear of all wargamers in those days was that people would mock them for 'playing with toy soldiers'. But this vast rules manual proved beyond doubt that we weren't playing. Playing implied fun and these rules were so complex you'd no more take them for fun than you would mistake a maths textbook for the *Kama Sutra*. We were not playing; the soldiers were not toys; Action Man was not a doll – our lives seemed defined by what things weren't rather than what they were.

The rules were dense, and to a newcomer whose experience of games ran the whole gamut from ludo to Monopoly, pretty much nonsensical. There were pages of explanations and equations and a whole section on scales. Here's the thing: most wargame figures are 20mm or 25mm tall. That is – roughly – $1/72$ scale. In $1/72$ scale one inch on the model represents seventy-two inches in real life. So a one-inch-high figure represents a six-foot-tall person. Simple. However, if we were to adopt $1/72$ as our ground scale, that is to say when measuring the area over which our model battle is to be fought, we run into immediate and obvious difficulties. At Waterloo, for example, the fighting took place on a front of approximately four thousand yards. In $\frac{1}{72}$ scale this is fifty-five yards. If you wanted to refight Waterloo in $\frac{1}{72}$ scale you'd need to hire a football field, but that would be no good because, aside from anything else, the grass would be in $\frac{1}{1}$ scale.

And so ground scale must be different from figure or height scale, usually something like one millimetre equals one yard. If we take that as our ground scale then suddenly Waterloo is shrunk down to a manageable four metres and can be refought on a fourteen-foot-long table.

But it's not as simple as that, because if you are using a $\frac{1}{1000}$ ground scale you are confronted with the problem of the width of your toy soldiers. Suddenly the shoulders of your models no longer represent – as they would in $\frac{1}{72}$ scale – something that is two-and-a-half feet across, but something more like ten yards across. Our model soldier is not occupying the space that one soldier would occupy but the space that more than ten soldiers would occupy. And so not only are we dealing with a problem of scales, but also one of ratios.

Initially the scale width of the figure and, more importantly, the base it stands on may seem like a big pain in the arse, but in actual fact it is a huge relief. At Waterloo the Allied, Prussian and French armies together numbered somewhere in the region of 220,000 men. That is a lot of toy soldiers. Wargaming it with one figure representing one man (or 1:1 ratio) would mean putting out three miniature metal armies with a combined weight of in excess of two metric tonnes. Even if you could find a table big enough for them the chances are it would collapse under the weight. Thanks to the ground scale though we are not looking at one figure representing one man, but representing a number of men. If we stick our figures on card bases that are in scale with the actual frontage occupied by Napoleonic soldiers in accordance with our ground scale, we can play around with this ratio quite a bit. For reasons largely connected with aesthetics and economics, 1:33 is the most popular.

And so from refighting Waterloo on a football field with getting on for a quarter of a million toy soldiers we are now looking at refighting it on a table fourteen feet by six feet with fewer than seven thousand.

Which is all very well. But what happens when you come to a battle like that at Rorke's Drift in which 120 British soldiers defended a fortified farmstead-cum-hospital against five thousand warriors of Prince Dabulamanzi's impi? If we use 1:33 we end up with three or four figures representing the British. And if we use a one millimetre to one yard ground scale the hospital compound would measure about four-and-a-half inches from end to end – which would hardly provide enough room for the two ¹/₇₂ scale buildings we need. And those buildings themselves are a problem, because they will measure a minimum of three inches by two-and-a-half inches, which make them accurate in terms of the height scale, but wildly oversized in terms of ground scale, occupying, as they do, an area equivalent to 270,000 square feet.

Have you got a migraine yet?

Despite the difficulty of the rules, Malcolm and I fought several dozen battles over the next few weeks. I was so overwhelmed by the joy these games brought me that I had soon made my own table by ripping up my Revell slot car racing track from its baseboard and painting the hardboard surface with green poster paint. I dug out all my old Airfix figures (all those, at least, that hadn't fallen dead or wounded during an earlier passion for air rifles) and stuck them on cardboard bases as the rules suggested. I persuaded Deano to join me in playing wargames. Deano had been experimenting with wargames of his own: he had been dousing old Timpo cowboys in methylated spirits and then firing lighted matches at them from a Britain's 155mm 'Long Tom' howitzer. Deano was a bit disappointed to find that my games replaced flaming missiles with dice, but I explained that, while on the surface the inferno option might seem more exciting, it was at heart puerile. What I was offering was something better, more grown-up. I quoted a review of Don Featherstone's *Advanced War Games* that had appeared in the *Manchester Evening News* and featured prominently on the dust jacket of *War Game Campaigns*: 'A fascinating book for the war games experts, who can now regard their hobby almost as a science.' A science, you see? Arson was juvenile; what we were about to embark upon was clever and adult. Deano remained sceptical until a fluky series of double sixes in a refight of Quatre Bras saw his single French howitzer decapitate the Duke of Wellington with shrapnel on the second move.

It was just as well that happened, or I would have been without an opponent. I had soon parted company with Malcolm. Under the influence of the Sven Hassel craze he had abandoned Napoleonic warfare in favour of the Second World War and painted up an SS Eastern Front division. 'I'm completely fanatical,' Malcolm said, his eyes burning with the kind of crazed glee that comes from a diet of Nazi pulp and glue fumes. 'If a company fails a morale test and have to retreat my other figures shoot them.' It was a step too far into the darkness for me.

Advanced War Games had come from the village library. I had, by now, borrowed every book on wargaming they had: *Introduction to Battle Gaming* by Terence Wise; Donald Featherstone's *War Games* and the follow-up cascade of *War Game Campaigns*, *Solo War Gaming* and *Wargames Through the Ages Volumes I, II and III*; *Practical Wargaming* and *With Pike and Musket* by Charles Wesencraft; *Charge!* by Brigadier Peter Young and Colonel James P. Lawford; and, my personal favourite and definite desert island book, *The War Game* by Charles Grant.

The fact that there were so many books on the topic in the

library of a small village in North Yorkshire indicates how far wargaming had come since TK and Rich had first met up and struggled to come to grips with the topic. By the early 1970s, wargaming was vying with model railways and wife-swapping as Britain's most popular indoor recreation. Where once there were only two hundred wargamers in the whole of the English-speaking world, now there were over two hundred wargame clubs in Britain alone and shops selling lead figures on every high street.

Part of this sudden expansion was down to the TV series *Callan*, which featured Edward Woodward as David Callan, a disillusioned common man anti-hero who spent his working life killing people for the secret service and his home life playing with model soldiers. Like all of us, Callan was particularly touchy about the T-word. If anybody made the mistake of saying 'toy' anywhere in the vicinity of his 20mm armies they were likely to find themselves staring down the silenced barrel of a Walther PPK 7.65mm automatic pistol.

Unlikely though it may seem given the subject matter of espionage and contract killers, wargaming played a central role in *Callan*. One episode was actually filmed at a wargame convention in Reading, though the producers cunningly avoided the anorak-clad, corduroy-wearing, carrier bag-toting reality by cordoning off part of the hall and decking it out like the campaign tent of an Ottoman field commander. Another episode was shot in the basement of the Tradition model soldier shop. With his natty haircut, three-button suits and amoral attitude to sex and violence, for a while Edward Woodward actually made the hobby seem pretty cool.

Wargaming was given a further patina of glamour by a number of celebrities, mainly actors, who had taken to the hobby, Peter Cushing, Stanley Baker and Charlton Heston among them. Arthur had got to know Deryck Guyler a bit through wargaming. Guyler was a British comedy-acting star.

He appeared in dozens of TV and radio shows such as *Sykes,
Please Sir!* and *The Men from the Ministry,* and gained international renown by playing a policeman in The Beatles movie *A
Hard Day's Night.* Guyler collected and wargamed with
German 30mm flat figures. He was once president of the
Society of Ancients (devoted to warfare in the ancient world
and founded in 1965) and plainly took his wargaming and
collecting seriously. 'A decent chap,' Arthur said, 'despite that
rather unsavoury moustache. Superb Romans. One of his
sons became a monk, though I doubt the figures had anything to do with that.'

By 1971 wargaming was so far into the mainstream it featured in an advert for Good News chocolates – possibly the
only sweets named after the Gospels, incidentally. The
adverts featured a sophisticated couple dressed as if they'd
just returned from a fondue party with the Galloping
Gourmet. The game, involving hundreds of very nicely
painted 30mm Stadden Seven Years War figures, proceeded
normally for about thirty seconds before the woman outwitted her moustachioed male opponent by use of a cunning
outflanking movement with a regiment of orange creams and
hazelnut clusters. For most viewers it was a lamentable ad for
some downmarket confectionery; for the hobby, though we
didn't realise it at the time, it was a high point.

In *Callan,* wargaming was shorthand for shrewd strategic
thinking and grace under pressure. Any enemy agent who was
a wargamer – and Callan discovered a surprising number of
them – was guaranteed to be cool, calculating and lethal.
There was a good reason why the writers of the series took
this attitude. Many early wargames writers had indeed displayed these qualities: Donald Featherstone had served as a
sergeant in the Royal Tank Regiment during the Second
World War, fighting his way across the Western Desert and up
through Italy; Charles Grant was a senior officer in Special

Branch while his teenage son, who featured in many of the books, later rose to the rank of brigadier in the Black Watch; and Peter Young served in No. 3 Commando, winning an MC during the raid of Vaago, a DSO for his part in the Dieppe raid and a bar for his MC during the invasion of Sicily.

That men who had fought in real battles should want to refight them as a game may seem peculiar, but in the end is it any odder than the fact that Richard Todd, the illustrator Denis McLoughlin and dozens of novelists should turn their experiences of war into adventure films, comics or thrillers? It was not uncommon, either. In the 1970s the letters pages of *Tradition* and *Wargamer's Newsletter* were peppered with letters from American servicemen in Vietnam seeking information about the uniforms of obscure Dutch units from the campaigns of the Duke of Marlborough, or discussing the use of shrapnel burst discs for calculating casualties caused by Seven Years War howitzers. 'I am interested in finding details of the lace patterns of the Württemberg Liebe-Garde *c.*1808,' they wrote. 'Please send all replies care of 525th Airborne Division, Da Nang.'

In his memoirs, John Cooke, a Lieutenant in the 43rd Light Infantry, recorded a wargame he and Thomas Wilkinson, a fellow officer, had fought after returning from the Walcheren Expedition in 1809. The two men made a baronial castle from wood, sheet tin and glass and carved an army of soldiers. The officers' accoutrements were gilded with gold leaf and the ensigns of each miniature regiment carried silk flags. Fire was provided by small brass cannon, loaded with swan-shot, and a siege of the castle played out:

> Before a breach was practicable, all the staff and superior officers were put *hors de combat*, where upon a sergeant who defended a round tower was promoted to the rank of Colonel and Lieutenant-Governor. There was a warm

wrangle between Wilkinson and myself at his skipping
over the grades of ensign, lieutenant, captain, and major,
but it was finally arranged that none under the rank of
Colonel could have the honour of taking charge of the
castle. The *ci-devant* [promoted] sergeant, armed with a tin
sword and repainted and covered with a profusion of silver
paper, cut a most dashing and brilliant appearance.
Having risen to this rank from the working soldier, we gave
him the post of honour, that is the hottest berth in the
castle, and the siege went on. Many fell by this side, but the
sergeant seemed endowed with a charmed exterior.

We were in the next room to the apartments of
Richards, the paymaster of our regiment, who was
exceedingly annoyed at the many loud reports of cannon
at this long siege. However, he eventually became so
excited that he would throw down his pen to see how
things were going on. Seeing the almost supernatural
escapes of the lieutenant-governor he entreated that the
fire of the brass cannon be directed to another quarter of
the castle, but without effect. When he heard that the
sergeant had at last fallen, he burst out of the room in a fit
of despair at the unfair way he had been treated. For days
afterwards he would enter the room and say, 'Really, I
cannot forget that poor sergeant.' Such was the force of
custom from the reports of the little cannon
day after day he protested that since the noise had ceased
he had failed to cast up his accounts with half the
correctness!

Years afterwards, whilst disembarking in England from
France, I had some of those little figures in a small case,
and a customhouse officer looked at them. I told him I
had made them. 'Oh, pooh,' replied he, 'they are of
French manufacture, but I shall not notice such trifles.'
Some of these little figures I possess to the present day.

Arthur had been acquainted with one pioneering wargamer, the roundly monikered J. R. Granville Bantock. Bantock's parents had been chums with H. G. Wells and he had played Little Wars-type games across the nursery carpet in the years leading up to the Great War. Military service in Flanders did little to curtail his wargaming. 'He once showed me his field service book from 1917,' Arthur said, 'page after page of notes on rules to recreate aerial combat – dogfights, Zeppelins and what have you. Even while he was fighting a genuine war in the trenches he was working out ways to turn it into a toy one.'

I asked Arthur why he thought Bantock had done that. 'Take his mind off things, I should imagine,' he said matter-of-factly. '"Man cannot stand too much reality" and all that. Especially when the reality is as bloody awful as that one was.'

As Anatole France pointed out, escape is a strong element of play. But, more than that, it seemed a kind of reflex. If writers see all experience as material, why shouldn't people who like making up games feel the same? Over the years I had come to realise that it was my interest in wargames that fuelled my interest in wars and not the other way round. I have never wanted to be a soldier.

It is true that I like history. And if you are interested in history it is very hard to avoid war. I once read E. H. Gombrich's *A Little History of the World* to my nine-year-old daughter. Gombrich was a humane and hugely decent man; *A Little History of the World* has a strong emphasis on tolerance, learning and justice and yet there is a battle on practically every page. War runs through the story of mankind like a spine. But it attracts me only in the same way that a deck of cards or a greyhound attracts a gambler.

It is very easy to turn war into a game, and equally easy to turn a game into a war. E. M. Forster once said that all drama stems from antithesis. The same is true of sports and games.

If there are only seven basic plots then there are, loosely, only three types of game: economic, racing and war. All but a very few (usually modern and generally, for historical reasons, German) are about beating other people, but since war is pretty much the acme of antithesis it is wargames that, over the centuries, have most exercised the human mind. Chess, Go, draughts and poker are all wargames. In poker, the army is the player's hand; he can reinforce, retreat (fold), attack or invite his adversaries to attack him and ambush them with a bluff. His casualties are money.

That combat and games should come together so success-fully is not surprising since they are both born of the same desire to prove that you are, in intelligence, strength, speed or perhaps ideology, superior to another person. The eighteenth century was the great era for gambling. Gentlemen would lose fortunes on matters of trivia: who could take his coat off fastest; which terrier could kill the most rats. Placing a bet makes any contest interesting, and the bigger the bet the more thrilling it becomes. It was also the era of duelling. These two activities are related. In one the stake is financial, in the other physical.

The most popular general amongst wargamers is Napoleon. This is because Napoleon actually *was* a wargamer, except he used real people and real landscapes and never had to worry about scales or ratios. Surveying the destruction after the Battle of Eylau in 1807, where twenty-five thousand of his army's dead and wounded lay freezing in the Prussian snows, the Emperor waved a dismissive arm and snapped, 'One drunken night in Paris will replace all these.' Yes, Boney, clear them off the table and put them back on the shelf and we'll all meet up for another set-to next week.

'All games aspire to the condition of war,' says the judge in Cormac McCarthy's novel *Blood Meridian*. True enough, but then war also aspires to the condition of a game. Combat and games are closely tied, they are symptoms of the same disease. Luckily, most of the time the symptoms aren't fatal. Wargames are mild palpitations – a real battle is a coronary.

10

The Effects of Terrain

'And we should never count the cost, or worry that we'll fall.
It's better to have fought and lost than not have fought at all.'
The Flashing Blade

When it came to the world of model soldiers, Arthur's enmities were the rule rather than the exception. Big Jim had gradually whittled down his Christmas card list until practically the only people on it were himself and Santa, and even Mr Claus was starting to get on his nerves big time. The longest-running and most bitter vendettas I have ever encountered occurred in the world of miniatures. It was as if a lifelong obsession with small things had left everybody with a skewed sense of perspective. Frequently I'd be talking to a veteran gamer or a dealer and mention someone else I'd met and they'd say, 'Never say that name in front of me again.' I'd say, 'Why, what happened?' and they'd snort and say, 'Don't get me started.' And then they'd start.

'Rather you than me,' Arthur said one day when I told him I was going to interview a man who, for a short while, had been the world's biggest manufacturer of lead soldiers. 'He's a terrible, bumptious little fellow, an absolute bounder. You know something: he pretends to be British, when he's really . . .' and Arthur paused dramatically to impress on me the infamy of what I was about to hear, 'an *Australian*.' He looked at me with one bushy eyebrow raised, as if the news was confirmation of some dark and hideous truth.

'Oh, *him*,' the retired figure-maker barked when Arthur's name cropped up in conversation, 'a real smaller-than-life character if ever there was one. I bet he told you I was from Australia, didn't he? Well I'm not. I was born in Basingstoke. So what do you say to that, eh?'

I thought of saying that if *I'd* been born in Basingstoke I'd have pretended to be Australian, but thought better of it. Instead I asked the man about his relationship with Peter Gilder. Gilder was a gifted figure designer, painter and modeller who also ran the world's first dedicated wargames holiday centre. In the 1960s he'd provided all the figures and scenery for the battles that were played out in *Callan*. Later he'd appeared on TV himself as one of the protagonists in *Battleground*, in which famous battles of history were refought as wargames. Edward Woodward was the presenter and the show ran for six episodes, at which point it dawned on somebody at ITV that maybe it wasn't going to displace snooker as the nation's favourite table-based television game experience. Gilder died in the 1990s. He was a hugely popular personality; nobody had a bad word to say about him. Well, almost no one.

'Relationship? I didn't have a relationship with him,' the man who wasn't Australian said, 'he was a crook. He *was*,' he said vehemently, as if I had contradicted him. 'He went to jail. Did time in prison. That makes you a crook in my book.'

Why Gilder went to jail was a matter of some debate. Some said he had taken the fall for his employer and gone inside in return for having his wife and kids cared for by his boss, others whispered that he had been fitted up by a bent accountant. It was hard to sift fact from fiction, but the most likely tale I heard came from Charlie. Charlie traded in second-hand soldiers, ran a company that made embroidered labels and appeared in the productions of the Driffield Amateur Operatic Society. Charlie was a small, dapper man who wore a bow tie and, unusually amongst toy traders, most of whom tended to be on the surly side of reticent, he seemed actually to enjoy talking to people. 'Peter was a smashing fella,' he said one day in a sports centre in Derby, 'lovely. Would do anything for anybody. He went down over some dealings with pie-heating equipment.'

Bitter and sometimes bloody disputes involving scale models have a long and rich history in Britain. They date back, in fact, to the early seventeenth century and the first recorded toy soldiers in England. These belonged to Henry Percy, 9th Earl of Northumberland. The rolls of Alnwick Castle show that from 12 February 1599 to 27 March 1602 the Earl commissioned four thousand 'leaden soldiers' cast in brass moulds, trimmed with verdigris and copper and furnished with wire pikes.

Henry Percy was nicknamed the 'Wizard Earl' because of his fondness for chemistry. He was a reclusive man with a pronounced stammer, who had renounced an early life of gambling, hunting and chasing women for the pursuit of knowledge. At his principal residence, Petworth in West Sussex, he had amassed a library of two thousand books – a staggering number for the time – and surrounded himself with a group of artists and men of science that included Sir Walter Ralegh and the playwright and possible spy Christopher Marlowe.

The rolls record that Percy's miniature metal army saw service at Alnwick Castle and then marched south to Syon House near Kew, another of the Earl's seats. Resident at Syon House was the Earl's principal scholar, the mathematician and astronomer Thomas Hariot. Many historians regard Hariot as the greatest scientist England produced prior to Sir Isaac Newton. He was an expert in algebra and optics, taught

Ralegh and his captains navigational skills and mapped the faces of the moon several years before Galileo. Hariot also carried out experiments with miniature cannons and gunpowder and, since Percy had been a commander during Elizabeth I's Irish Wars, it seems likely that Northumberland's toy soldiers were being used as part of a tactical military game. It also makes sense historically, because this was one of the great eras of military theorising.

Hundreds of treatises on the topic were published, all promising certain victory to those who employed the complex systems they outlined. In the early part of the seventeenth century strategy and tactics seemed likely to replace alchemy and astrology as the chosen preserve of the conman and the crackpot.

It may well have been Percy of whom John Webster was thinking when he wrote of a character in *The Duchess of Malfi*:

> He hath read all the late service
> As the City-Chronicle relates it:
> And keeps two pewterers going, only to express
> Battles in model.

Because he was rich, powerful and a Roman Catholic, Henry Percy had tried to remain as inconspicuous as possible, hiding away indoors with his books and toys. Unfortunately, one of his senior staff, grandson Thomas Percy, was not so circumspect. He got involved with Guy Fawkes and was named as one of the five plotters attempting to blow up the Houses of Parliament. Thomas fled to Holbeche House in Staffordshire, which was quickly besieged by government troops. The plotters attempted to go out with a bang, quite literally. But the powder they'd stored in the house was damp, the fuses were badly laid and so, instead of blowing up, it simply burst into flames. Badly scorched, young Percy fled from the burning building and was promptly shot dead by a marksman.

The Wizard Earl had had nothing to do with the plot, but the chance to get rid of a potentially dangerous foe and raise a bit of cash at the same time was too much of a temptation for the forces of the crown. Henry was locked up in the Tower of London for sixteen years and fined £30,000. The sum was raised by the sale of part of his estate. One of the things that went was the miniature army, which is next recorded in the possession of Henry, Prince of Wales, James I's son. And so Britain's first wargame army changed hands because one man accused another of treason.

Britain's next great model army was also the cause of acrimony and ruin, though this time it had a more central role. In 1830 Captain William Siborne was commissioned by Lord Hill (later 1st Viscount Hill), a former general in the Duke of Wellington's army who then succeeded Wellington as Commander-in-Chief of the Forces, to make a large model of the Battle of Waterloo to be displayed in a proposed new museum devoted to Britain's armed forces. Siborne, who was then assistant military secretary to the Commander of the Forces of Ireland, was advanced £350 of a proposed budget of £1400 and immediately set to work.

The thirty-three-year-old officer, who had served in France as part of the Army of Occupation from 1815 to 1817, would not be the first to construct a replica of a battlefield. That honour fell to a rather stylised representation of the 1743 Battle of Dettingen which had been made according to a plan drawn up by a French general of military engineers named Le Seigne and built in 1787 by a figure recorded for posterity as only 'a former guards officer'. The model then went on display at the French Army Museum in Les Invalides in Paris.

However, it is likely that the inspiration behind Siborne's commission came directly from Napoleon himself, a man whose life defined that of the Iron Duke in much the same way Joe Frazier's did that of Muhammad Ali. Like boxers or matadors, generals come to be measured by the quality of the opponents they have defeated, so that a great marshal's reputation is inseparable from that of his enemy. Certainly, for an apparently bluff and no-nonsense Englishman, Wellington was weirdly preoccupied with his old adversary, having an affair with one of the Emperor's former mistresses and spending many hours staring at Bonaparte's effigy in Madame Tussaud's Waxwork Museum.

Though by no means certain, it is likely that while Wellington was in Paris after the conclusion of the first war against Napoleon he would have come across a $^1/_{144}$ scale model of the decisive moments of the Battle of Lodi. Bonaparte had commissioned this in 1804, when he was still First Consul of the Republic. The Battle of Lodi had taken place on 11 May 1796 (or as the plaque on the model had it 'The 21st of the month of Floreal in the year IV'. The French revolutionaries took a Pol Pot-like attitude to time. They even attempted to introduce a decimal clock.) It was one of Bonaparte's many victories during the Italian Campaign. Though it was neither his greatest battle, nor his most dazzling strategic feat, nor anywhere near as famous as the Battle of Marengo which followed it, Napoleon looked upon the combat as a turning point. Lodi, he said with that humility for which he was noted, was important because it was there that he had truly recognised his own capacity for greatness.

The model of Lodi was made by Martin Boitard who based it on the recollections and watercolours of Louis-Albert-Ghislain Bacler d'Albe, a member of Napoleon's general staff and the man tasked with training the artists attached to the quartermaster section of *La Grande Armée*. It shows French troops streaming across a bridge over the Adda River to attack the Austrian forces that are massed on the opposite bank. The figures were cast in slate moulds and tweaked into lifelike positions using forceps. Despite the fact that the infantrymen were just 10mm high, each had belts and ammunition pouches made of tracing paper. The horses had reins and traces made from silken thread and saddles of thin card; the whole force of several thousand figures were finely painted using gouache. Unfortunately, nobody thought to varnish them. As a result the figures gradually oxidised and, one by one, like the real soldiers they so precisely represented, they crumbled into dust.

Captain Siborne – who had earned his commission by producing a now long-lost model of Napoleon's clash with Kutuzov at Borodino – set about his new project in a most methodical manner. He visited the battlefield, talked to local farmers and spent eight months mapping out the terrain in minute detail. Then he returned to his base at the Royal Hibernian Military Asylum in Dublin and made a model in $^{1}/_{600}$ scale on thirty-five wooden boards measuring a total of slightly over four hundred square feet. (I should say that $^{1}/_{600}$ was the ground scale. In the interests of aesthetics, a 1:180 height scale was used.) The battlefield, fashioned from a mix of plaster of Paris and papier mâché laid over a framework of boxwood and ivory, was complete in every topographical detail. Hedges made from green chenille lined roads paved with cobbles cast in lead and fields of corn fashioned from stiffened towelling. Smoke of painted cotton wool rose from cork-walled buildings of the Hougomont, La Haye Sainte and Papelotte farms. It was a magnificent sight.

Now all he needed were the soldiers to put on it – one hundred and ninety thousand of them. By this time, Siborne had long since spent all the money Lord Hill had advanced him, so he went back for more. The general told him that since it was public money he would have to apply to Parliament but, unhappily for Siborne, the Whigs had just ousted the Duke of Wellington's Tory party and refused to offer financial support to a project designed to glorify the leader of the opposition. Siborne cajoled and pleaded and begged, but no cash was forthcoming. The Captain might have given up, but by now he too was gripped by a mania to finish the project. He borrowed money from a bank, he took advances on his pay and he scrounged from friends and acquaintances. He was sure he could make the money back when the model was complete, by putting it on public display.

Siborne's confidence was well-founded: at that time public exhibitions were big business. In modelling circles it's common to refer to the sort of model Siborne was engaged in making as a diorama. That is a mistake. Real dioramas are a different, if equally elaborate, affair and in the 1830s they were a major moneymaking venture. The diorama had been invented in Paris by Louis Daguerre, who combined the singular pursuits of theatrical design and physics with breakthroughs in photography. He later worked with Nicéphore Niépce, who was also a pioneering photographer. Their diorama combined the black-and-white photographer's knowledge of light and shade with scene-painting skills: huge pictures measuring seventy feet by forty feet were painted onto translucent silk and suspended in ranks from the walls of a purpose-built circular pavilion lit only from the roof. By the use of vast Heath Robinson contrivances, mirrors, skylights and coloured filters were manipulated in such a way as to create an illusion of three dimensions and suggest the gradual passing of the day from dawn to dusk.

Daguerre's first diorama, which opened in Paris in 1822, consisted of two paintings, one by Daguerre and another by Charles Bouton, and attracted eighty thousand visitors in a year, netting a profit of two hundred thousand francs (about £8000). The Frenchmen promptly set about expanding the franchise by opening a diorama in London. This was built in Park Square on the edge of Regent's Park at a cost of £10,000. Britain was still hostile to France following the Napoleonic Wars and soon a rival attraction named, with bludgeoning lack of subtlety, 'The British Diorama' was opened in the Queen's Bazaar, Oxford Street by Clarkson Stanfield and David Roberts. Unperturbed by patriotism, the British public flocked to both.

If so many people would go to see a bit of flummery with silk and sunlight, how many more might be expected to pay to see a fine collection of figures on sculpted terrain? Siborne was certain that, when his model was finished, not only would he pay off his debts, he'd make a small fortune.

For several years he commissioned and painted the figures for his model. Half-an-inch high, each tiny man represented two actual soldiers. They were lacking in detail but convincing displayed en masse. Who made them is not recorded; Siborne kept meticulous accounts but the receipts for the miniature soldiers are missing. Perhaps, like many wargamers in later years, he burned them before his wife could see what he had spent. In 1838 the model was finally completed. It had cost in excess of £3000, then Siborne spent another £400 transporting it to London to be exhibited in the Egyptian Hall in Piccadilly.

Siborne had expected to make a bundle, but he was disappointed. The problem was that he had incurred the disapproval of the very man the model was supposed to celebrate. The Duke of Wellington took a dim view of military history, regarding it as a hopeless and frivolous pursuit. 'You may as well try and write the history of a ball as of a battle,' he had replied curtly when Siborne appealed for his recollections of the events at Waterloo. Wellington's opinion was based on experience; the Napoleonic battlefield was not a place where anybody could take a general overview. Owing to the topography of the field and the clouds of dark smoke produced by the black powder of the muskets, rifles and cannons, no single man could ever observe more than a tiny fraction of the battlefield. Siborne was attempting to stitch together those fractions to create a complete picture. In Old Beaky's view, attempting to synchronise one with another was – as at a dance – more or less impossible.

Wellington may have had a point, but others were not so laconic. The Prussian high command in particular offered their wholehearted assistance to the Englishman, though the evidence they supplied painted a rather different picture of the events of 18 June 1815 than the one given in Wellington's official despatch written on the morning after the battle. The Prussians of Field Marshal Gebhard von Blücher had, it appeared, arrived on the right flank of the French Army several hours earlier than the Duke had credited.

The model reflected what Siborne had discovered. It showed the conflict at its point of crisis, late in the afternoon with Donzelot's division in possession of the farmhouse of La Haye Sainte and Napoleon's Imperial Guard advancing up the ridge toward Mont St Jean. It all looked splendid, but, as far as Wellington was concerned, there was far too much Prussian blue in evidence. The Duke had always praised the efforts of Blücher and characterised the victory as an allied, rather than purely British, one. (Even the 'British' Army at Waterloo was comprised largely of Germans and Dutch.) But there seemed to be a degree of magnanimity in this verdict because, according to his own report, the Prussians had turned up rather late. The positioning of the dark blue soldiers on the model suggested that, far from simply aiding Wellington in the final push for victory, Blücher's arrival had been the turning point. Indeed, one might even conclude that damned old 'Marshal Vorwarts' (as Blücher was known) had actually rescued the Iron Duke. This simply would not do. The model not only challenged Wellington's reputation but also his veracity. He refused to make a public visit to see it, or to voice his approval, and, though he remained resolutely silent on the topic, privately word was quickly spread that the great man was furious that Siborne had allowed himself to be 'humbugged' in such a manner by the Germans. This had a marked effect on the success of the exhibition: it was as if J. K. Rowling had gone into print to slaughter a forthcoming Harry Potter movie. Siborne recouped some of his investment and, in a pitiful attempt to regain the Duke's favour, even went so far as to remove forty thousand Prussian figures from the landscape, but to no avail. The exhibition closed and another venue could not be found for it. Siborne's offer to present the model as a gift to the nation was turned down by the authorities, his prospects of military advancement reduced to nil.

Over the next few years Siborne published a detailed account of the battle based on the letters he had exchanged with the combatants, and even embarked on another scale model of an altogether less controversial moment in the affair – the charge of the Union Brigade around La Haye Sainte. But despite his determination, hard work and skill he never made his fortune from Waterloo and died of intestinal disease at the Royal Military Hospital in Chelsea in 1849. He was fifty-one. The large model, unwanted and homeless, was shifted from one place to another before coming to rest in a dusty Irish warehouse where it remained for over sixty years, forgotten save by mice and moths. Thankfully it was eventually saved and now, fully restored, is on display at the National Army Museum, Chelsea.

*

'So,' Arthur said when I had returned from seeing the man who wasn't Australian, 'what did you make of him? Hope you counted your fingernails after he shook your hand.' I said he had been very pleasant and most informative. 'Was he now?' Arthur said with a malevolent grin.

'It doesn't really matter,' I said in a bid to stave off an argument.

'Nothing really matters,' Arthur growled. 'About 99.99 per cent of everything a man does in his life is totally irrelevant. And that's if he's a ruddy genius. The rest of us are chaff, cannon fodder. What matters is what you decide matters, and these things matter to me.'

I didn't like Arthur's tone, but I knew that what he was saying was true. For some years I'd worked in the upper echelons of the hotel trade, where people got very vexed when a new waiter set the wrong spoon for the consommé. It was trivial, it was insignificant, but if you pointed that out to the banqueting manager you'd be picking up your P45 before you could say 'asparagus tongs'. If a man can commit himself fully and with complete seriousness to something that is totally without importance, then he is halfway to riches. If you don't believe me, try watching *Match of the Day* some time.

'And was his wife around?' Arthur asked after a momentary silence. I said she was, and that she had brought us tea and lemon drizzle cake in the conservatory.

'Well let me tell you something that might amuse you. Once, back in the sixties, I went round to that old scoundrel's house to collect some 30mm Franco-Prussians I'd ordered. A big old place it was, set well back from the road. I rang the door-bell and got no reply, though the lights were on inside. So I wandered round the back. There was light streaming out across the lawn from the French windows of the drawing room so I strolled over and peeked in. Good Lord, what a scene! There was that fellow, as fat then as he doubtless is today, absolutely starkers, chasing his equally plump and no less naked lady wife round the sofa attempting to tickle her with a big red feather duster. Five o'clock of a winter's afternoon, can you imagine it?'

I said that I'd rather not. Though, to be honest, I suspected Arthur was doing enough imagining for the both of us.

11

Unit Status – Elites to Militia

'The human heart is the starting point for all matters relating to war.'

Hermann-Maurice, Comte de Saxe

'In the 1860s the French Army was acknowledged to be the finest in the world,' I said.

'Ah well now,' Arthur replied, 'I think if you make a study of history you'll find that the French Army has *always* been at its most invincible during times of peace.' He let out a snort that sent the foam from his cappuccino spraying across the table. We were sitting in an Italian café near Golders Hill Park, and Arthur was expatiating on the centrality of France in the world of the little men.

Even the most devoted Francophobe would have found it hard to argue the point. There had, for example, been no systematic or detailed study of military uniforms until the French took it up in the latter part of the nineteenth century. It was the success of the Army Pavilion at the Paris Universal Exposition in 1889 that sparked a group of artists including Lucien Rousselot and Édouard Détaille to form a society, *La Sabretache*, with the specific aim of studying the subject. The society issued a monthly magazine, *Carnet de la Sabretache*, which proved an instant success.

In truth, the French had always loved military things: the

elan, the swagger, the glory. The only trouble was that for France the glory didn't necessarily follow the other two. By 1890, however, the French Army had recovered from the debacle of the Franco-Prussian War and the public were ready to embrace it again and, following the appearance of the *Carnet*, the country's passion for uniforms and militaria was rekindled. A new army museum opened in Paris to great fanfare, and Commandant Bucquoy began publishing his epic works on the uniforms of the First Empire. The mania has continued more or less unabated ever since.

When I was a small boy I loved butterflies and birds, particularly those from the tropics. I had books filled with pictures of Rajah Brooke's birdwings, blue mountain swallowtails, purple-crested turacos and Leadbeater's cockatoos. I'd sit on my bed studying them in detail, trying to decide which I'd rather see, the southern carmine bee-eater or the lilac-breasted roller; the Bhutan glory or the gaudy commodore. They were so much more colourful than the birds and butterflies I could see in my own garden.

Military uniforms offered a similar glimpse of a brighter, showier life. My father, who had begun painting 54mm figures in breaks between model yachts and radio-controlled aircraft, had a number of books on the topic. My particular favourite was *Military Uniforms in Colour* by the Danish writer and artist Preben Kannick. *Military Uniforms* was published by Blandford, who produced dozens of books on uniforms, aircraft and armoured fighting vehicles. They had hard blue covers and measured 7¼ inches by 4¾ inches. They were chunky yet pocket-sized, the big brother of the Observer series. Most books concentrated on a particular army or conflict, *Uniforms of Waterloo*, *Medieval Military Dress*, *Fighter Aircraft 1914–1918* and so on, but Kannick's book covered every conflict from the Dutch Wars to Korea. If you wanted to know what a trooper of the Venezuelan General Bolivar's

Bodyguard (1820) looked like, you only had to reach for Kannick. And when I did the same questions always arose. Which looked finest, France: Chasseurs d'Afrique, Trooper, 1870; or British West Indies: West India Regiment, Lance-Corporal, 1926? And which was silliest, the extremely short shorts of Germany: Afrika Korps, Infantryman, 1943, or the ridiculously baggy red pantaloons of France: 3rd Zouave Regiment, Zouave, 1854?

I made endless lists, hit parades on military couture in which Australia: New South Wales Lancers, Trooper, 1900, was a surprise entry at four, while Denmark-Norway: Fyn Light Dragoons, Trooper, 1813, was down five places at number eight. To this day, I can't pick up a copy of *The World's Great Regiments* by Vezio Melegari or a volume from the classic Éditions Casterman series on Napoleonic military fashions without spending half an hour trying to decide which is nicer, the outfit of the Chasseurs à Cheval of the Imperial Guard or that of the Lanciers de Berg.

Up until the Great War, soldiers were the birds of paradise of the masculine world. In Victorian England, the ordinary middle-class man went about his business in black trousers, a black coat, a white shirt, a black tie and a black hat. His counterpart in a hussar regiment, meanwhile, might be seen swanning about in crimson breeches, a blue fur-trimmed jacket with brocaded front, a tunic with gold lace and embroidery and a bearskin with a scarlet top. While the rest of the world was in monochrome, the army was in Technicolor. Even Oliver Cromwell dressed his soldiers in red coats.

The finery didn't arrive by accident, either. In the masculine world vanity and violence often swagger down the street hand-in-hand. Many military commanders showed a commitment to design and tailoring that makes Beau Brummel look like Barney Gumble. Napoleon's cavalry commander,

Marshal Prince Joachim Murat, King of Naples, was so concerned with his personal appearance that when *La Grande
Armée* rumbled into Russia in 1812 its baggage train included
one cart filled with his clothes and another entirely devoted to
his headgear and make-up. Murat's attention to grooming
was exceptional, but hardly without precedent. There were
Austrian officers in the eighteenth century who, even when
on campaign, did their best to preserve silky smooth skin by
soaking regularly in baths filled with warm milk, while at the
Prussian Military Academy in Berlin cadets spent the first
hour and a half of every day dressing their hair, then devoted
another thirty minutes to buttoning their boots correctly.

The cut of the cavalry's uniforms, meanwhile, owed much
to the proclivities of one of Murat's predecessors, Marshal
Maurice de Saxe. The Comte de Saxe was a brilliant Polish
commander who led the French to victory after victory
during the War of the Austrian Succession. He was also given
to high living: the French expression *soul comme un Polonais* –
'pissed as a Pole' – was coined in his honour. Saxe liked food
and he liked wine, but his principal addiction was to actresses
and ballerinas, and he had a corps de ballet attached to his
staff in a semi-official capacity. The uniform of his troops was
influenced by the theatrical fashions of the day. The brass
helmet with horsehair crinière he introduced for his dragoons
was a direct copy of those being worn by actors in the
Roman plays that were all the rage in Paris. This helmet, with
various modifications, swiftly became the accepted headgear
for heavy cavalry in all nations (fashion trends swept through
the armies of the world as quickly as through haute couture.
One minute only the Hungarians had hussars, the next every
country had them.) Later, the horsehair was removed and the
metal that had held it, *le cimier*, reduced until all that was left
was a ridge – a vestigial crest. This style of helmet was subsequently adopted by various fire services. So we can say that

the headgear worn by the New York firefighter is the direct result of the Comte de Saxe and his affection for dancing girls.

When I was in London in the eighties there was a big international newsagent's shop round the corner from where I was working that sold hundreds and hundreds of newspapers and periodicals from all around the world. It had been there for many decades. 'Two brothers came over from Silesia before the war and started it,' Arthur, who also knew the shop well, told me. 'A rum pair. One of them had a big nose and the other was a dwarf. And the dwarf died.'

The man who ran the shop now was the son of the big-nosed Silesian. He had thick glasses that made his eyes look like those of some vast aquatic invertebrate, hair even less life-like than that of Action Man and skin the colour of rendered mutton fat. He sat behind the counter all day, watching and waiting. He was a hawk and his prey was anybody with the temerity to take a magazine off the shelf and start glancing through the pages. 'Strictly No Browsing!!!!' said the signs, and they weren't just there for decoration. The exclamation marks looked like a flight of arrows and that wasn't a coincidence. Pick the magazine up, check the date or the issue number and pay for it. That was what a customer was expected to do. If you lingered too long over the illustration on the front you'd hear a loud, sarcastic whine: 'Sign above the door says "Public Library", does it? I'll tell you what, don't stand there in discomfort. Take it home and bring it back when you've finished with it. Or would sir, perchance, like me to photocopy the relevant pages for him? All part of the service. It's not like I'm running a fackin' business, or anything.'

Big-nosed Silesian junior was rude, cantankerous and ill mannered, but that didn't bother me too much. Compared to the men who ran most model soldier shops he was a regular

Pollyanna. The men in charge of model soldier shops were
routinely monosyllabic, curmudgeonly and totally disinter-
ested in the vulgar routines of commerce. They had the
manners of a moose and the customer care skills of Sweeney
Todd. As soon as he saw you approaching the counter, the
average model soldier shop owner would miraculously discover some task that involved disappearing behind the
banked counter display of painted 15mm Samurai armies, or
turning his back to tinker noisily amongst the drawers stuffed
with modern micro-armour AFVs. You'd stand, waiting for
him to give you his attention. And you'd wait. And you'd
wait, while he scuffled pointlessly about. You'd cough. You'd
fumble noisily with your change. And briefly you'd actually
consider flinging the figures aside, yelling, 'Sod you then, you
miserable bugger!' and storming out. But you knew, and he
knew, that you couldn't do that. Because this was the only
place in London where you could get a blister pack of RAFM
Iroquois Indians (standing, firing muskets) and you really
needed them, desperately. And he knew that too.

   Besides, this rudeness was tradition. The Swiss writer and
toy soldier collector Jean Nicollier recalls 'a dealer in lead soldiers named Coisel' who ran a business in the rue de
Dunkerque, Paris, in the years before the outbreak of the
Great War. Monsieur Coisel used to organise huge battles in
his shop, which were played out during opening hours. 'He
would delve into his boxes, ostensibly on sale to the public,
and even show some ill-temper if an unfortunate customer
should appear and interrupt his consideration of the next
move.' Wearing a large Alpinist's beret, M. Coisel gave short
shrift to anybody, even the most loyal buyer, who failed to
show consideration for him when he was mid-battle and as a
consequence, Nicollier relates sadly, 'The unfortunate shop-
keeper soon became bankrupt.' And so, it must be said, did
most of his British counterparts.

The big-nosed Silesian's son hence did not unsettle me. I went in to his shop once a month to get a copy of the French military history magazine *Campaign*, which specialised in large illustrations of the uniforms of the Premier Empire, coloured plates in the style of the great Gallic military artists Rousselot, Détaille, Chartier and Myrbach. I had limited French, poor CSE standard bulked up by the terminology I'd learned at catering college. Now I added to that the fastidious yet lyrical vocabulary of military fashion: *dolman, pelisse, ganse de cocard, raquettes, bourdalou, cadenette, retroussis simules, chaperons doubles* and, my particular favourite, *chabraque*. And then there were the colours: *bleu celeste, bleu de roi, cramoisis, paille, jonquille, rose vif, vert gazon, ponceau, garance, gris cendre, lilas, bleuet, chataigne, violet*. The words had romance; reading them was enough to make you feel like you'd just danced with a pretty girl. Plus I was not only feeding my hobby, but also improving my French. Though admittedly the chances of me ever having to visit Paris to buy a lawn green saddlecloth are somewhat limited.

So significant were uniforms to the French that their collective name for the conflicts of the mid-eighteenth century (The War of the Austrian Succession, the Seven Years War and so forth) was *la guerre en dentelle* – the war in lace. This name came from the fancy embroidered tape that edged the soldiers' buttonholes and cuffs; each regiment would have its own unique lace. I often wondered how these were chosen. I imagined the colonel of the regiment sitting at a table, sifting listlessly through designs before crying, 'No, these are too, too busy. Can't you get me something a little more, you know, Coco Chanel?'

The most elaborate uniforms of all belonged to the hussars. An adaptation of the costume worn by the horsemen of the Hungarian plains, hussars wore thigh-length boots and tight breeches, a short fitted brocade jacket and had a fur-trimmed jacket slung nonchalantly over the shoulder. The

Prussian hussars of Frederick the Great even had hearts embroidered on the upper thighs of their breeches. The hussar's accoutrements extended beyond just clothing: he also wore a long moustache, and had the locks of hair at his temples plaited. Not until the arrival of Elvis Presley would any male capture the same wild, rebel swagger.

The new interest in military uniforms in France was soon reflected by an increase in the sale of toy soldiers to French grown-ups, or 'collectors' as they chose to style themselves. The first toy soldiers from the German city of Nuremberg (to which my uncle had escorted Rudolf Hess) were made by local goldsmiths for their children, but their fame quickly spread. By the early 1600s Maria de Medici, wife of Henry IV of France, was giving vast armies of them to her son, the future Louis XIII. This army was gradually added to until by the time Louis XIV was a youth the collection was said to be worth fifty thousand *écus*. In the true spirit of the toy soldier enthusiast, on reaching adulthood the Sun King promptly ordered an even bigger army. Ostensibly this was for his own son, though I think we can guess who played with it most.

The new model army was such a massive undertaking that Louis handed responsibility for organising its recruitment to his illustrious finance minister Jean Baptiste Colbert, who immediately passed it on to his brother Charles. Charles Colbert saw that this was no job for an amateur and so gave the brief to Sébastien le Prestre de Vauban, arguably the greatest designer of military fortifications in history (just about the only part of Ypres that survived the onslaught of the First World War were Vauban's earth and stone bastions, built nearly two centuries earlier). Vauban commissioned the Nuremberg goldsmith Johann Jakob Wolrab to make the figures, and a clockwork mechanism that made them move was added by an instrument maker named Gottfried Hautsch. The resulting army was such a big hit with the French royal household that in Florence the Medicis immediately commissioned an identical one.

Louis promptly raised the ante by commissioning an army of card soldiers consisting of twenty squadrons of cavalry and ten battalions of infantry from a French maker named Pierre Couturier. Numbering some eight thousand figures, it cost fifty thousand livres. And there the Sun King's model soldier mania was allowed to rest. What happened to his armies after he died is a matter of conjecture, for they have never been seen since. If modern precedent is anything to go on, my guess would be that his widow gave them to the Boy Scouts jumble sale.

Like Maria de Medici, the *nouvelle vague* of French collectors also favoured figures from Germany, in this case two dimensional 30mm soldiers made from tin. Only these would do; they mocked those who collected three-dimensional lead soldiers, such as those being produced at that time by Britain's, as 'les plombiers', a punning name meaning 'the plumbers' – reflecting the same snobbish attitude I would take to plastics. Flats were artistic; all else was kids' stuff.

The French collectors took their hobby seriously. A series of articles in *L'Illustration* in the first months of the twentieth century recounted the efforts of a Parisian doctor, Camille Laumonnier, to refight the Battle of Austerlitz on his drawing room floor. The medic had used over four thousand figures. Luckily his drawing room measured twelve metres by twelve metres so there was enough space for his family to walk through without stepping on the Imperial Guard reserve. Laumonnier spent days setting the scenery up, sprinkling the floor with icing sugar to represent the frost of that cold Austrian morning. Unfortunately the drawings in *L'Illustration* clearly show that he was using a sheet pinned to a washing line suspended between two stepladders as his back-drop, adding a domestic touch that spoiled the grand tone somewhat.

One of the greatest collectors in Paris at that time was an Englishman, Samuel MacGregor Mathers, a former officer in the territorials. (Any number of ex-military men were involved in the figure collecting scene in France. The same was true across Europe: the Belgian model soldier society had for decades been presided over by General Deleuze, while the man dubbed 'the father of Austrian collectors' was the splendidly named Colonel Willy Teuber-Weckersdorff.)

According to the French author and figure collector Marcel Baldet, Samuel MacGregor Mathers had more than twenty-five thousand figures and fought battles with them to rules of his own devising, *le jeu des soldats de plomb*, that extended to several dozen pages.

Mathers had adopted the middle name of MacGregor when he was a young man to give himself a whiff of Highland glamour, though he was born in Hackney, and he later adopted the style Comte de Glenstrae. His wife also changed her name, from Mina to the more Scottish-sounding Moina. She was the sister of the Roman Catholic philosopher Henri Bergson, and Mathers had 'philosophical' interest of his own. 'He had two ruling passions in his life,' wrote the Irish poet W. B. Yeats, 'magic and the theory of war.' In pursuit of the former, the Count co-founded the Hermetic Order of the Golden Dawn, an occult organisation that mixed freemasonry with cabbala, astrology, alchemy, the arcane mysteries of the ancient Egyptian priesthood and a faint hint of devil worship. I imagine when the Bergson clan got together at Christmas this must have created quite an atmosphere.

Members of the Order included Yeats and the Welsh writer of weird tales Arthur Machen. Machen was to have his own indirect influence on the world of wargaming: it was his work that inspired the likes of Robert E. Howard and H. P. Lovecraft, and led inexorably to blokes sitting in student flats painting dwarves, elves, Atlantis fish-men and improbably muscled barbarian heroes.

Through the Hermetic Order of the Golden Dawn, Mathers also formed a friendship with the notorious Aleister Crowley, the self-professed 'Great Beast' and world's most evil man, an infamous devil worshipper who boasted of drinking human blood and copulating with goats.

A chap I knew had made a TV documentary about Crowley so I got in touch with him and asked if he knew anyone I could talk to about Samuel Mathers. He gave me the number of a man in Braintree. 'He's a warlock,' he said. 'I wouldn't advise going round his house.'

'Bit spooky, is it?' I said.

'Not really. It's just he's a vegetarian. The food's atrocious and there's that veggie farty smell everywhere.'

So I telephoned instead. The warlock was very keen to talk of Mathers, a vegetarian himself, incidentally, despite his passion for artillery. He regarded him as one of the fathers of the revival of Paganism, which had begun in the 1880s. 'He saw the links between many things,' the warlock said, 'the foot prints of the natural path . . .'

'It's not really the occult side of his life I'm interested in,' I said. 'I wanted to talk about the toy soldiers.'

'The *toy soldiers*?' the warlock said with a tone of what I can only call horror.

'Yes,' I said. 'Apparently he had thousands of German 30mm tin flats and he used to fight huge battles with them. I'm not sure, but it seems likely that when he wasn't dressing in Egyptian regalia and sending exhortations to Isis-Urania he was knocking around with a Parisian doctor named Camille Laumonnier who did Austerlitz on the drawing room floor. Anatole France wrote about it. Mather was one of the first wargamers. He had complex rules and everything. I wondered if you could shed any light on that.'

There was a long silence, then the warlock said in a very quiet voice, 'No, I think you must be mistaken. I don't believe Count Mathers would ever have been involved in anything of *that* sort.'

'Why not? After all, he played Enochian chess with cardboard pieces representing the deities of ancient Egypt . . .' But I was talking to myself. The line to Essex had gone dead.

Mathers and Crowley eventually fell out. Mathers sent a spectral vampire to feast on Crowley's blood and Crowley responded by despatching a demon army to scourge his former friend's flesh. Mathers died in 1918; his grave has never been found. Crowley went on to become the world's leading Satanist and an inspiration to a generation of drug-addled heavy rock guitarists. There was no record of the Great Beast himself playing wargames, I should add. It's possible, though, that all the talk of blood sucking and goat fucking was just a beard and he actually spent his evenings refighting the Crimean War in 15mm.

The wargaming efforts of Samuel Mathers and Dr Laumonnier were followed by those of Léopold Marchant, Jean Besnus, Dr Kouchnir and Jacques Laurent of the venerable French model soldier club *La Société des Collectionneurs de Figurines Historiques*. As a result of the kind of reverse stereotyping to which the English are prone, I had always imagined the early French wargames scene to be rather dashing.

There was good reason for this. One of my favourite British figure designers, Marcus Hinton, had begun by making figures for the Sentry Box. I remembered the adverts for the Sentry Box that appeared in *Tradition*. They were quite plain and simple but the thing that stuck in my mind was the bracketed note (Prop. Miss Y. Edmonds. Callers by appointment only), which gave the whole thing an air at once genteel and yet slightly seedy. Miss Edmonds had begun running the company as a sideline with her daytime employer Dr Lovel

Barnes, a London psychiatrist and model soldier enthusiast. In an interview she confessed that the business now took up so much of her time that she could no longer find a spare minute to make curtains for her small flat. Holidays, meals in restaurants and nights in the West End were also out of the question. 'The only luxury she allows herself,' the interviewer noted, 'is the ownership of a colour television set.' In her spartan devotion to the little men, Miss Edmonds put me in mind of a character from a William Trevor short story.

The French figure-makers, by contrast, were a mysterious and romantic breed. There was the fiercely exacting General Paul Angenot, a divisional cavalry commander in the Great War who ran a riding school and spent his spare hours carving immaculate equestrian models from basswood. Such were Angenot's standards it was said that he destroyed 50 per cent of all the models he made because they did not match his aesthetic vision. Roger Berdou was a reclusive genius whose remarkable 54mm Premier Empire figures were furtively hoarded by a few equally retiring collectors. One of these was an Austrian baron, another an Englishman who would not allow his name to be published for fear of attracting burglars, a third was a wealthy Californian with the unlikely name of Elton L. Puffer. Josianne des Fontaine was a shy and reserved lady from Boulogne-sur-Seine who worked purely to commission. The widow Madame Metayer had begun her career painting figures for Paul Armont, the prolific dramatist whose work was adapted for Hollywood musicals by Rodgers and Hart. The gallant journalist Marcel Baldet had been wounded four times fighting for his country in the trenches during the First World War. Undeterred, he had signed up for a second crack at the Germans in 1939 and been shot again. After that Baldet confined his military duties to producing figures and advising the film industry on uniforms in a vain bid to stop retired colonels writing angry letters complaining that the buttons on the Prussians' cuffs were the wrong type of metal.

I imagined that some of this intrigue and panache would have been carried over into French wargaming. I pictured something akin to the ballroom scenes in *L'Éducation Sentimental*, with men in tailcoats manoeuvring vast armies across billiard tables while coquettish young women in hussars' uniforms distributed glasses of Chateau d'Yquem and canapés.

I came across Claude-Victor in cyberspace. He was a veteran French wargamer and a man of some wit and erudition, even in a language that was not his own. It was Claude-Victor who told me of the Marshal de Saxe and his theatrical frolics, and it was plain he was the man to question on the original generals of the *jeux de guerre*. So I emailed him. He replied, congratulating me on my knowledge of French history before severely disabusing me of my romantic notions.

'I was myself a member of the extremely venerable *Société des Collectionneurs de Figurines Historiques et Amis de l'Histoire Militaire*,' Claude-Victor wrote. 'My experiences suggest that the wargames played by its esteemed members would have been rather different from the hobby as we know it today. I joined the society in 1961; at this time most of the members were still looking down their noses at the best *ronde-bosse* lead soldiers, which they derided as toy soldiers, only tin flats being worthy of the holy label of "miniature militaire". This was characteristic of their general attitude, which was devotedly archaic, hyper-conservative, self-congratulatory and scornfully sectarian. An attitude related in part, of course, to the average age of the members (most of whom were over seventy) and also to their sociological recruitment – generals, bishops, judges, doctors (provided they were at least *professeurs d'université*), obscenely rich notaries and so on. Their games were burdened by the obsessive pedantry so typical of secluded, closed and haughty micro-groups everywhere. They did not seek to expand their hobby; they did not want it to be popular. Indeed, I'm sure the mere word popular made most of them nauseous. All those I encountered were haunted by nostalgia, not for their childhood games with toy soldiers, but for the grand old days of feudalism.'

Claude-Victor was a biology teacher. He said he had begun to worry for the education of France. Last week, he said, he had received an essay in which a boy had written that 'the giant squid captures and crushes prey using its gigantic testicles'.

Arthur would, I think, have enjoyed this joke. But by the time I met Claude-Victor, Arthur was dead.

12

Organising and Basing your Armies

'You do not stop playing games when you get old; you get old when you stop playing games.'

Oliver Wendell Holmes

Wargaming may not have featured much on television or in movies but it turned up an awful lot in literature, if only in the background. Goethe wrote about it, so did Sterne, but the first literary giants to really explore the potential of the hobby were the Brontës: Charlotte, Anne, Emily and Branwell.

The Brontës' obsession with toy soldiers began when their father returned to Haworth from a trip to Leeds bearing a box of the carved wooden figures known as biffins. The effect of the arrival at the parsonage of the little men was immediate and galvanic. In her memoir *The History of the Year 1829*, Charlotte records:

When Papa came home it was night, and we were in bed, so next morning Branwell came to our door with a box of soldiers. Emily and I jumped out of bed, and I snatched up one and exclaimed, 'This is the Duke of Wellington! This shall be the Duke.' When I had said this, Emily likewise took one up and said it should be hers; when Anne came down she said one should be hers. Mine was the prettiest of the whole and the tallest, and the most perfect in every part. Emily's was a grave looking fellow, and we called him 'Gravey'. Anne's was a queer little thing, much like herself, and we called him 'Waiting Boy'. Branwell chose his and called him 'Buonaparte'.

The soldiers became part of an elaborate game, which grew bigger as more and more figures were added to the children's collection. One box of a dozen new soldiers was named 'The Young Men' and sent immediately to explore West Africa where, amongst other adventures, they encountered 'An immense and terrible monster his head touched the clouds was encircled with a red and fiery Halo his nostrils flashed forth flame'. An imaginary kingdom, Angria, was called into being and the figures were each assigned a part in the politics, culture and military life of this fantasy nation. Battles and rebellions abounded, the history of which was recorded in tiny hand-made books – the first wargames journals – by Angria's own historian, a carved soldier the Brontës christened Captain John Bud.

Branwell's passion for the Premier Empire evidently continued, since one of the later figures that belonged to him was named Young Soult in honour of one of Bonaparte's greatest marshals. Nicolas Jean de Dieu Soult had been a decent strategist on the battlefield, though it is said he showed more initiative and daring when it came to accumulating money, using the Napoleonic Wars to amass a huge fortune by a combination of extortion and plunder. In Angria, his namesake had an altogether less worldly role as the national poet.

After the wargames finished, the sisters directed their imaginations into writing fiction. Branwell, meanwhile, took to opium and strong drink, and became a teacher. The former are not requirements for the British educationalist, but they help.

While the Brontës were playing with their soldiers in Yorkshire, across in Copenhagen Hans Christian Andersen was also drawing inspiration from the little men. Andersen wrote several stories about toy soldiers, the most famous of which is *The Steadfast Tin Soldier*. The steadfast tin soldier and the rest of his platoon were made from the metal of a melted-down spoon. That kind of recycling wasn't uncommon; Astrid Lindgren mentions Swedish boys doing it in *The Children of Noisy Village*, and there were companies in London at the turn of the century that knocked out whole divisions of infantry from old sardine cans.

Thousands of figures were home-cast in that way. Arthur told me that before the Second World War he and his best friend Peter had home-cast their own toy armies using zinc moulds they had bought through the *Exchange and Mart*. A few white metal ingots had come with the moulds, but when this ran out they had decided to make a saving to their defence budget by cutting the lead flashing from around the neighbours' drainpipes and guttering and using that instead. Peter's mother worked during the day, so they had the kitchen to themselves. They would melt the lead in an aluminium pan on the gas cooker, pour it into the moulds and have the pan washed and back in the cupboard before Peter's mother returned home and started boiling the potatoes in it. Everything went well, and they were turning out thirty or more figures a day, when disaster struck.

'The pan was on the draining board,' Arthur said, 'and we were in such a hurry we didn't bother to dry it.' Lead has a very low melting point, which makes casting easy. However, like all molten metals, it has to be handled carefully. If even so much as a drop of moisture gets into it, hot lead is likely to react violently. 'We heated it as normal and, just as it began to bubble, KERBAAM!'

The lead exploded. Molten metal flew up, blew a hole in

the ceiling and then fell back down again in shiny slugs, smashing several plates and a glass bowl. Worse still, the force that had powered the lead up into the air had the opposite effect on the pan, blasting it downward, straight through the top of the cooker and into the oven. 'What I always remember is that I turned to my chum and said, "Crikey, Peter. We're lucky that didn't kill either of us." And he, poor chap, surveyed the damage to his mother's kitchen and said, "To tell the truth, Arthur, I rather wish it had."'

Home-casting was popular in England for a long time, largely because most toy soldiers were imported and thus very expensive. The epicentre of the toy soldier world was the German city of Nuremberg (which still hosts Europe's largest toy fair). Nuremberg owed this status to its pewterers. Pewter had been invented by the Egyptians and introduced into northern Europe by the Romans. By the late thirteenth century Nuremberg was established as one of the world's great centres for pewterers, and it was from this metal amalgam that toy soldiers were (and quite often still are) made. Originally pewter had been an amalgam of tin and lead. Lead tarnishes, however, while tin does not. Unfortunately in terms of cost tin lags behind only platinum, gold and silver in the table of precious metals, making it impractically expensive to use in pure form. So gradually a new form of pewter was developed using tin, antimony and copper. This came into common use in the 1750s, which, perhaps coincidentally, is when the *Zinnfiguren* started to appear in greater and greater numbers in Nuremberg, led initially by a company run by the Hilpert family (whose output was much admired by Goethe).

Making the figures was entrusted to workers, usually women (who could be paid less than men), who lived on site and slogged away for sixteen hours per day in the mephitic fumes wafting from molten lead, tin, antimony and bismuth.

The figures were sold in painted sets, usually in split pine boxes. Outworkers did the painting. Some were women, but, initially at least, most were children – as late as 1898 the workshops in Nuremberg and Fürth were recorded as employing 151 schoolchildren aged between six and thirteen to colour the *Zinnfiguren* in their spare time. Working in poor light for hours at a stretch, many of the child workers went blind.

Tin is resilient and tough. The singular thing about it, though, is that when it is bent the crystals of the metal rub together and produce a high-pitched squeak, like the alarm call of a small mammal. If you drop a box of *Zinnfiguren* on the floor, above the metallic rattle you will often hear what sounds like a tiny cry of protest.

Thanks to the success of the Nuremberg figures, toy soldiers were soon being made commercially across Europe. Makers are recorded in Sweden and Denmark in the 1760s, and Italy, Switzerland and Portugal in the 1770s. But Britain and the Colonies were reliant on imports, as indicated by an advert in a New York City newspaper from 1777 offering German-made soldiers packed in sawdust in light wood boxes at a price of eighteen shillings per dozen.

The reason for the lack of toy soldier manufacturers in Britain was simple: British men had not, by and large, been soldiers and British boys did not, generally, play with soldiers. An edition of the *Graphic* of 1871 notes: 'Our boys are now being introduced to a new delight. There are model steam engines, locomotives and fire engines worked by steam. Just as military playthings are sold in France to bring up young soldiers, these beautiful models serve in England to train up young engineers.' As if to prove a point, Frank Hornby invented Meccano a few decades later, and in 1898 the first issue of the world's longest-running hobby magazine, *Model Engineer*, hit the shelves. Construction, not destruction, was the future of Britain.

Despite that, by the 1880s large numbers of solid 30mm and 40mm figures were coming into England from Germany. The principal makers were Johan and Konrad Allgeyer of Fürth and the father and son operation of Heinrichsen in Nuremberg. Allgeyer figures were particularly splendid, and had first come to the attention of the British public at the Great Exhibition of 1851. The range they produced was massive, covering a wide variety of eras and featuring every conceivable troop type, from the common infantryman to camel-mounted light artillery. Amongst their products was a marvellous British armoured train, packed with soldiers in sun-helmets, their rifles sticking out above the riveted steel sides of the train like the spines of a porcupine. A regimental colour fluttered from the rear carriage and a rotund billow of sooty smoke puffed from the chimney of the chunky engine. Like all Allgeyer figures, it came in a red box decorated with a label displaying illustrations of all the medals the company had won at the trade fairs of Europe. Incidentally, Allgeyer's are the only make of toy soldier named by Thomas Pynchon in his novel *Gravity's Rainbow*.

Three of the major buyers of these figures were Charles, Robert and George Trevelyan of Wallington House, Northumberland. The Trevelyans were one of England's great aristocratic and intellectual families. The previous occupants of Wallingford had included their aunt, Pauline, Lady Trevelyan. Lady Trevelyan had created an artistic coterie at the house and was regularly visited by John Ruskin, Dante Gabriel Rossetti and Algernon Charles Swinburne. Her husband, Sir Walter, was a botanist and temperance crusader. He was also a man of eccentric habits. When the writer and antiquarian Augustus Hare (whose own interests tended towards the obscure – he is best remembered for writing a biographical note on a gentleman who repeatedly married women with wooden legs) visited Wallington Sir Walter served him a meal consisting entirely of artichokes and cauliflowers.

While Pauline collected Pre-Raphaelites, her nephews had their own interests. Over a period of five or six years the brothers acquired nearly four thousand Allgeyer and Heinrichsen figures from a dealer in the Burlington Arcade. These were used to fight huge battles on the floor of an upstairs room set aside for the purpose. One of their most fondly remembered engagements was a refight of the Duke of Marlborough's great victory at Blenheim in the War of the Spanish Succession. This clearly required a considerable suspension of disbelief because the figures the Trevelyans owned were predominantly drawn from the Franco-Prussian War.

Many of the figures in the current collection of Wallington House are still labelled as they were by the Trevelyans, a piece of inaccuracy which has caused many a military hobbyist to storm out without viewing the rest of the house on the grounds that 'if they label a group of French 1870s Zouaves as British foot of 1715 then when you get upstairs you'll probably find a melamine picnic plate labelled as a Ming vase'.

The Trevelyans were only doing what most wargamers had done at some point in their careers. Deano and I, for example, had once fought a bloodily attritional recreation of the Siege of Delhi using Airfix French Foreign Legion as British troops and Airfix ACW Confederates as the mutinous sepoys. The walls of Delhi were made out of Lego. The battle raged for an entire day, from sunrise to sunset. When General Havelock's men had finally stormed the city Deano picked up the wall, which was about four feet long and three inches high, and we smashed it into its component blocks by clubbing one another round the shoulders with it. Afterwards Deano said that, like the troops in the real battle, we had plainly gone into a frenzy because our blood was up. This was indeed true, though it has to be said that our frenzy was as nothing compared to that of Deano's granny, whose back bedroom we had used for the battle, when she came in and saw the mess we had made.

The Trevelyans doubtless didn't suffer such problems. If they made a mess the servants cleared it up. The brother's battles were elaborate affairs lasting for several days and apparently fought out to complex rules based on those of the Prussian game kriegspiel.

George Trevelyan went on to become one of Britain's most eminent historians. He attributed his ability to describe military campaigns to the days spent wargaming with his brothers on the carpets of Wallington. His siblings made less obvious use of their hobby. Charles joined the Fabian Society, hung around with Beatrice Webb and George Bernard Shaw, became a Liberal MP, fell out with Lloyd George after campaigning vigorously against Britain becoming involved in the Great War and then joined the Labour Party instead. Robert became a poet, his works being published alongside those of Rupert Brooke and Edward Thomas in anthologies of the Georgian poets. Both Brooke and Thomas would die in the war that Charles opposed.

The German toy soldiers had made an impact on the British market but they remained beyond the pocket of most children. William Britain junior would change all that. His father had moved from his native city of Birmingham to Hornsey Rise in North London in 1845 and founded Britain's Ltd. Britain is described as a stately yet active man; his specialism was complex automata – clockwork metal machines that performed an elaborate series of functions and manoeuvres. Britain's made a bear that walked on its hind legs, a circus elephant and a moneybox featuring a sailor who tipped his cap whenever a penny was dropped through the collection slot.

The toys were clever and inventive, but they were too difficult to manufacture and too expensive for the mass market.

It was Britain's eldest son who hit on the idea of making toy soldiers. Allgeyer and Heinrichsen's soldiers were solid cast. They were heavy and each figure contained a lot of expensive metal. Britain's developed a new process of casting soldiers in two hollow halves and sticking them together like an Easter egg. These hollow-cast soldiers were cheaper to make because they used less alloy and they were lighter, which made them cheaper to ship too.

The first Britain's toy soldiers, 54mm in size, were made in 1893. It took some while to convince retailers to stock them, however. To most shopkeepers, toy soldiers were German; trying to persuade them to sell a British version was like trying to convince people to drink English wine. Eventually Gamages, a singular department store in Holborn, London, that was noted, amongst other things, for hosting an indoor circus during the festive season, was persuaded to stock a few boxes. Success after that was more or less instant. Soon Gamages had a whole department devoted to William S. Britain and the hollow-cast figures in their bright red boxes were the biggest-selling toys on the planet.

Despite the sudden emergence of numerous domestic rivals – among them John Hill Co. (founded, confusingly, by a man named Wood), Crescent, Charbens, Kews, Renvoize, Russell, Hanks, Turnbull and Abel and Fry – Britain's kept it that way for over half a century by constantly updating and upgrading their catalogue and with frequent court battles against makers they accused of copying their products.

It was the advent of Britain's figures that inspired H. G. Wells to write *Floor Games* and then *Little Wars*. Wells wargamed with his brothers, as well as the publisher Frank Palmer and the writer Jerome K. Jerome. None of the men had any military experience, though Jerome's middle name was Klapka in honour of General George Klapka, young hero of the 1848 Hungarian War of Independence who had once stayed with his family in Walsall.

Palmer suggested the idea for the book *Floor Games* to Wells. Wells had written a brief description of battles with toy soldiers in his novel *The New Machiavelli*, and the publisher was so taken with the topic he asked the author to expand it into a book. Wells himself may have taken the initial idea from a pamphlet issued by Britain's in 1908.

Wells quickly became a keen wargamer. His other hobbies were cycling, politics and fathering illegitimate children. He seems to have come up with *Little Wars* with two aims in mind: first, to foster a spirit of pacifism in British youth by demonstrating to them the reality of war and, secondly, to bring a greater sense of stability to his own family life. It was a noble sentiment, but within a year of *Little Wars* being published the Kaiser's armies were rolling into France and Wells was rolling into bed with Rebecca West.

The first book about hobby wargaming was published in England. The next book about fighting battles with toy soldiers came out in Sweden. *Hur Man För Krig Med Tennsoldater* appeared just two weeks before the Kaiser's armies rumbled across the border into Belgium. It was written by Ossian J. D. Elgström, an artist and writer whose self-illustrated studies on life in Lapland were regarded as minor masterpieces in his homeland. I knew of Elgström's book through a friend of mine in Sweden, Benny Solberg. Benny had been working on a set of wargame rules that could be used for every period of warfare from ancient times to the present day. It had taken him five years but he felt happy that he was at last getting somewhere. 'It is hard,' he said, 'to find mechanisms that can accommodate every martial form and action from Bronze Age warriors mounted in chariots to nuclear missiles and other modern unpleasantnesses.'

Benny lived in the Old Town district of Stockholm, though he had another house out in the countryside. He said he liked to go there at weekends because then he could play his bagpipes without the neighbours complaining.

Wells used Britain's cannons, firing metal rods to knock his figures over. Elgström invented a whole arsenal of missile weapons, including the splendid *bombe kastore*. This is a sort of miniature medieval catapult that launches a missile made of cocktail sticks stuck into the side of a cork. Looking at it now, I am forced to conclude that the phrase 'you could take someone's eye out with that' has no Swedish equivalent.

At just about the time Wells and Elgström were writing their books, in Germany Karl Floericke was producing something very similar, *Strategie und Taktik des Spieles mit Bleisoldaten*. Floericke's work is now very rare, but my friend Uwe borrowed it from the Bavarian State Library. It is printed in dense Gothic script and illustrated with line drawings from the catalogues of various makers of *Zinnfiguren*. Like Wells and Elgström, Floericke's book suggests simulating firing by the use of actual missiles – in this case different sized rubber balls rolled across the terrain. In tone, though, his book is quite different. In his introduction, Floericke informs us that since all German boys play with soldiers it is the duty of adults to instruct them in the reality of war not just the romance of it. It quickly becomes obvious that when Floericke talks about the reality of war he does not mean brutality, mutilation and death, but discipline, drill and troop formations. Wells was hoping to convert boys into pacifists; Floericke to turn them into army officers.

Wells was not the first literary figure to be attracted to wargaming, nor would he be the last. We already know about the Brontës and the Trevelyans, and you can add Robert Louis Stevenson, whose battles in the attic with his nephew Lloyd Osborne using German tin figures were documented by the Scots novelist in a home-made newspaper, the *Yallobally Record*.

A. J. A. Symons was a dandy, bon viveur and gourmand. He founded the British Food and Wine Society with André Simon and wrote *The Quest for Corvo*, an extraordinary biography of novelist, conman and eccentric Frederick Rolfe, aka Baron Corvo. It's a book that, in terms of form, structure and content, may fairly claim to be forty years ahead of its time. Symons might have gone on to great literary fame, but as his brother, the crime writer Julian, has noted, he easily got distracted by trivial things: musical boxes were one, wargames another.

Symons began playing Little Wars-type games with Britain's soldiers, but after a spell in the Artists' Rifles toward the end of the Great War he met up with Captain Harold Fisher. Captain Fisher had won the Military Cross for his bravery on the Eastern Front and, like Granville Bantock, seems to have spent much of the time when he wasn't really fighting thinking about pretend fighting. He had come up with his own version of kriegspiel, played out on Ordnance Survey maps with specially cast pieces representing the various arms. The rules must have been complex because it apparently took him a fortnight to explain them to A. J. A. Symons, and Symons was a very clever chap. The campaign the two men played lasted more than a year; which of them won is not recorded. A decade later, as Hitler marched into the Sudetenland, Symons tried to revive the game, but was disappointed to find that none of his friends had the wherewithal to grasp the rules.

Born in Buffalo, New York, in 1897, Fletcher Pratt was a small, busy man with a ginger moustache. He fought as a professional flyweight boxer, worked as a librarian, news reporter and restaurant reviewer, translated Icelandic sagas and French novels into English and wrote dozens of historical works on every topic from Ancient Rome to the Second

World War, as well as hundreds of sci-fi and fantasy stories (many illustrated by his wife, Inga) for the sort of pulp magazines that published H. P. Lovecraft and Robert E. Howard. Such was his prodigious output, it is said that he was often writing half a dozen books more or less simultaneously. Despite his workload, Pratt also found time to develop a set of rules for naval wargaming that are still widely used today, found one of the first wargames clubs and hang around chewing the fat with Isaac Asimov. Asimov must have been involved too, because when Wells' *Little Wars* was reissued in the 1970s he wrote the preface to it.

It was through his wargame group that Pratt met another sci-fi writer, L. Sprague de Camp. De Camp was busy editing and rewriting Robert E. Howard's Conan stories, but he found time to collaborate with Pratt on a couple of dozen novels, the most famous of which are the Enchanter series. Though if you're not the sort of person who is happy to spend two hours in Forbidden Planet you are unlikely ever to have heard of it.

What attracted these literary people to wargaming? I'd say the brilliance of the toy soldiers and the narrative any game with them suggests. Handling the Meissen figures might, in the opinion of Bruce Chatwin's Utz, bring them to life, but it is really the imagination. Like the Brontës, Robert Louis Stevenson recorded in detail the bravery and cowardice of individual soldiers in his attic battles. He wrote back-stories for generals and heroes and poltroons that motivated their deeds and actions. It's easy to dismiss it as whimsy, but there is more to it than that. As children we form a bond with our toys and a residue of that feeling remains. We give them life and in return, as Anatole France notes in *On Life and Letters*, they give us joy and forgetfulness.

Wargamers in France such as Samuel Mathers were contemporaries of Wells and Jerome, but their motivation for playing was very different. J. M. Barrie's *Peter Pan* had first appeared on the London stage in 1904 and was an instant hit. *Little Wars* and *Floor Games* (and later *Charge!*) reflected some of that same spirit of wilful masculine infantilism. Mathers was playing with soldiers because he wanted to be a general; Wells because he wanted to be a boy, or at least to be boyish. It has been said that the success of *Peter Pan* was to do with the spirit of the age, that masculinity had come to carry such weighty responsibility men shrank from it.

I don't believe that, though. A few years ago taking the train from Brussels to Bruges I looked down the Belgian railway carriage and noticed that practically every adult I could see – male and female, tourists and natives alike – was reading a Harry Potter novel. There is a universal desire to retreat into a world of simple childhood certainty.

Once when I was round at TK's house he was rooting about in one of his many cabinets looking for some Renaissance stradiots when suddenly he popped up clutching a little 1960s Airfix British infantryman. 'Bloody hell, H,' he said, 'it's Little Audie. I thought our old bull terrier got him years ago.'

Little Audie, TK said, had been the hero of many Second World War battles he'd fought with his mate Rich. He was their equivalent of Lieutenant John Cooke's gallant sergeant. 'He's one of the unarmed figures. Look,' he said, holding Little Audie up for inspection. 'But that never stopped him. Stormed the $\frac{1}{72}$ scale Bellona gun emplacement single-handed one time. Panzer grenadiers, the lot.' TK held the little plastic figure up in front of his face, squinting to get a better look. 'Good to see you again, buddy,' he said with a big grin, and he placed Little Audie up on a high shelf where the new dog Kipper couldn't grab him.

All imaginative games create their own world, whole and hermetically sealed, filled with adventure and yet ultimately totally safe. This, as Alan Bennett has pointed out, is what the riverbank of *The Wind in the Willows* and Sherlock Holmes' residence at 221B Baker Street have in common. Here was excitement, sure enough, but when the adventures are over and the London fog has cleared we return to a warm house and familiar things, where the kettle sings and Mrs Hudson has toasted fresh muffins for our tea.

13

Charge Reaction and Counter-Charge

'The first thing they heard in the world, when the lid was taken off their box, had been the words "Tin Soldiers!" These words were uttered by a little boy, who clapped his hands with delight.'

Hans Christian Andersen, *The Steadfast Tin Soldier*

I wasn't much good at modelling, but I soon discovered that I had some skill at painting. I had a steady hand, good eyesight and the only child's infinite capacity for loneliness and futility. During school holidays I sat for hour after hour at my desk, surrounded by figures and little tin pots of enamel paint made by Humbrol, who billed their colours as 'authentic' despite howls of protest from military hobbyists.

The exact nature of colour preoccupied military hobbyists in ways most professional artists would frankly have found disturbing. The plethora of uniform books that had followed the initial publication of *Le Carnet* back in the 1890s hardly helped. New research kept changing things.

Uniforms weren't the only things that had suffered in this way, of course. Dinosaurs too had changed like chameleons over the past thirty years. When I was a boy they were all the same shade of sludge, whereas nowadays they are as brightly tinted as *DC* comics. People said this was because modern thinking on the topic had taken on board the pigmentation of

lizards and other reptiles. Maybe so, but I couldn't help thinking it was a big PR stunt for palaeontology and a good way of
keeping book illustrators busy.

The constant shifting of the ground on uniforms stirred up
a dust storm of controversy. Letters pages, message boards and
discussion groups were filled with fierce, and at times acrimo-
nious, debate over what precise shade American Second World
War olive drab was, or whether British khaki was lighter or
darker than the person before had just said, and if rifles green
had originally been black and, if so, how many washes had it
taken before the uniform had faded to a dark grey, and
whether that grey would have been a blue-grey, a green-grey or
simply and prosaically a grey-grey. Even men who had worn
the uniforms seemed incapable of agreeing on what hue they
were. On and on it went with not so much as a hint of an out-
come. The whole tedious pedantry of it was neatly summed up
in the 1970s by a cartoon in *Military Modelling*. Two men are
inspecting a 54mm model of an Ancient Greek hoplite and
one says to the other, 'Very nice, but I think you'll find the dirt
under his fingernails is a little too dark for Corinth.'

I never cared much for this sort of thing myself. As far as
I was concerned, American olive drab was Humbrol 86 and
that was that. Besides, I was far too busy painting. Someone
once asked me how long it took to paint a figure. Like an idiot
I decided to find out. The next time I began a regiment (The
Earl of Manchester's Foot, 1645) I carefully noted down the
start and finish time of each painting session. When the regiment was completed I added up the hours I'd spent on it.
Twenty-eight 20mm soldiers had taken forty-three hours and
twenty-seven minutes – an entire working week plus a bit of
overtime on Saturday morning. I thought of all the figures I
had painted in my life. How many years it had taken to complete them. If I had put it into some sensible activity I might
now be a lawyer, architect or neurosurgeon and you'd be

reading a book by somebody reasonable like John Grisham, Bernard Cornwell or Alain de Botton.

'I bet you get all kinds of ideas for articles and books while you're painting those figures,' kindly friends would remark. I smiled in a manner that I hoped was enigmatic, though it probably looked like I had wind. Because the truth was that when I was painting I was concentrating so hard on the brush tip and the figure that I didn't think about anything at all. And that was quite a relief.

Despite the volume of figures and the length of time spent on them, I could remember the time I'd painted just about everything in the cabinets. There were colonial British infantrymen I'd painted when I was fourteen, living in a rented house because we were having a kitchen extension done at home. A horde of Gauls I'd finished when I took a week off after delivering the manuscript of my first book, sitting at my desk, brush in hand, for seven hours a day listening to talking books, colouring the shields of four hundred warriors while acquiring a fondness for the quirky short stories of Alastair Gray. Iroquois Indians painted in a flat in Clapham so cold I had to work on them wearing fingerless gloves and warm my hands regularly over the gas stove to stop them shaking; the fact that the flesh tone is much too dark I blame on the lack of a decent anglepoise lamp. And here amongst the Victorian Naval Brigade is a figure of a rating with a white number three painted on his grass green base. This is Mick McMahon the Irish sailor who took part in dozens of skirmishes throughout the 1970s, was wounded repeatedly but never fatally, until one too many reckless charges saw him gunned down by Jihadiya riflemen lurking amongst the rocks near El Teb. The paint on his hat is flaking, he's got metal fatigue round the ankles and his bayonet is broken, but you can't hold that against him – the little guy is a veteran, my answer to Little Audie.

*

It wasn't long after my first games with Malcolm that I abandoned my plastic Airfix figures for the more adult pursuit of
white metal. There were many reasons for swapping to metal
soldiers, not least because the adverts carried a series of dire
warnings about the effect that the lead content would have on
the brains of small children which proved beyond doubt that
these were *not* toys. Though not as well modelled as the plastic figures, the lead soldiers seemed more characterful and
human. Plastic figures came attached to a long sprig of polystyrene like the leaves on a plant. Lead figures came
individually. A little plug on the bottom of the base where the
molten metal had been poured into the mould was their
equivalent of the umbilical cord.

The main thing in the lead men's favour, though, was that
thousands more troop types were available from dozens of
conflicts that Airfix got nowhere near to covering. I dipped
my toe in the water by buying a few Napoleonic French, and
then went after Zulus. By now it was becoming obvious that,
like my father with model kits, I had an obscurantist bent
when it came to the armies. In the 1980s, for example, I
decided on a whim to reproduce the French and Indian War
on my tabletop. This was so deliciously arcane that I had to
send off to a company in Canada to get the figures. The only
place I could find any books on the topic was the reading
room at the National Army Museum. Painstakingly over four
years I pieced together and painted two armies and a horde
of natives and collected a library of volumes picked up in
second-hand bookshops and by kindly relatives during trips to
America. Then Michael Mann's film *The Last of the Mohicans*
came out. Suddenly you couldn't move for 25mm woodland
Indians. There was an apparently unstaunchable flow of figures, books and videos devoted to Montcalm and Wolfe,
Rogers and de Bougainville (after whom, incidentally, the
bougainvillea is named). I felt as sickened as I had when I was

a teenager and a favourite punk band had a top-ten hit. The French and Indian War had let me down. It had gone commercial; it had sold out. Disgusted, I offloaded my entire collection on a bloke in Berkhamsted for eight hundred pounds and went off in pursuit of Imperial Russians for the Conquest of the Akhal-Tekke Turcomans.

Zulus were hard to trace, even in metal. But I eventually tracked some down to a model shop in Harrow-on-the-Hill, a mere three hundred miles from my house. This didn't bother me at all. In fact, it just added to the excitement: the difficulty of locating the figures you wanted added to their mystique. Mail order in the UK thirty years ago was an erratic and long-winded process that often ended in disappointment. It was the retail equivalent of a blind date. You sent away for a catalogue enclosing a stamped addressed envelope. In order to deter timewasters and dilettantes, the makers then waited a month before returning it to you with their lists, which were invariably printed on paper the texture of an ancient shroud, in ink so pale you really needed some expertise in Braille to read it, and featuring, if you were lucky, one illustration of a figure you were not interested in and which had been discontinued three years earlier anyway. But it was worth it, because a catalogue is a holiday for the mind. You could sit for hours with the Hinton Hunt lists (dozens of pages held between mustard yellow covers by the combination of two rusting staples and a giant paper clip) pondering whether to buy Brunswick death's head hussars or Nassau grenadiers, making unit inventories, tallying up the cost and seeing if you had enough money in your post office savings account to qualify for the 100-500 figure discount. You could start lists and scrap them and start again. Abandon the idea of Norman Conquest in favour of the American Civil War, and then toss that aside when Tel-El-Kebir arrested your attention. After weeks of agonising you finally settled on a compromise that would see Saxon fyrd, Louisiana tigers and Egyptian fellaheen lining up together on the battlefield and sent off your order, block capitals only, postal order enclosed. A month later the parcel arrived and you opened it with delight and expectation, only to find that half the figures were not there because despite having spent every waking hour staring at the catalogue you had somehow failed to notice the little asterisks and the footnote 'Not available until October 1974'.

A company called Jacklex had made Mick McMahon; the dervishes who killed him had come from Les Higgins and Hinton Hunt. Twenty-five years after buying Mick and his adversaries, I began trying to piece together the story of the men who had designed and made the figures. In the case of Jacklex that proved fairly easy. Jacklex was one man, Jack Alexander, and he was still alive and sprightly, and happy to be kept on the phone for hours at a time describing how he had fashioned his 20mm colonial range using liquid solder and gardening wire. The rest were considerably more difficult. All of the designers were, without exception, dead, and published details of their lives were confined to catalogues and adverts. Gustave Flaubert declared, '*L'homme n'est rien, l'oeuvre tout.*' This was nowhere truer than in the world of toy soldier making, where a designer's output was often left to serve as biography and obituary. Determined, I tracked down people who had known them, or worked for them, or bought from them regularly, or bumped into them once or twice at trade shows in Brussels and Kulmbach. Constructing the stories of their lives from talking to people was difficult. Fragments emerged, old animosities flared up; some people made things up to fill in what they had forgotten, others did it out of a sense of mischief or grievance. I felt like somebody trying to work out the personality of the owner of a house by studying the books on the shelves, not knowing whether some of the novels I found hadn't simply been left behind by absent-minded visitors.

I had wanted to know about the man behind Hinton Hunt, Marcus Hinton, who died in 1986. I had bought Zulus and Hadendowah warriors from him when I was a teenager and now owned several thousand of the Napoleonic and English Civil War figures he had designed. A man I spoke to in Littlehampton said the person I ought to talk to if I wanted to know anything about Hinton was Colonel Anders Lindstrom in Stockholm.

Colonel Lindstrom was a retired Swedish cavalry officer who ran a company making 30mm figures designed in the 1950s by Holger Eriksson of Karlstadt. I phoned Colonel Lindstrom. He was an extremely courteous man who spoke lightly accented English in the cautious yet charming manner of Sven-Göran Eriksson. He said, 'I think you have been misinformed, Mr Pearson. I never actually knew Mr Hinton, though I was familiar with his productions, of course. The person you should speak to is . . . wait one moment, I will check my papers.' I heard a filing cabinet open and the rattling of files. 'Ah yes,' Colonel Lindstrom said, 'it is a lady named Mrs Fenella Brill. Will you take down her number?'

I think it is fair to say there isn't a man alive who wouldn't take down the telephone number of a woman named Fenella Brill.

Fenella Brill worked as a figure animator and painter for Tradition, the company that had promoted Charles Stadden's work. Once they had a shop in Piccadilly, then it had moved to Shepherd's Market, Mayfair, and lately it had taken up an even swankier station in Curzon Street. Roy Belmont-Maitland founded Tradition in the 1950s after he discovered some of Stadden's models in a shop in the Burlington Arcade, the near legendary Hummel's House of Miniatures. Roy Belmont-Maitland was not his real name. He was, according to some people anyway, a German Jew who had fled the Nazis in the 1930s. During the war it was said he had worked in intelligence. His past was either shady or shrouded in mystery, depending on who you asked. 'He never drove a car,' somebody muttered, 'because in the 1940s he'd run a chap over during the blackout and damn near killed him.' I had no idea whether this was true or not.

I called Fenella Brill. She couldn't really talk now, she said, as she had friends round and they were watching the racing from Cheltenham. She sounded very jolly and I felt I could hear the noise of gin in the background. I asked if she'd known Marcus Hinton. 'Oh my goodness yes, I should say so,' she replied. 'He was the original one-off. Dressed like an Edwardian dandy. Always wore a bowler hat. Went every-where by bicycle. He idolised Robert E. Lee, you know? He had a flagpole in his garden at Taplow and every year on the anniversary of the Battle of Gettysburg he raised the Confederate flag.' She said if I wanted to know more I should phone again on Saturday and speak to her husband, Peter.

Peter Brill was an expert on British naval uniforms and, along with Marcus Hinton and Brigadier Peter Young, he had helped found The Sealed Knot English Civil War re-enactment society. Mr Brill made a living running a firm in High Wycombe that manufactured Masonic regalia. Another founder of The Sealed Knot was the model maker Edward Suren.

As Arthur had known practically everyone who made fig-ures back in the 1960s I tried to get him to tell me something about Les Higgins. Les Higgins had his own company making 20mm figures, but he still worked full-time as a designer for Mettoy. Higgins was the man who designed the model figures for Corgi cars. The little Sean Connery in the dinner jacket pointing his Walther PPK that went with the Aston Martin DB6 was one of Les's; so was the man in the ejector seat. Higgins had died in 1970 aged forty-two from a combination of all sorts of complicated reasons. The metal figures he made representing the soldiers of the English Civil War and the armies of the Duke of Marlborough were just about the loveliest toy soldiers ever made. I liked them so much I spent two years tracking down the original master figures (the tiny sculptures fashioned out of tin from which the rubber centrifugal moulds are made), so that TK, Rich and I could buy the company.

Arthur knew Higgins pretty well, but he had got sidetracked on the subject of Suren. Suren was a retired Indian Army cavalry captain who made a range of daintily capricious 33mm figures which was now owned by Colonel Lindstrom. 'There isn't anyone around like Ted Suren these days,' Arthur grunted. 'He was a character. A lot of people nowadays don't know what that word means.'

This had become something of a refrain of Arthur's lately, largely, I suspect, because he had recently suffered a small tailoring disaster. Arthur had bought a rather natty summer-weight suit from a shop in Swallow Street and had taken it to the dry cleaner round the corner from his flat to have the trousers altered. Arthur had wanted the hems finished at a slant so that the back of the trousers were longer than the front. The woman had never heard of anything like it, got confused and finished them the other way round. When Arthur put the trousers on the laces of his shoes were smothered in fine wool and his ankles exposed to the world. Anyone else might have laughed about it, but Arthur had entered that phase of life when every error, however minor, seemed to presage the collapse of civilisation as we know it.

'Modern Britain is a nation of oafs,' Arthur said. I had no wish to hear about the trousers again, so I tried to change the subject. Suren must have done well from his model soldiers, I said, because he had a shop in Lower Sloane Street in Chelsea and when he retired he sold up and moved to a villa on the Cap d'Antibes.

'Oh, he didn't make his money from the soldiers,' Arthur

said, 'he made his money from . . .' There was a pause, and I got the distinct impression that, mentally at least, Arthur was looking from side to side to check nobody was listening. 'The stuff in the basement,' he whispered.

'*The stuff in the basement?*' I said.

'You could only go down there if Ted knew you or you came with an introduction,' Arthur said. 'It was where he kept his subjects,' he lowered his voice again, 'for the *gentleman connoisseur*.' Then he said, 'Have you heard of Phil Stearns?'

I had. Philip Olcott Stearns had been educated at Princeton. He'd graduated with honours in art and archaeology, joined the Office of Strategic Services (OSS, precursor of the CIA) and spent most of the Second World War in London. Philip O. Stearns collected model soldiers. He was also a professional photographer. Nearly every book about toy soldiers that was published between the 1960s and the 1980s had photographs in it by Philip O. Stearns. The patrician American lived in a lavish apartment in Mayfair, and model soldiers were Stearns's hobby. His day job was working for *Penthouse* magazine.

'His apartment was a real eye-opener,' an old figure designer who had called in on Stearns in 1974 had told me. 'It was wall to wall toy soldiers and naked girls.' Oddly enough, at the time that was pretty much what the inside of my head looked like.

'Well,' Arthur said, 'put it this way, it was the sort of stuff Phil Stearns would have known all about.'

'Did you ever go down into the basement?' I asked.

'A couple of times.'

'And?'

'It was all done with a bit of wit, style and panache,' Arthur growled. 'It wasn't like nowadays with these foul so-called alternative comedians.'

Arthur had known Marcus Hinton too. He didn't much care for him, though that may have been down to the designer's corpulence and the facial hair rather than any character defect. 'He lived,' Arthur said, 'on the banks of the Thames in a lane that was known locally as Gaiety Row because at one time a lot of the houses in it had been rented out to chorus girls from the Gaiety Theatre. Lillie Langtry, Edward VII's fancy piece, had lived there.

'I went only once,' Arthur continued, 'and a bizarre place it was too, halfway between Miss Havisham and the Hammer House of Horror. Hinton collected militaria and his wife, Cynthia, collected cats. The whole place was jam full of moggies and suits of armour. Good God! You lifted up the visor on a Thirty Years War hobilar's helmet and a cat jumped out. Hinton never showed, sleeping probably, so I left empty-handed.'

I was interested that Arthur had mentioned Mrs Hinton. 'His wife was a model. Well, of course she was. That's how he met her,' Fenella Brill had said when I spoke to her. As with much of what Mrs Brill told me, I wasn't exactly sure what this meant. 'One thing's for certain,' Arthur said, when I reported the remark to him, 'she wasn't modelling for Marcus's figures!' He let out a big, choking guffaw.

'The joke that went around was that God made man in his own image and Marcus made *his* men in *his* own. Oddly shaped fellows, you see? I can believe Cynthia was a model of some sort, though. I remember her very well. Hard to forget, actually. An ample lady fore and aft. Fondness for tight velvet dresses, too. The British Model Soldier Society meetings in those days were held at the Caxton Hall and the sight of her coming up the front steps carrying several boxes of lead figures was something to behold. It became a source of keen anticipation amongst the members, I can tell you. Not many women around in those days,' Arthur said. I assumed he was speaking of the BMSS meetings, though he may have meant in England generally.

14

Hand-to-Hand Combat

'I can think of no sport that is the peer of escape.'
Major Pat Reid, MBE, MC

The BBC TV series *Colditz*, which ran from 1972 until 1974, was so popular it spawned a travelling exhibition; Airfix made a model of the glider built in the attic by pilot officers Jack Best and the appropriately named Bill Goldfinch; and Action Man had a full Colditz set, including a prison guard and an escapee complete with forged ID card, documents and maps.

Looking at it now, I can see that the BBC drama was a gritty portrayal of the grim reality of life as a POW in Oflag IV C. Certainly there was little to laugh about here, though the more puerile may have tittered at the character named Lieutenant Dick Player, and an air of menace and uncertainty hung over the grey walls of the shadowy castle.

As a boy, however, all that was lost on me. The trouble with a prisoner of war camp, whether it was Colditz or *The Wooden Horse*'s Stalag Luft III, was that all the things that made it hell for an adult – lack of freedom, being ordered about, not having a say over what you ate or when you turned your bedroom light out, getting ousted out of bed and forced to put on a uniform on a freezing cold morning by unreasonable fascists – were everyday reality for a child.

Other aspects of POW life, meanwhile, were clearly better

than ordinary life. The prisoners didn't have to go to school or work, they simply mooched about all day, playing football or chess (clearly a Subbuteo football game or a Scalextric slot car racing set would have brightened things up even further – an application to the Red Cross would surely have put that right?); there were no girls, a deprivation for a grown man, but a positive boon for a boy; the people in charge were clearly baddies and therefore there would be no recriminations from your mum and dad no matter how cheeky you were to them. If I'd given my headmaster the sort of lip that was regularly handed out to Kommandant Bernard Hepton I'd have been sent to bed with no supper and a clap round the arse, I can tell you – and to cap it all, large parcels filled with treats arrived from Switzerland every week.

As far as I could see, being in Oflag IV C was like a particularly brilliant Christmas holiday. Certainly things were made uncomfortable for David McCallum, a POW veteran who'd started tunnelling a decade earlier in *The Great Escape*, Robert Wagner and co. by the appearance of merciless and sadistic SS officer Major Horst Mohn (played by the actor Anthony Valentine, who also turned up as the merciless and sadistic MI5 operative Toby Mears in *Callan*), but so what? Every walk you took past the older kids on bikes on your way back from the sweet shop ran a similar risk of random brutality. Like most boys I spent my entire day anticipating a slap on the back of the head. And I was rarely disappointed.

I mentioned this to my friend Will. He said, 'I know what you mean. I was at prep school at the time. It even had the same turrets, though there was a bit less barbed wire and no machine gun posts to speak of.' He said boarding school had been the ideal place for playing Colditz games. He and his school chums had even nicknamed the matron Horst in honour of the Anthony Valentine character.

In fact, so exciting did *Colditz* appear to youngsters that it spawned not one, but two board games. The first one was called Escape from Colditz Castle and was designed by an eighteen-year-old schoolboy named Adrian Wild. That was the original game, and though it sold 130,000 copies it's not the one everyone remembers today. (When I say everyone I obviously don't mean it literally. I mean it in the same way that newspaper writers mean 'everyone' when they say 'these days *everyone* is going to Umbria'.) The game everyone remembers – Escape from Colditz – came out a year later and was designed by Colditz escapee Major Pat Reid himself. It was a tie-in with the TV series, and very fine it is too.

Escape from Colditz was made by Parker Brothers and later by H. P. Gibson and, oddly enough, was also produced under licence in Spain. The Spanish rather took to the game they know as *Fuga de Colditz*. So much so that they even had Major Reid design a follow-up, *Después de Colditz* (After Colditz), in which the POWs have to make their way across Europe and try to get to Switzerland, Spain, Sweden or across the Channel to dear old Blighty – something which *Después de Colditz* itself conspicuously failed to do.

Escape from Colditz was hugely popular, but it had one major defect – someone had to be the Germans. While the allied players got to run around the castle hoping to nick the staff car, collecting skeleton keys and wire cutters and hoarding Red Cross cigarettes with which to bribe the guards, the German player just marched around with his dogs hoping to fall into a tunnel. His one moment of excitement was playing a 'Shoot to Kill' card. This was plainly a role for the disaffected, the outcast or the simply odd. Or your dad.

I mentioned *Colditz* to a Chilean friend of mine. As soon as he heard the name Enrique's eyes lit up. '*Colditz*! Oh, fantastic,' he said. 'I watched it always as a little boy in Concepćion. It was on twice weekly at seven o'clock. It was very, very popular in Chile. At school, you know, we played Colditz games.

Some were guards. Some were POWs trying to escape. Bernard Hepton! David McCallum! Oh, yes, *Colditz*, I like it very much.'

I told Enrique that the series had been really popular in Spain too. I said I was surprised it had been taken up in countries that had not been involved in the war, in which the history behind it didn't have the same resonance it did in Britain. I asked him why he thought people in South America had liked it so much. 'Well,' he said, 'in Chile, and also in Spain, at that time we had military governments; there were secret police everywhere. We were all sneaking about trying to get the better of them. Maybe we were living in a kind of Colditz ourselves?'

Enrique and Will are both part of the board-game group. We have played everything from Ave Caesar to Zombies!!! We have not yet got round to Colditz. This is not because we consider it infantile, but because the game is now so collectable that getting a complete set on eBay is harder than wrestling a leg of ham from the mouth of an alligator. And considerably more expensive.

I got some games off eBay and quite a few more from a dealer in Germany named Norbert Frings. Germany is the board-game nation par excellence: 160,000 people attend the board-game fair in Essen each year. Germany's most popular game, The Settlers of Catan, had sold thirteen million copies in ten years and spawned a novel written by a woman who was described as Spain's answer to Umberto Eco. Mathias had played board-games all his life; it was part of the national culture. German companies such as Ravensburger, Uberplay and Hans im Glück churned out dozens of new titles a year. There were games of Polynesian exploration, art dealing, Hanseatic trading, medieval city building, mammoth hunting and motor racing. One thing the German companies rarely touched was war. War, as Mathias said, was *problematic* for

Germany. In German games victory tended to be achieved by oblique influence rather than direct belligerence; economic, political or cultural power rather than military might. The games were even-handed, logical and rarely called on the players to do anything truly cruel to one another. They promoted harmony and, as such, they reflected modern Germany. British and American games tended to be nastier and noisier. And as such . . .

Mainly, though, when I wanted new games I rooted around in the basement of Forbidden Planet. And, believe me, no basement is more basement-like than the basement of Forbidden Planet. Forbidden Planet always looks as if a particularly messy bomb has just hit it. There are boxes everywhere, the aisles are narrow and the carpet is a tawdry splattered mess the colour of a cow's spleen. In Forbidden Planet, there is always someone talking to the bloke behind the counter and, strangely, it always looks like the same someone. He has shoulders that slope so dramatically that on anyone else they'd be elbows, and long wispy hair which he tosses out of his eyes every few seconds in a gesture that is dramatically at odds with everything else about him. His voice is like the thrumming of a distant generator.

At first I used to think that Forbidden Planet could do with a dynamic marketing and retail brain to give it a shake-up and sort it out a bit. Then it gradually dawned on me that they already had. For Forbidden Planet's customers something that looked like the shruddiest teenager in the world's bedroom just before his parents told him to tidy it up right this minute or they were sending him to military school was just the environment they were looking for. This was the most cunningly designed shop ever, and I spent hours in its shadowed fastness assessing the relative merits of Princes of the Renaissance, Kung Fu Fighting, Condotierre and Railroad Tycoon.

Games Club was a dream come true for me. As a boy I had loved board games. My problem was that I was an only child, so there was no one to play them with. My mum and dad would occasionally agree to a reluctant game of Waddington's Battle of the Little Big Horn or Sir Brian Horrock's Combat Game. But their hearts weren't in it. They had come to hate all parlour games during the Second World War when they had been forced to play them for hours on end largely because there was nothing else to do. If you waved a copy of Monopoly at my dad he hissed like Dracula in front of a crucifix. The war had left many emotional and psychological scars. My parents wouldn't buy a German car, they wouldn't eat pilchards and they wouldn't play board games. This was a blow because the 1960s and 1970s had been a board-gaming golden age.

Board games had been around for a long time without really doing much until then. Waddington's House of Games, Parker Brothers and H. P. Gibson had been knocking them out since the Great War. Most were simple children's games, but some had an adult appeal.

The most long-lived and popular military game was L'Attaque, a simple and elegant two-hander first patented in Paris in November 1908 by a Mademoiselle Hermance Edan who described it as '*un jeu de bataille avec pièces mobiles sur damier*'. According to some accounts, it is actually a version of a much earlier Chinese game called Jungle.

L'Attaque was sold commercially in France from 1910 onwards. It says something for Anglo-French relations that, despite having been allies for over fifty years by that stage, and the mounting antipathy towards the Kaiser, the makers still decided that the two armies pitched against one another should be those of the British and French.

Variations of the L'Attaque system have appeared regularly ever since. A naval version, Dover Patrol, came out shortly after the First World War, Aviation and Tri-Tactics followed in the 1950s and 1960s and, recently, a Napoleonic version featuring Bernard Cornwell's Napoleonic rifleman Sharpe has hit the toy-shop shelves.

In Holland in the late 1950s, L'Attaque was given a Premier Empire makeover by the toy manufacturer Jumbo and issued as Stratego. The game quickly became so popular in Holland, Belgium and Germany that leagues and regional knockout competitions were organised. The annual world championship now draws Stratego experts from all over the globe eager to get their hands on the £5000 first prize, though the Dutch usually win it.

L'Attaque was popular in Britain, but it wasn't the only military game available. Battleships was first issued commercially in the 1930s under a variety of names including Broadsides, Combat and Salvo, whose producers claimed that the game was invented 'by soldiers in Russia' shortly after the First World War. Whether Whites or Bolsheviks it didn't say.

The mounting fear of war in Europe seemed to give military board games a lift. Waddington's came up with GHQ, which featured a map of France and the Low Countries with the armies of the opposing forces represented by flags – including the black swastika of Nazi Germany – pinned into cork blocks.

Around the same time writer Dennis Wheatley – author of *The Devil Rides Out* – designed a series of military games for Hutchinson. Hutchinson published maps and atlases as well as Wheatley's output. Like A. J. A. Symons, Wheatley was a man with a penchant for fine food, wine and games. Unlike Symons, he was a prolific writer and prodigiously popular; his books sold a million copies a year from 1960 to 1975.

Wheatley had fought in the First World War, being wounded at Passchendaele and eventually invalided out after being caught in a gas attack. He was a fanatical anti-communist, having become convinced that socialism and Satanism were one and the same. His belief was based on the somewhat shaky linguistic ground that socialism was called 'the left wing' while devil worship was known as 'the leftward path'.

Though Wheatley wrote about the occult he did not include magic in any of his games, preferring to concentrate on more corporeal matters. Invasion (1938) promised 'attack and defence by land, sea and air' and was billed as 'a thrilling battle of wits for two, three or four players'. Blockade followed a year later. In Blockade victory went to the player who succeeded in sinking his opponent's merchant ships, forcing him to surrender or face starvation. So nothing the children of the UK could relate to there, then.

When the real war started Wheatley went to work for British Intelligence. It would be nice to think that the author of *To the Devil a Daughter* was taken on because of his strategy games, but actually he owed his job to his wife, who worked as a driver for MI5. Wheatley's contribution to the allied victory was varied to say the least. He came up with the idea of a double for Field Marshal Montgomery – the scheme filmed as *I Was Monty's Double* – and also suggested dropping leaflets on Germany saying that Britain had invented a death ray that would shoot Luftwaffe planes from the skies. Another of his schemes involved spreading a rumour throughout Europe that a pacifist Messiah had arrived in the Fatherland. Mostly, though, he seems to have eaten a lot, drunk a lot and spent his afternoons asleep on the couch in his office, which is presumably where he dreamed up these last two plans.

The Yanks were slow to get involved in the Second World War and just as slow getting involved in the board-game side of the conflict, but quickly got the hang of things once they did, with Parker Brothers issuing Ranger Commando in

1942, presumably in celebration of the coming fun. The game recreated a commando raid on the coast of Europe. Unwilling to encourage deviancy by having one player take the role of the Germans, Parker opted to make all the players Americans and have them compete for victory points with the highest-scoring platoon being the winners.

Parker continued to issue military games thereafter. The Civil War Game, which came out for the centenary of the start of the American Civil War, was followed up in 1968 with Situation 4, a game of modern military conflict that bizarrely combines wargaming with a large jigsaw puzzle. Situation 4 (and its follow-up Situation 7) was promoted as ideal fun for all the family. Instead of the usual box art of tanks, jets and rockets, Parker went for a living room scene in which a typical nuclear family were enjoying a game of Situation 4. Dad and daughter were ranged on one side, Mom and son on the other. Whatever was happening on that board was clearly pretty thrilling, as daughter wears the spaced-out expression of someone who has just downed a forest glade of magic mushrooms and Mom is wide-eyed and waving her arms about in a manner that suggests she is midway through recreating the orgasm scene from *When Harry Met Sally*.

Undoubtedly Parker Brothers' biggest contribution to the board-game boom came in 1959 when they issued Risk – The Game of World Conquest. Its sales quickly began to outstrip even Monopoly. After all, as the advertising strapline put it: Why stop at Mayfair when you can own the whole globe? By the 1970s the game was so popular that *Playboy* was running articles on winning strategies. I have no idea what these were, though wearing a G-string and pausing during tense moments to rub baby oil into your breasts might work.

The Parker Brothers' version of Risk wasn't the original version of the game. Risk was invented by a Frenchman and had first appeared as *La Conquête du Monde* two years earlier. The inventor's name was Albert Lamorisse and 1957 was a rather good year for him: not only was his game of world conquest published but he also won an Oscar for his movie *The Red Balloon*. As far as I know Lamorisse didn't invent any other games, but he did make plenty more films, including *The Lovers' Wind* – a title that probably sounds a whole lot better in French.

Risk is still one of the world's biggest-selling board games, and has recently become a bit of a franchise with variations – Castle Risk, Risk: Edition Napoleon, Risk: 2210AD, Risk: Godstorm, Risk: Star Wars and, inevitably, Risk: Lord of the Rings – rolling off the production line in an apparently unstoppable torrent. More than that it sparked a whole raft of other designers and companies producing world conquest games, not least Supremacy, a spin-off set during the Cold War which comes with a set of spiffy, brightly coloured plastic mushroom clouds.

According to an article in the *Guardian* of 30 September 2005, playing Risk is the best way to discover the personality dynamic within your family. Maybe so, but it is arguably the most boring too. Risk, frankly, is rubbish. 'All those infernal bits of wood or plastic. You only had to sneeze and you'd scatter your armies to all corners,' Arthur said dismissively when I mentioned it to him once. 'All of the boredom and maths with none of the pageant – a wargame for accountants.'

Arthur didn't have much time for Diplomacy either, which also appeared in 1959. And Diplomacy was something you needed a lot of time for. Despite appearances, this was not so much a board game as a lifestyle choice: games could and often did go on for months, even years. People played by post (play-by-mail games, or PBMs, originated with Diplomacy), sending their moves by letter to a central umpire or gamesmaster who informed the players of the results of their

actions by return of post. Middle-aged veterans of these massive games, who played against opponents they never saw or
even knew, vividly recalled every detail of campaigns fought
during their student days. 'Of course, I realised straight away
I should have supported Serbia and reinforced Switzerland,
but, gaargh!' they yelled if you brought the subject up.

Risk and Diplomacy kick-started a whole new wave of
board games aimed at adults, from massive military games
featuring stacks of hundreds of cardboard counters to risqué
party games that Hugh Hefner might have produced after
everyone at the Playboy Mansion had tired of trying to capture the last bit of South America.

One of the best games to emerge in the 1970s, and one of
Games Club's all-time favourites, was undoubtedly
Waddington's Game of Nations. Aimed at an international
market, this came with its French name, *Le Jeu Des Nations –
Un jeu de stratégie politique*, emblazoned across the box. To
ensure no one who picked it up thought they were getting the
indoor equivalent of *Jeux sans Frontières* with a chance to play
the joker on the person who could carry a tray of jellies up a
ladder quickest, the box also carried a quotation: 'Skill and
nerve are the principal requirements in this amoral and cyn-
ical game in which there are neither winners nor losers – only
survivors.' These words, which really should end with a clash
of thunder and the cawing of crows, were written by Miles
Copeland, former head of the CIA and father of the drum-
mer from The Police.

Copeland was well acquainted with the Game of Nations
because for a long while the US Office of Strategic Services
(employer of Philip O. Stearns and America's original over-
seas espionage agency) had used an elaborate umpire-driven
version of the game as a way of selecting section heads for the
exacting job of attempting to destabilise Cuba by poisoning
Castro's milkshake and making his beard fall out.

The idea of using games to assess character wasn't new. Bismarck had played chess with every crowned head in Europe in a bid to find out something of his or her psychology. General Eisenhower played bridge with his generals throughout the Second World War and made promotions and assignments based on the way they performed. Edgar Allan Poe shared Eisenhower's belief in the power of card games to hone the mind and reveal the character of the participants. According to Poe, whist was the pre-eminent game when it came to testing a player's powers of analysis. 'The best chess player in Christendom *may* be little more than the best player of chess; but proficiency in whist implies capacity for success in all these more important undertakings,' he notes in *The Murders in the Rue Morgue*. Eisenhower could hardly have put it better. That being said, it's hard to imagine Ike writing *The Fall of the House of Usher*, or Poe organising the Normandy Landings.

The Game of Nations followed a long and noble line of military planning games. Sun Tzu, author of *The Art of War* – currently required reading for all budding entrepreneurs and international sports coaches – had designed a game called Wei Hai, which to be honest sounds more like something a little bald chap would shout in *The Benny Hill Show*. It caught on in China, though, and ever since then toy soldiers and games have been used to instruct military commanders.

In the sixteenth century Junellus Turianus built a small army of automata that mustered and moved 'according to the discipline of war'. Turianus displayed his invention before Emperor Charles V and his court, but was promptly denounced by a watching bishop 'unskilled in the mathematik' as a witch and a heretic.

In 1614 a wooden army was made for Philip IV of Spain. It was a massive host complete with pontoon train, sutlers, armourers and even a corps of military barbers. Manufactured by Alberto Struzzi, the set also featured lakes, trees and a castle. Further north, William of Orange, in company with Netherlands historian Everard van Reyd, was using Nuremberg tin soldiers to plan the reforms of the Dutch army that he would later lead against the Spanish.

Louis XIV had his army of silver and cardstock soldiers, but by far the greatest collection belonged to the Duke of Brunswick. This had been made for him by his master of pages, Helwig, and featured thousands of figures on a terrain board of 1666 squares.

Not to be outdone, one Georg Vinturinus came up with something called *Neues Kriegspiel* in 1796. This featured no fewer than eighteen thousand brigades of infantry and cavalry and eight hundred artillery batteries fighting across a board representing Northern France and the Low Countries. Unfortunately Vinturinus's rules for the game ran to sixty pages and were so infernally complex even those skilled in mathematik took one look at them, sighed and said, 'Is it really worth it?'

In 1824 a young Prussian lieutenant named von Reisswitz invented what was arguably the most influential military game of all time, kriegspiel. According to historical accounts, it was played using wooden blocks on a map based on the German-Belgian border (though, confusingly, Belgium didn't actually exist in 1824). The Prussian high command were so taken with von Reisswitz's game that they had sets sent to every Prussian regiment and for the next seventy years playing it was compulsory for all officers and aspiring other ranks. Kriegspiel was credited with helping formulate the strategies that led to the unification of Germany via the military defeats of Denmark, Austria and France.

Not everybody saw kriegspiel's influence as helpful, however. The game enjoyed a vogue in Queen Victoria's army

too. One of its greatest exponents was Lieutenant-General
Lord Chelmsford, whose mastery of the game was considered something of a wonder. In 1879 Chelmsford led the
British invasion of Zululand. The Zulu army surprised the
central column of the invading force – to which Chelmsford
himself was attached – at Isandlwana and in the ensuing
battle all but totally annihilated it. Chelmsford had been off
on a reconnaissance trip when the attack occurred and so survived. His reputation did not, nor, in Britain at least, did that
of kriegspiel. The historian Joseph Lehmann noted sardonically, 'As a player of kriegspiel at Aldershot, Chelmsford had
won an enviable reputation; unfortunately Cetshwayo and his
Zulu warriors, knowing nothing of this sophisticated table
game, did not play by the rules.'

If kriegspiel was all strategy, the CIA's Game of Nations
tended towards pure psychology. In any session the key to the
process was judging the ability of players to maintain a 'game
attitude', to see events and actions as having no external con-
sequences. By maintaining the principle that you are playing
a game you can divorce yourself from factors that might
cloud your judgement. In a game odds of 5:1 in your favour
would seem like very good odds indeed. But if you knew
everyone you loved and held dear would be wiped off the
face of the planet on a die roll of one, would you make the
throw? That was the question the Game of Nations asked of
its participants. Those who cast the die without hesitation got
picked for stardom and those who wavered went back to central casting. I suspect that Major Pat Reid, who clearly viewed
running from the Gestapo as a bit of a lark, would have done
rather well at it.

The Game of Nations is set in a fictional oil-rich region
called the Kark Peninsula. Players attempt to seize control of
oil production by setting up and maintaining puppet admin-
istrations. In short, the game has so much contemporary

resonance the box practically vibrates. Games Club has played it many times, and though I always seem to get stuck with the little white plastic tank with no gun barrel and end up landlocked and reliant on handouts from the IMF to keep my guerrilla campaign against the Imperialist lickspittles and running dog forces of the UAR going, I rate it very highly.

It had passed more significant tests, too. The game was designed by a Harvard psychologist during the Second World War and survived for several decades afterwards as a principal means of testing and – and I really think you need to pay attention to this bit – *predicting the actions of existing heads of state and national leaders.* Yep, you got it. For a large portion of the Cold War the world's most powerful nation was basing its foreign policy decisions on a board game. Wars had been used as the basis to make games and games had been used as the basis to make wars. And since the world didn't go up in an irradiated cloud, and the Soviet Union collapsed, you'd have to say that – from an American point of view at least – in this case the game did a damn fine job.

PART THREE

COMBAT FATIGUE

'I don't know what they do to the
enemy, but by God they frighten me.'

THE DUKE OF WELLINGTON

15

Specialist Troop Types

'It should be noted that children at play are not playing about; their games should be seen as their most serious-minded activity.'

Montaigne

'Women just don't get it. They just don't,' the man on the train said. I had bumped into him and his mate at York Station. I was carrying a yellow carrier bag from the Varnaptapak wargame show and they had recognised it and homed in on me. There was nothing more guaranteed to put you off wargaming than a visit to a wargames show. Yet I was drawn back to them like a salmon to its spawning ground. Or a dog to its own vomit.

'My mam thinks I'm nuts,' the man said, and grinned rue-fully. He was in his mid-thirties, wearing Marks and Spencer's slacks. He had the vulnerable look of someone who has worn spectacles all their life and has just changed over to contact lenses, as if his face was naked in a public place for the first time and he wasn't sure whether to feel pleased or embar-rassed. 'I've tried her on AWI, ECW, ACW, SYW. Just doesn't get it,' he said again, shrugging his shoulders.

She was probably bemused by all the acronyms. Military hobbyists are mad on acronyms. Nearly all the major conflicts of history were reduced to three letters: AWI was the

American War of Independence, ECW the English Civil War and so on. Sometimes you'd hear men at conventions sitting earnestly on the steps talking and one would say, 'I know you're doing EIR but what rules are you using, WRG 7th, DBM, DBA or WAB?' And the other bloke would reply, 'To be honest I've been doing my own set based on TSATF. The LHI and HC definitions in WRG are outdated IMHO and the D6s in WAB are way OTT.'

The acronym thing reached its lyrical height in the Second World War, which featured more machinery than had ever before been used in armed conflict. Wherever there are machines there are, inevitably, jargon, initials and code numbers, and so we find AFVs (armoured fighting vehicles), some of which are SPGs (self-propelling guns) dodging HE (high-explosive) rounds fired by an 88mm AA (anti-aircraft) gun while an NCO from the HLI waves his MLE and wonders if it it hasn't all gone a bit OTT. Things were made even worse by the fact that the German military shortened long compound nouns by removing all the vowels, and some random consonants too, just to be on the safe side, so that *Panzerkampfwagen*, the German for tank (literally 'armoured battle vehicle'), became PzKpfw. I should add here that the English word tank refers to the fact that the vehicles were built in top secret and transported to the front line disguised as water tanks. The original code name the MOD had given them was water carriers, but the acronym of that was WC and it was changed at the last minute to save embarrassment. One million men dead and they were still worried about making ladies blush; that's proper manners for you.

On top of that, the German AFVs and SPGs were painted in camouflage that was all coded. The date of the introduction of camo and the exact theatres it was used in was as serious a matter to many Second World War gamers as etiquette was to the Samurai. Fail to bow the requisite number of times and to the requisite angle before a daimyo and you were likely to be decapitated. Paint your tanks in the wrong shades and you were likely to be subject to the derision of men from Penge and Rickmansworth called Rick, Sime or Nige. 'Look at that,' they'd say. 'See amongst those AFVs, there's a Panzer IV Ausf H Sd.kfz 161/2 Pz. Div 12 in pattern T4G75Y. But – heh-heh-heh – this is supposed to be Eastern Front, 1942 and [pause like Perry Mason about to catch witness in a lie] T4G75Y was Normandy, 1944!'

'He's right,' his mate said. 'Women don't. They don't get it.' His friend was shorter, stockier and dressed from head to foot in black. His T-shirt advertised the last but one tour by Metallica and looked like he had bought it ready stained. Up until that point he hadn't said anything. On his lap was a box file of second-hand figures he'd bought at the bring-and-buy stall and he was preoccupied with them. Every once in a while he'd lean forward, open the lid slightly and peep in, grinning like a boy with a beetle in a matchbox.

'Tell him about the AFVs, Craig,' the first man said, and he nodded at me and smiled in a 'this is a good 'un, this is' kind of way.

'I showed this lass my Second World War Eastern Front 1944 German Armoured Division,' the short man said. I tried to picture the scene. I imagined the lass being invited back to his house and the short man saying 'Wait here, I've got something to show you' before disappearing off upstairs. She was probably worried that he would return wearing a leopard-skin posing pouch and a Thai silk bathrobe, but instead when he came back he was carrying a plastic baker's tray filled with Panzers, Tigers and half-track APCs.

'You know what she said?' the short man said, but he was still too worked up about it to wait for an answer. 'She said,

"Oh, they're really little, aren't they?"' His friend raised his eyebrows. The short man shook his head. 'Really little! They're $\frac{1}{72}$ scale,' he said indignantly, 'they're not bloody micro-armour.'

Micro-armour was $\frac{1}{285}$ scale. A $\frac{1}{72}$ scale tank was about three inches long; a micro-armour tank was the size of a thumbnail. 'Really little!' the man snorted. He didn't speak again until we reached Durham.

'They just don't get it,' his chum said, shaking his head.

It was true, of course. During love's first golden bloom many women take a deep interest in their boyfriend's hobbies. I had seen young women at wargames conventions trying to work up a spark of enthusiasm for a unit of 15mm Ashigaru or 10mm Marlburians, or to stifle a yawn when some bloke entered the twenty-first stanza of his epic account of the day he had triumphed in a WRG seventh edition ancients tournament thirteen years ago in Derby by judicious use of a unit of Scythian horse archers. It soon wears off, though.

Men, by contrast, rarely try to take an interest in their partner's hobbies. Well, not all the time anyway. Sometimes it works the other way round. That at least can be the only reason imaginable as to why I have ever been to the opera. It was in London and the ENO, and what a night it was, loads of hugely fat people bawling their lungs out and pretending to be half their real ages. And that was just in the pub in Covent Garden beforehand. When we got into the opera house things were even worse. We had gone to see *The Marriage of Figaro*. Figaro is supposed to be in his mid twenties. The only thing about the bloke playing the part that was in its mid twenties was his weight – in stone. At one point he had to hide in a wardrobe. It was touch and go whether he'd get out, I can tell you. I am too much of a gentleman to comment on the shape of the female lead; suffice to say that if she ever lay on a beach Greenpeace would turn up and try to roll her back into the sea. Apart from that it was rubbish. It was my last effort to engage with this area of Catherine's life. I have so far avoided taking up yoga, too.

Catherine, meanwhile, has never played a wargame, nor have I ever encouraged her to. Call me old-fashioned, but I believe there are some things a woman just shouldn't do. Piloting a fighter aircraft, working down a coal mine, the Catholic priesthood, serving in a combat regiment in the front line – all that I can accept, but geekdom, no way. That must be a male-only preserve.

Seven years ago when Catherine was pregnant I secretly hoped for a son. This was not only for the obvious reason (I'd be able to buy lots more toy soldiers and pretend they were a present for him) but also because I felt that, while the workings of the female mind would forever remain a sweet mystery, I would be able to understand what a boy was thinking.

This is a popular misconception amongst men. Though it is true we don't know what is going on inside a girl's head, we don't know what is going on inside a boy's head either. Men, in fact, don't know what is going on inside anybody's head, including their own. If they did they wouldn't spend so much time arranging their CDs in alphabetical order, or set fire to their eyebrows trying to light a barbecue with siphoned petrol.

In the end we had a daughter, Maisie. And I am grateful we did, even as I struggle to put her hair into plaits, or sit in the bath trying to forget that the eyes of the fourteen naked Barbies she has left perched around the rim seem to be staring straight at my groin (well, let's face it, it's a bit of a shock after Ken or indeed Action Man, isn't it?).

My friend Will has a son who is a year older than Maisie. One day Will and I took Maisie, his son and his son's best friend to the cinema. The children sat on the back seat of the car. The two boys began to talk about a video game, a topic that slid effortlessly into what they would do if threatened by an evil criminal mastermind who wanted to capture and torture them to death: 'I'd throw massive great poison darts at his bottom and then lasso him and tie him to a stake and bash him with a . . . Dad, what's that spiked ball on a chain thing knights have?'

I glanced at my friend and raised an eyebrow. He grinned sardonically. 'Oh yes,' he said, 'I forget, you're safe from all this, aren't you, in your little pink world.'

He was right, of course. Those without small children might imagine that sexual equality has blurred the gender roles of infants, but if anything the lines of demarcation are even more firmly drawn than they were when I was growing up back in the sixties. There is a little pink world, where I hang out, and there is camo-zone, an explosive, belligerent place I only occasionally glimpse, usually during the commercial breaks on Saturday morning TV.

The adverts for boys' toys feature thrashing heavy metal, over which a man with a voice so deep he makes the Carlsberg man sound like a dolphin on helium bellows, 'RICKY ROCK! The all-new all-action toy that chops, hacks, smashes and fires lethal meteorites of molten iron from his NOSE. But watch out! Here's BEASTMAN with alligator-action teeth that literally bite through toughened steel!'

The noise of kerrrranging guitars and explosions subsides and is replaced by the tinkling of a piano and a woman so resolutely feminine that compared to her Nanette Newman is Tony Soprano. She advises us to, 'Say hello to Dainty Daisy Doosie, the cuddly little doll who's as bright as a kitten's eye.' The whole confection is filmed through a Vaseline-coated, rose-tinted lens, and at the end, when little Dainty Daisy Doosie chortles, 'Bye-bye to my bestest friend,' any sane person will have to battle very hard to stop themselves rushing out of the room and strangling the nearest puppy.

Both are obnoxious in their own way, of course, but from my biased perch I content myself with the thought that while Dainty Daisy Doosie is so sugary just watching her rots your teeth, at least she doesn't blow things up or saw anyone's head off.

Perhaps I am over-reacting. My daughter takes an altogether more sanguine view of the situation. When we got back from the cinema I asked if she had been all right in the back of the car. 'What were those boys banging on about?' I asked. Maisie cocked her hip and adopted her best Valley Girl drawl. 'Oh, y'know, it was like, "I'd shoot a bazooka in his eye and push him in a vat of boiling poo blah, blah, blah." I mean, as if.' She sounded dismissive, but in her eye there was a glint of excitement, something that signalled trouble ahead.

At some point during the seemingly interminable time it took for Maisie to be born her umbilical cord got wrapped around her neck. The crisis quickly passed, but it left me shaken. Afterwards the midwife, a sturdy Geordie, looked at me and said, 'If you think that was nerve-racking wait till she gets a boyfriend with a motorbike.'

One day the camo-zone will noisily burst in on us. It is not something I want to think about. That is for the future. For the next few years I intend to remain safe and happy in my little pink world. Then I'm going to buy a gun. A real one.

The two men on the train were called Kev and Col. Kev was the taller one. I started bumping into them at just about every show I went to. (Kev and Col didn't call them shows, though. They called them 'exhibitions'.) Kev and Col were in their late forties; they were both bachelors and they both lived with their mothers. Over the years they'd spent so much time together they'd become like an old couple.

That's not to say there weren't differences between them. Col, for instance, liked the War of the Austrian Succession and Kev didn't. Col was also definitely the more gruesome of the two. To hear him tell it, his life was marked by a trail of gore and accompanied by maniacal laughter. Practically every anecdote Col told ended in a grotesque or bloody scene. If he left the house on a sunny summer's morning to visit his lovely Aunt Doreen in Ventnor you could guarantee that the moment he stepped out onto the street the sky would darken, one-legged dogs would howl, there'd be a chalk outline on the tarmac, a severed thumb in the teapot and a wall-eyed child talking in tongues and wearing a beard of bees. He was a one-man Addams Family. Or that was what you thought until you met his mother, a woman so filled with foreboding she made Jeremiah look like Forrest Gump.

Kev and Col reiterated one another's comments, finished each other's sentences and had a way of excluding the listener from their conversations so completely that after a while you began to feel as if you were actually observing them through a two-way mirror. When I met them at FIASCO in Leeds they offered me a lift to the station, but I couldn't get into the back of Kev's Renault Clio because there was a huge picture of a dark-haired female pop singer on the seat.

'It's Sharleen Spiteri,' Kev said.

'From Texas,' said Col.

'And Scotland,' Kev said, 'which is a slight paradox.'

'We are very fond of Sharleen,' said Col.

'And not just her music,' Kev said.

'Though she's got a canny voice,' said Col.

'Oh aye, she's got a canny set of pipes,' Kev said.

'That's enough about Sharleen's pipes,' said Col.

'Eeh give over, you,' Kev said.

*

Kev had downloaded the picture of Sharleen Spiteri from the Internet and enlarged it on the photocopier at the local library at a cost of thirty pence, which he considered a bargain. He carefully lifted it off the seat and put it on the back window ledge. I'd been about to do the same thing myself, but I sensed that neither Kev nor Col wanted me touching Sharleen Spiteri in their presence. Or indeed at any other time.

I asked them what they had been up to.

'Crisis,' Kev said.

'In Belgium,' said Col.

This was not as dramatic as it sounded. Crisis was a wargame show organised by the Tin Soldiers of Antwerp. Belgium – or at least the Dutch-speaking part of it – was pretty much the epicentre of continental wargaming.

There were a number of highly thought of wargame clubs in Flanders, including TSOA, the Red Barons of *Waregem* and *Schilde und Vriende*. The latter was named after the phrase that Flemish patriots in Bruges had used as a test of nationality when they rebelled against their French overlords in the Middle Ages. If they came across a stranger the patriots demanded that they enunciate *schilde und vriende*. The combination of slurring Ss, hard Cs and rolling Rs was just about impossible for any foreigner to pronounce. Which was unfortunate, because if you couldn't say it properly the Flemish patriots killed you. Clearly medieval Bruges was not a good place to be a Francophone. Or to be a Flandrian with a speech impediment either.

The Belgian society of model soldier collectors was also very old. For years it had been presided over by General Deleuze. Jean Nicollier – who seemed to make a specialism of eccentric shopkeepers – records a gentleman's outfitters in the Rue Haute, Brussels, presided over by the rotund and amiable Monsieur Seldenslagh. 'Seldenslagh would first attempt the sale of a jacket or a pair of trousers, but on seeing the customer's puzzled expression, he would give a sign of understanding and conduct his visitor upstairs, where masses of model soldiers were kept.'

Kev and Col had been to Crisis in Antwerp and it turned out they had had a minor *crise* of their own while they were there.

'We stayed at a hotel,' Kev said.

'A three-star establishment,' Col said.

'There was a bit of an incident,' Kev said.

'There was a contretemps,' said Col.

'Our bedrooms had these little fridges in them,' Kev said.

'There were drinks in them,' said Col.

'Alcoholic beverages, fruit juices and a range of sweet and savoury snacks,' Kev said.

'Minibars,' I said.

Kev and Col exchanged astonished glances.

'You know about them?' Kev asked.

'Fridges in the bedrooms?' asked Col.

I said that, yes, I did.

'Did you know you had to pay for the contents?' Kev asked.

'For the beverages and snacks?' asked Col.

'Because we thought they were free,' Kev said, not waiting for an answer.

'We thought it was complimentary,' said Col.

'Like those dishes of nuts they have on the bar top,' Kev said.

'Or the little biscuit they give you with a coffee,' said Col.

'We helped ourselves on that basis,' Kev said.

'Assuming it was gratis,' said Col.

'We didn't go mad,' Kev said.

'We were practically abstemious,' said Col.

'But when we checked out . . .'

'The lassie presented us with an enormous bill!'

'We said, what's this?'

'The lassie said, "It's the bar bill."'

'We said, we haven't been in the bar.'

'The lassie said, "The bar in your rooms."'

'We said, *the bar in our rooms?*'

'She was a South-eastern Asian lassie.'

'Immaculate English.'

'Very attractive.'

'We saw a lot of her.'

'There was a lot of her to see.'

'But she had a nice personality with it.'

'Which is the more important thing.'

'She said, "The fridge in your room – the minibar."'

'*The minibar?*'

'Well anyway,' Kev said.

'To cut a long story short,' said Col.

'We had to pay.'

'But not before we'd given them back the miniatures we'd put in our bags,' said Col.

'Oh yes, we made them deduct those,' Kev said.

'Which was a pity really,' said Col.

'Because my mam would have enjoyed that cherry brandy,' Kev said.

'And the advocaat,' said Col.

At this point it dawned on me that we had set off ten minutes ago and had now just turned a corner back into the street we had started from.

'We seem to have gone in a complete circle,' I said.

'Eeh, look,' said Col.

'We've gone in a complete circle,' said Kev.

'I think you should have turned left at the traffic lights,' I said.

'How did we get back here?' Col said.

'I think we should have turned left at the traffic lights,' said Kev.

'Crisis was good,' Col said, when we had found the ring road.

'The Antwerp exhibition,' Kev said.

'Nice demo games.'

'Plenty of traders.'

'Excellent bring-and-buy stall.'

'I got myself a few 15mm Franco-Prussian units.'

'Bavarians foot and mounted.'

'I'd have liked a few more.'

'But we didn't have any euros left.'

'Because of that fridge-bar business, you know.'

I didn't see them again over the winter, then I bumped into Kev at the spring show in York. Col wasn't with him, so I asked where he was.

'Not coming out at the minute,' Kev said. 'Bad news, to be honest.' I noticed that even without Col he spoke in short bursts, like automatic fire. Maybe he had always spoken like that, or perhaps he was now speaking for two.

'He's lost his mam. Passed away in February. He's looked after her since his dad went. Twenty-seven years together,' Kev said. 'He's a bit down. He said to me, "Kev, she wasn't just my mam, she was my best friend."'

I'd assumed Kev was his best friend, so I said, 'What about you?'

'Oh,' Kev said, 'been getting into these new 40mm SYW figures from the Russian Federation. Lovely detailing.'

16

How To Test Troop Morale

'Maybe I don't want to meet someone who shares my interests. I hate my interests.'

Seymour, *Ghost World*

The wargame show was in a big community hall. The fluorescent tubes in the ceiling hummed and so did quite a lot of the paying customers. Traders' stands were lined around the perimeter. In the centre a dozen demonstration games were going on. There was a ¹⁄₄₈ scale Stalingrad skirmish complete with two hundred ruined buildings and aircraft flying over the rubble, mounted on car radio aerials so you could adjust their altitude; a 15mm Relief of Gordon with a slice of the Nile snaking along one table edge between wafting palms and a large pile of Kit-Kat wrappers and Coke cans; several involving space hulks and mechanoids; one steam-punk in Africa sort of thing, in which Victorian explorers in coal-powered AFVs were being menaced by herds of dinosaurs as they fled back towards a large Zeppelin; a vast micro-armour Desert Storm in which hundreds of thumbnail-sized Abrams MBTs and Soviet-built T72-M1s inched towards one another across a sand-coloured tablecloth at scale speeds so low that if you came back two hours later they'd have moved slightly less than the average glacier; and, in the centre, a massive sixteen foot by six foot table on which one of Julius Caesar's victories in Gaul was being re-fought with several thousand 28mm figures. I paused to have a look at it.

''Allo, 'allo!' the man running the game said the second I glanced at the charging warbands. 'Gallia 57BC – if we're allowed to say Before Christ these days without the political correctness mob swooping down and taking away the children heh-heh-heh. Caesar's legions are scattered gathering forage and materials for their marching camp when Asterix and his mob burst forth from the forests on the other side of the Sambre . . .' The people who run demonstration games at wargame shows fall into two main categories: those who bend over the table continually for eight hours refusing to make eye contact with any member of the general public for fear they will be forced to break a lifetime vow to their mum and talk to strangers; and those blessed with an evangelical zeal for communication and so much bonhomie that if you could bottle it you'd certainly do so. And then take it to a secret location and bury it deep beneath the earth.

'Figures are a mix of OG, BT and GB. Rules are WAB. The terrain boards we make ourselves,' the man continued; his voice was slightly high-pitched and his delivery made it sound like the words were squirting out from his lips like pumpkin seeds. I felt certain that if he ever mentioned his wife he'd call her 'the memsahib', or 'she who must be obeyed', or 'my better half', all delivered with a slight raising of the chin and cocking of the head to suggest that he wasn't being entirely serious. He was a fellow whose life was lived in inverted commas.

'They've proved such a hit we've started to produce them commercially. Very reasonable price too IMHO. Sixty centimetres by sixty centimetres, MDF base, individually sculpted extruded poly, topcoat with PVA, sprinkle with sharp sand, spray coat of standard car-coat British racing green, dry brush with jade, hay, and straw acrylics, a wash of antelope brown artist's ink IIRC, fill in the rivers with a mix of gloss blue-green and linseed-based resin and *Monsieur Robert est votre oncle* as they say in *la belle Gallica*.'

'Great,' I said.

'How much d'you think per tile?' the man asked. 'Go on.'

'I don't know,' I said.

'Well, put it this way,' the man said, 'ATE are doing the same size tile, without – without, mind – our interlocking cherry-wood dowel rods, for £27.99 a pop. TTT are asking £25. Now, what d'you reckon for one of ours?'

'Twenty quid,' I said.

'£23.99,' the bloke piped, completely undeterred, 'and if you take a dozen or more there's a discount of 10 per cent. Hang on, I'll get you a price list and contact details.' He darted off to the other end of the table. The moment his back was turned I made off. I realise this was rude, but I suffer from Anti-Sales Deficiency Syndrome. I can't say no to people who are trying to flog me stuff. My house is filled with aerosols of suede protection spray and extended warranties for electrical goods. I have more accident insurance cover than Michael Schumacher. Our car is double-glazed. Even our coal shed has a conservatory.

Once I knew I was safe from the terrain boards I wandered around, stopping at the second-hand bookstalls and looking along the rows of Osprey Men-at-Arms uniform guides. Many dealers had several shelves of them. The Osprey books were about as thick as a pre-cut slice of bread and the covers were white. The titles on the spines of the 1970s and 1980s volumes were printed in a kind of copperplate script 7mm high. By the time I'd scanned five or six hundred of them for a copy of number 129, *Rome's Enemies: Germanics and Dacians*, I'd started to feel dizzy, so I went to the coffee bar for a sit down.

The coffee bar was in an annexe just by the front entrance.

It was presided over by a burly, blank-eyed woman in a blue
nylon tabard. There was a touch of gravel in her voice and
the same was true of her caffè latte. The cappuccino looked
like dishwater topped with cuckoo spit, though it was probably less nourishing that that. I took my Styrofoam cup and a
Twix, and sat down at a table to watch the world go by. Or at
least that aspect of the world that comes to a wargame convention. Men in dust-coloured blousons, easy-fit jeans and
World of Warcraft T-shirts shuffled by, yellow carrier bags
slapping against their knees. Some of the visitors were
cheery, heads up and surveying the scene; others stared at the
ground, glancing furtively through fringes of lank hair like
fugitives from the undergrowth. Some looked as if they knew
all the people in the hall, others like they didn't know anybody at all. In the whole world. There were other types too,
but I am tired of description. If you want to know what they
look like, walk into the nearest IT department or hi-fi shop
and take a butcher's at the people who work there.

Snatches of arcane conversation wafted through the air:
'He had these mouthwatering Pechenegs . . . Well, he was all
Void at one point but now he's drifted in the direction of
Necromunda . . . He takes the morale test for his Sipahis and
he only goes and rolls a double one! . . . There was no way
elephants should have stood against enfilading staff-
slingers . . . The bloke said they were FAW but the Turcos
looked more FPW to me . . . I'm not knocking them generally. I just think they overrate the mêlée power of the
Tercio . . . D'you see the turnbacks on those AWI Hessians?
What the hell was all that about, then?'

The men behind me were arguing about scarlet, the exact
nature of which was proving a vexation in the pursuit of a
correctly coloured force of 28mm Sikh War British. I was
trying to concentrate on the scarlet conversation but it was
difficult because I was having real problems opening my

Twix. A couple of days before I'd been trying to prise the lid off an aerosol of gloss varnish with a craft knife, the knife had slipped and the tip of the blade had jabbed into my left index finger. It was one of those cuts where the blood takes a little while to come to the surface, just long enough in fact for you to mutter the words, 'Bloody hell, that could have been nasty.' Soon it was spurting from the wound and dripping all over the carpet, which, I noted, sparkled slightly as a result of all the tiny shavings of white metal I had dropped onto it since it was last Hoovered. Eventually I had staunched the flow by strapping an Elastoplast around the finger and pulling it so tight that when I removed it two days later the skin was the colour and texture of damp suet.

I was just trying to bite the wrapper open with my teeth when two blokes approached and asked if they could share my table. Well, they didn't ask exactly. They nodded at the two spare chairs and mumbled, 'Er, you know, is it . . . ?' and I – fluent in the language of Nerd, having been domiciled in that God-forsaken land for many moons since the iron crown of Shrud fell to the Norkbrood – in turn waggled my right hand slightly in their general direction and grunted ,'Nobody, yeah.'

'I've tried florists' wire, but it's not rigid enough for anything longer than a javelin,' one of them said when he sat down. 'I could use piano wire, I guess. Piano wire's rigid.'

'And how,' his mate said grimly.

Piano wire was what most wargamers used for spears and pikes. It was hard for the makers to cast these weapons as an integral part of the figure; either they made them realistically thin, in which case they snapped the moment anyone breathed on them, or they were practically and robustly proportioned and your Spartan hoplites looked like they were armed with a steel-tipped caber. Piano wire is the thing that makes the sound when the hammer of the piano strikes it. It comes in a variety of diameters, though whether these are to fit different sized pianos or to make higher or lower notes I don't rightly know. I guess there must also be harpsichord and spinet wire too, but they don't sell that in the Newcastle Model Shop. Unfortunately, like the second bloke said, piano wire has its disadvantages, not least that when you cut it to length using wire cutters it tends to fly off across the room with a ping and embed itself in the dog.

'You wanna use the bristles from a nylon yard brush,' the second man continued. 'It's easier to cut and it's cheaper.'

It was a trait of wargamers to use unlikely materials. During my time I have sprayed pine cones green to make trees, cut up brown corduroy trousers for ploughed fields, made a Second World War gun emplacement from an egg carton and sawn ping-pong balls in half and covered them in garden twine to make Zulu beehive huts. Beer mats are particularly useful because, unlike most other card, they don't warp when they get wet and that means you can paint them with water-based acrylics. For years the first thing I did when I sat down in a pub was collect all the beer mats off the table and stuff them in my pocket. If one of the bar staff replaced them later I felt like I'd got a right result. To civilians, an offcut of fun fur was just a piece of tat; to a wargamer it was something that could be fashioned into a very nice thatched roof if you first soaked it in a runny Polyfilla solution and then brushed it with a curry-comb.

'When I was doing Marston Moor,' the second bloke continued, 'I got the pikes for both armies from a single broom. And I still had enough for the phalanxes of Antigonus One-eye.'

'I didn't know you had Macedonian successors,' the first man said.

'Well, I didn't, but I had all those bristles left over so I had to do something with them.'

'You could have chucked them out.'

'What, and waste them? That's not very ecological.'

They paused in conversation. Two re-enactors from a Napoleonic British light infantry regiment had come into the coffee bar to forage for Kit-Kats and prawn cocktail-flavoured Skips. I had seen them earlier, standing by a Ford Fiesta unloading Brown Bess muskets from the roof box. One of them had left his shako on the bonnet and I noticed it had a spectacles case and a packet of Victory V lozenges in it. As they walked past one of the blokes at my table raised his eyebrows and his mate smiled and mouthed the word 'Wankers'.

Wargamers generally divided into two camps when it came to re-enactment: either they were re-enactors themselves, or they thought re-enactors were pompous and pitiful idiots. I wasn't a re-enactor, but I was reluctant to start calling people names because of their niche interests. Except if their niche interest was fantasy gaming, naturally. But that was different because fantasy gamers really are pitiful idiots. Not, I should add, that re-enactment and Tolkien are mutually exclusive: there is, as it happens, a Middle Earth Historical Re-enactment Society. The question of how something that is made up can be historical or how you re-enact events that never actually happened I will leave to the philosophers to answer.

The first re-enactment society in Britain was The Sealed Knot. It was formed by the dashing Brigadier Peter Young in 1968, more or less as an excuse for a fancy dress party and a few bottles of claret, but subsequently took on a more educational function. The Sealed Knot proselytised on behalf of the English Civil War. Fearful that their share of the lucrative battle market would be seriously eroded, the adherents of other armed conflicts soon began to hit back. Nowadays, there are people re-enacting the Middle Ages, the Anglo-Scots Wars, the Anglo-Welsh Border Wars, and the two World Wars. There are people recreating noted riots in the history of London and the defence of La Haye Sainte. There are Celts, Saxons, Romans of all types, Greek hoplites, Elizabethans, eighteenth-century militia, Jacobites, Crimean War hussars and Zulu War infantrymen. Geographical location is no impediment either. There are Vikings in Australia, Louisiana tigers in Berkhamsted, Roundheads in Wisconsin, Old West gunslingers in SE1 and knights in New Zealand.

The idea is to bring history alive. Children always love re-enactors. I think I would have done too when I was young. They have plenty of weapons and they are keen to let you handle them. At wargame shows, where the re-enactors were generally hived off in some separate area like plague victims – a wise precaution in the case of the Star Wars Re-enactment Society – you could guarantee you'd see at least one small boy come barrelling along the corridor from the squash court squeaking, 'Dad! Dad! It's really good. If you ask they'll even let you touch their bayonets!'

Some re-enactors have achieved a certain degree of fame. In what Northumberland County Council chooses to dub 'Hadrian's Wall Country', the Roman re-enactor Jefficus is quite a celebrity nowadays. When my local garage opened its new mini-mart the ceremonial cutting of the ribbon was carried out by Jefficus in tandem with Newcastle United legend Malcolm Macdonald. They got equal billing on the publicity posters.

A few months later my daughter's first school class got to visit the site of the Corstopitum Roman fort where they had the double thrill of meeting both Jefficus and the deputy prime minister John Prescott. Asked which of the two men they had found most interesting, the children's answer was spontaneous and unanimous: John Prescott.

Only joking.

Despite, or maybe because of this, a lot of wargamers did not like the re-enactors. They thought they were bumptious, with a tendency to regard themselves as the fount of all knowledge on the period they re-enacted. They also accused them of drifting dangerously close to delusion. Certainly there was a tendency amongst some to become a little too immersed in the role: officers tended to strut about in rather too realistic a manner, Greek hoplites looked to have spent a little too long rubbing olive oil into their thighs. Once, in Sweden, Catherine, Maisie and I visited a very good Viking camp. The Vikings were blowing glass, making swords, weaving cloth and roasting a pig. Occasionally they stopped to have a sword fight. We talked to a Viking silversmith. 'Where have you come from?' he asked. We told him Northumberland. The man thought for a moment, then he smiled. 'Ah yes,' he said, 'Lindisfarne. I have not been myself. But of course we went there many times in the tenth and eleventh centuries.' A couple of days later we saw him again, on the Gotland ferry. He was still in costume. He was holding his wooden shield on one arm, but he had had to lean his spear against a bulkhead because he was busy sending a text message.

'We went there many times.' There is a tendency towards that sort of thing in all areas of study. Many years ago Catherine and I visited Charleston in East Sussex. One of the things that most sticks in my mind about the place, along with the fact that many people who adore the Bloomsbury Group actually dress like them (as if, in fact, they were part of a re-enactment society – The Sealed Woolf, perhaps – and spent their weekends re-fighting their heroine's battle against clinical depression), was that the people who took the guided tours always referred to the former residents and guests by their first names. 'This door panel was painted by Duncan,' they said. 'Vanessa always sat at this window. Leonard was on the sofa by the fire – Leonard always felt the cold.' 'They think they know them,' Catherine whispered as we were

shown baths that Lytton reclined in and closets that John
Maynard burst forth from. To which I, made melancholy by
the sight of all the earnest young women in wide-brimmed
hats and ankle-length skirts, could only respond, 'Poor bas-
tards.'

Despite that I was indulgent towards re-enactors. I felt that
as a wargamer I shouldn't point a finger at anybody else and
sneer. I felt a bit like Lenny Bruce: 'After suffering two thousand years of oppression you'd think Jews would be tolerant.
But what happens? The phone rings. It's my mother. She
says, "Lenny, you'll never believe what's happened to the
neighbourhood. It's terrible. The Puerto Ricans have moved
in."'

I believed it was beholden upon the wargamer to cast a
kindly eye over other people's hobbies. If folk wanted to go to
conventions of milk bottle top collectors, make butterflies out
of feathers or watch an episode of *The Waltons* every Monday
night at eight o'clock just like in the seventies, then that was
fine by me. And if they wanted to put on chain mail and form
a shield wall with fifteen of their mates in a muddy field once
a month then that was OK by me too. Though I must say
that if I really wanted to see an epic recreation of medieval
times I'd not bother with historical pageant societies. I'd just
go down to the Newcastle Quayside on a Saturday night.

Maybe I was more tolerant than most non-re-enactors
because TK had once served in a regiment of Napoleonic
French cuirassiers with half a dozen blokes from Nuneaton.
'Can you ride a horse, then?' I asked him when he told me
about it.

'Of course I can ride a horse,' TK said. 'I'd be hard
pressed to be a cuirassier if I couldn't ride a horse, wouldn't
I? What did you think, that I charged into battle on a
moped?'

He said it got expensive because they had to hire ex-police

horses that wouldn't be scared by the popping of enemy muskets. He'd given it up after one last hurrah, at a recreation of
the Battle of Waterloo in a field near Carshalton. 'Did the
historic charge of Marshal Ney's heavy cavalry brigade,' TK
said with some pride.

'All six of you?' I asked.

'No, Mr Sarky,' TK said, 'we were joined by other
Napoleonic French heavy cavalry units from all over Europe.'

'All over Europe?'

'Well . . .' TK said, 'there were some carabineers from
Wakefield, and a dragoon from Bangor. Anyroad, it was more
than six, is what I'm saying.'

'How many more?'

TK shook his head as if refusing to dignify this question
with an answer, but then he relented. 'There were sixteen, if
you must know,' he said. 'There would have been seventeen.
But one of the lads from Wakefield had to cry off with Delhi
belly after a dodgy biryani the night before. You don't want to
be sat on a galloping horse in button-fronted britches if
you've got diarrhoea I can tell you, H, mate.'

After a decade on campaign TK knew nearly all the
Napoleonic re-enactors in Britain. Whenever there was a history programme on TV he'd phone and say, 'See that lad
who's playing Marshal Soult, Duc de Dalmatie? He's a
newsagent in Crewe, he is.'

TK said they'd done some filming for the BBC once, stock
footage that had turned up on screen in dozens of programmes for decades afterwards. I said, 'Did you get repeat
fees?'

'No,' he said, 'we just got a one-off payment – twenty-five
pounds for the day. Well, that was what most of us got. Andy
got thirty quid.'

'How come he got the extra fiver?' I asked

'He's only got one arm,' TK said.

Travelling to a wargame convention in Newark once I found myself sitting on the train opposite a man who spent his summer weekends being medieval around Britain. He was a longbowman in the army of Henry V. He only had time for wargaming in the winter, he said, and only then when he'd finished his fletching. His wife accompanied him on his escapades as a scullery maid-cum-camp follower. He explained that there was a re-enactors convention in Northamptonshire every year. 'It's brilliant,' he said, 'you've got everyone from Ancient Rome to Vietnam, Rebels, Yankees, Ironsides the lot.'

. He said that on the final day of the re-enactment festival there was a huge free-for-all in which everyone took part and afterwards they all went to a big tent and got pissed. 'You look down the tables in that marquee and there are warriors from all of human history drinking flagons of ale together. There's Border Reivers sitting next to Second World War American paratroopers, Icenii next to Prince Rupert's cavalry, knights and Norsemen. It's like Valhalla,' he said. 'There was even a U-boat crew last year.'

'They've got a submarine?'

'No,' he said, 'they just re-enact shore leave.'

He took out a wallet of photos and started showing me pictures. 'Ah, hey,' he said as he pulled one out, 'now this one's good. Our lass got friendly with some blokes out of the Wehrmacht – from Swindon they were, good lads – and they let her try on some of the gear. Here she is, look, got up as a Panzer Grenadier.'

He handed me the photo. I tried to show an interest, but I found the whole business a bit disquieting. Apart from the Nazi element, there was the whole weird thing of another man showing you pictures of his wife in jackboots.

Actually there were a surprising number of female re-enactors. Usually they were cast in the roles of camp followers. A woman I knew said she'd got into re-enacting through her ex-husband who was a Viking bondi from Pontefract. Actually he was a woodwork teacher from Pontefract; he was only a Viking bondi during the holidays.

She said that during the blissful happy days of their early married life they had toured all over Europe meeting up with other Vikings. Once, at a get-together at a re-created Danish settlement near Copenhagen, some American tourists, on finding the Vikings could speak English, had said, 'Well, we sure have enjoyed watching your craft activities and learning about your life-ways. Do you know if there are other Viking reservations we can visit in Europe?' Her husband had replied that there weren't, but that he believed there was an Ostrogoth tribal territory near Frankfurt they might like to stop in on.

She said that she'd enjoyed being a Viking, though it wasn't all plain sailing. They'd gone to another Viking shindig in Poland once and a company of Teutonic knights from the former East Germany had turned up. 'They had some fairly dodgy political views, as you can probably imagine,' she said. Her husband and his Viking band, being from South Yorkshire, were all ardent socialists and the weekend had passed under the threat of anti-fascist combat.

Things had gone from bad to worse when a group of Vikings from Kiev appeared. Kiev had once been the capital of the Russ lands, the settlements of Vikings from Sweden who went across the Baltic and then down the river Volga. During the years of the Soviet Union, displays of Ukrainian nationalism were forbidden and Viking activity frowned upon. The Vikings in the UK risked mockery; the Vikings in Kiev risked the Gulags. As a consequence they took their Viking-ness very seriously indeed. 'They came striding over to us,' the woman said. 'Dead excited, they were. And then they started speaking to us . . . in Norse. Well, my husband and his mates didn't have a clue what they were saying. They couldn't speak Norse. They were a bunch of fellas from Yorkshire who were more in it for the battleaxes and the mead. The Kiev Vikings were really vexed when they realised the situation. They started shouting at us . . . in Norse. I thought things were going to get nasty, but eventually they just turned and stomped off.'

I said that maybe they didn't like the idea of 'bloody weekend Vikings'.

She said that was pretty much the case. 'Later on, though, we bumped into them at a picnic site near Stettin and we all had a beer and a game of football and that seemed to smooth things over.' She said she often wondered what the picnicking Polish families made of the sight of two dozen Vikings playing three-goals-the-winner with spears for goalposts.

17

Rallying Broken Troops

'If some dispute over the rules arises, then let the dice decide.'
H. G. Wells, *Little Wars*

I was always cautious about reading *Wargames Illustrated* on the train. Originally this was because I didn't want people to think I was a gun-crazy sad sack. Then the magazine started taking adverts from companies selling fantasy stuff. Like comic – sorry, *graphic novel* – artists, fantasy designers always talked up the maturity and breadth of their vision, but however much psychological background, darkness and subtle moral shading they might invest in their work, when it came to women they just couldn't get away from breasts and lingerie. Suddenly you'd turn the page from a double page spread on the Battle of Chickamauga and find yourself looking at a full page photo of 30mm nuns in suspenders brandishing MAC Ingram machine pistols, or semi-naked sylph built in a manner that recalled Dudley Moore's description of his ideal woman, gazelle-like, but 'with Jayne Mansfield overtones'. If anyone looked over your shoulder and saw this stuff they'd think you were a pervert. Now, at one time the term pervert had a certain continental, aristocratic and sophisticated whiff to it. Perverts were people like the Marquis de Sade and Count Leopold von Sacher-Masoch. In recent times, though, perversion had gone downmarket. Now it was all seedy fat men in their Y-fronts downloading stuff from the Internet. It was certainly preferable to be a nerd than a pervert. But a pervy nerd (a nervert?), that was something else entirely.

'Are you a wargamer?' the bloke opposite shouted. The bloke wasn't even sitting next to me. He was sitting across the aisle. The train was busy and, up until that point, it had been very noisy. Now it suddenly seemed to go very quiet indeed. I looked at the bloke. He was extremely corpulent and, combined with the fact he was dressed entirely in black, it gave him the look of a mobile car park. If you'd wanted to kill him you'd have had to carpet bomb.

I should have said, 'No, this is for my son. He's just turned eleven so I'm hoping he'll soon drop this foolish toy soldier lark in favour of solvent abuse and masturbation.' But these things never come to you until after the event, do they?

The man I now saw was, besides his girth, displaying many of the other tell-tale signs of shrud-dom – a comedy slogan T-shirt ('Suits you, Sir!'), a rucksack so stuffed with, well, stuff it bulged like a Strasbourg goose, and a goatee and sideburn arrangement that was the hair equivalent of a wacky bow-tie. Unfortunately, he also proved to be that most rare of beasts, an extrovert geek. He wanted to talk. Loudly. He began to discourse at immense volume about his gaming activities. 'I'm not much into wargaming myself,' he said, 'a bit of Warhammer 40K, some D&D, Call of Cthulu. More RPGs, I guess. What I'm up for big style is LARP. You do any LARPing?'

Whatever was left of my self-esteem shrivelled to the size of a walnut and attempted to throw itself from the window. 'No,' I said.

RPG was an acronym for role-playing games, LARP for live action role-play. In RPG you acted the part of a character in what was, more or less, a board game. In LARP you acted the part of a character in what was, more or less, the real world. The classic RPG was D&D (Dungeons and Dragons – honestly, you really must stay in more), which in my limited experience generally involved sitting round on the floor smoking dope while some bloke who was holding the rule book said, 'But as you enter the inner sanctum of Flock, Baldo Forkiegash, your keen dwarfish eye is arrested by an eerie, glimmering light. Could this be the sacred sword of Poof the Mothslayer glinting in the candle flame? Throw a score of ten or more to find out.' The game went on for many, many hours ending only when Baldo Forkiegash or Forkie Balderdash, or whatever he was called, had located the gilded tuffet of Angina, or everybody had got so stoned they could no longer tell if they were the right way up and had fallen asleep with their heads in the left-over pizza. LARP was altogether less urbane.

Once I went with a non-wargaming friend to a massive wargame show in West London. Mat worked in film and theatre, and he was curious to see what species of people such a show would attract. We went in past hordes of men with carrier bags and then, foolishly, I allowed him to go off on his own while I took care of important business. I arranged to meet him an hour later by the bring-and-buy stall. When Mat returned he was plainly feeling very unwell; his skin had gone the colour of some poisonous plate fungus. 'Can we go home now?' he stammered. Mat was no lily-livered weakling. He had sailed across the Atlantic on a yacht, battled severe asthma and worked for Michael Winner. Yet something he had seen had set his nerves twanging like stretched catgut with the cat still attached. I agreed to leave. I'd already bought a Frontier stockade, two uniform books about Russian cavalry, six blister packs of Ojibway Indians, a cutting mat, two waterline 1/72 scale Dutch barges and a second edition of Terry Wise's 1968 classic *An Introduction to Battle*

Gaming, which I hadn't seen since I last got it out of the village library when I was fifteen. My credit card was emitting a burning smell; my wallet looked like *La Grande Armée* had passed through it.

We forced our way through the scrum around the bring-and-buy stall, out into the fresh air and hopped on a bus bound for Peckham. 'Men,' Mat said when we got on the bus. 'Men. Video.' He had come across some darkened corner of Olympia in which some men from Deptford who LARPed were showing a video of themselves LARPing in Epping Forest. 'They had capes on,' Mat said as the threat retreated down Kensington High Street, 'and these laser guns. And foam swords. And they were running about shooting at one another and shouting, "In the name of Tharklerodd First Porker of Mangle I arrest thee!" It was . . .' He stopped speaking. Words were not enough. He had witnessed something so unsettling, so hideous that, to borrow a phrase from one of the RPGer's favourite authors, H. P. Lovecraft, 'only poetry or madness could do justice to it'.

'LARPing's my top thing,' the bloke sitting opposite me bellowed. 'Love LARPing.'

'Live to LARP, LARP to live,' I suggested.

'Whoa, nice one,' the bloke said. 'I could put that on a T-shirt.'

That would be an idea, I told him.

'Is that the new issue of *WT*?' the man asked. 'Haven't got it yet. Bit pricey at £3.50, to be honest. Those laser pistols don't come cheap and there's the space marine armour too. We get it from a firm in Cramlington that have it made in China, but even so . . .'

I handed him my copy and told him to keep it. My interest was at a low point. We had a mortgage to pay, a small child, a dog. I hadn't had time to paint figures for months, and the more days passed the weaker the grip the figures held on me became. I hadn't actually fought a wargame for over a year. I didn't altogether miss it.

In my view, the aspect of wargaming that was most like real war was that it was never quite as thrilling as you hoped and imagined it would be. The little men looked splendid, the terrain was lovely, the strategic planning was great fun, but once the fighting started it all dissolved into a chaotic slogging match. Few, if any, battles were ended by master strokes of strategy, or brilliant tactics; the vast majority came down to a grim attritional pounding, from which ultimate victory would go to the commander who could go on adding and subtracting factors and concentrating on the minutiae of the morale rules long after his foe was applying an ice pack to his throbbing temples and mumbling, 'They told me it would all be over by five o'clock but it's four forty-five already and we've only completed four moves . . .'

The aspect of wargaming that still excited me as much as it had done when I clapped eyes on those figures in Malcolm's loft when I was twelve was the sight of the figures on the table before the action commenced. But if you skipped the battle, what was the point of the figures? If you took the wargame out of wargaming, what you were left with was a collection. And I couldn't do with that.

When Napoleon assembled *La Grande Armée* at Boulogne in 1805 in preparation for the invasion of Britain, they were considered – and justifiably so – to be the most delightfully coutured of any army in history. Under the Little Corporal's watchful eye, they carried out drills on vast parade grounds and the watching public were astonished by the splendour of it all. Then came the Battle of Trafalgar and the news that Russia and Austria, incensed by Napoleon's decision to crown himself emperor, had declared war on France. The wonderful

spectacle marched off in perfect order to the carnage of
Austerlitz, Eylau and Friedland.

In his book *Adultery and Other Diversions*, Tim Parks notes of
a friend who has embarked on an affair: 'For those of us looking on, those still safely within wedlock's everyday limits, it's
hard not to feel a mixture of trepidation and envy to see a
friend in this state. Clearly it is very exciting when you start
destroying everything.' A boy, the child psychologist Erik
Erikson observed, carefully builds a tower from wooden
blocks and then takes delight in knocking it down. War was
another form of *amour fou*, another skyscraper of toy bricks.
An army was meticulously assembled and then sent crashing
to the earth in a mangled heap. But what else was there to
do? If an army doesn't go to war, all it is is a bunch of dumb
blokes in fancy costumes. Once it's assembled it must be used.
The one thing wargaming genuinely teaches you about war is
this: if you don't want to fight, don't get an army. Did I want
to fight? I was no longer sure.

One morning a month before, the phone rang. A female
voice, well spoken: 'Is that Harry Pearson?' I said it was. 'My
name is Margaret Brown,' the woman said. From her tone
and manner I assumed she was someone from the Women's
Institute phoning to ask if I'd give a talk on fairs and markets.
I was already preparing an excuse when Margaret Brown
said, 'You don't know me, but I'm Arthur's daughter. I'm
afraid I have some bad news.' Arthur had died suddenly of a
heart attack.

It was a shock, though to be honest in many ways the really
shocking news was to find Arthur had a daughter. He had a
son too, as it turned out. He'd married during the war, but
things hadn't worked out. Mrs Brown didn't hold it against
him. Her father's childhood had hardly prepared him for
normal life, she said. His own father's printing business had
collapsed when Arthur was a teenager and, distraught and

disgraced at his failure, he'd committed suicide by laying his head on a railway track in Clapham.

Arthur's mother had taken to drink, wandered off one night and turned up years later in a lunatic asylum. At fifteen Arthur had been bringing up two younger sisters. The war had come and Arthur had dropped into the Burmese jungle. 'But I guess you know all this. He was very fond of you,' she said. But, of course I didn't know any of it. I had never talked to him about his life. All we had talked about was toy soldiers.

Arthur once told me that there were times in his life when he thought about nothing else but figures, the games he had just played and those he was about to play. 'Sometimes I'd leave the house in the morning and the next thing I knew I was sitting at my desk and no idea how I'd got there,' Arthur said. I thought of Lloyd Osborne's comment on his uncle Robert Louis Stevenson: 'The tin soldiers most took his fancy; and the wargame was constantly improved and elaborated, until from a few hours the war took weeks to play, and the critical operations in the attic monopolised half our thoughts.'

Arthur's was my second death in a fortnight. One of my other wargame friends, Anthony Garcia, was a captain in the US Army. Tony collected the same sort of $1/72$ scale figures that I did, old Hinton Hunt and Les Higgins miniatures. We swapped figures and sent each other photocopied catalogues. We emailed once a week. We wittered on to one another about figures and armies, films, books, rule sets and documentaries. We rarely touched on anything that wasn't directly related to our hobby. Though I knew that his painting style was neat and simple and the details of every army he owned, I had no idea what he looked like. I knew he had a wife and a young son, but not their names.

It was a busy time for American military personnel. His

opportunities for wargaming were limited. His regular opponent, an army chaplain with a fixation on the Persian Army of Cyrus the Great, had been posted 250 miles away. I sent him accounts and photos of the battles I fought and he responded enthusiastically, initially from Fort Dix and later Baghram airbase.

Later the US army embarked on what Tony dubbed 'The Second Mesopotamian Punitive Expedition'. He emailed me sporadically after deployment. He had become interested in the Indian Mutiny and was ordering figures of General Havelock's army from a company in Yorkshire and having them delivered to his house back home in Pennsylvania. He was looking forward to getting started on them; his son had been detailed to shake his tins of enamel paint once a week to stop them separating and solidifying. 'Keep sending news of your wargaming activities,' he wrote, 'they are a welcome dose of sanity in all this craziness.' And I did. But when the reply came to my account of a re-fight of the Battle of Marathon it was not from Tony, but from his wife. There'd been a suicide bomber at a checkpoint. You know the story.

So now I knew her name and that of Tony's son. I thought about them sometimes and about the parcels of 20mm sepoys and highlanders that will never be painted, and will sit in a cupboard until one day his wife grits her teeth, takes them out and drops them in the dustbin.

At this point I suppose I should say that I look on this lack of knowledge with regret. But the truth is that I don't. We knew each other in the way we did.

'There is no greater sport than the sport of escape,' Major Pat Reid noted enthusiastically in the pamphlet that came with the Escape from Colditz board game. Every once in a while you need to go over the wall. And when Arthur and Tony needed to I had abetted them, and they had done the same for me, though all I was ever ducking was the dull mess of the everyday, like those people reading Harry Potter on the train to Bruges, or you reading this now.

A month later I was round at TK's house in Cannock. We had spent four hours sitting in his wargame room, an extension he'd built himself over the garage, talking about a huge collection of 20mm figures we were considering buying off a bloke in Gravesend. I said, 'Jeez, TK. I think I'm going to have to sell Catherine to pay for this lot.'

'Don't be stupid,' TK said. 'Don't sell her. Put her on the street. That way you'll have an income stream. Pete says he might have some TYW for sale in May.'

I said, 'God, what a pair of sad gits we are.'

TK said he didn't know what I was talking about: 'A lot of people say that, but I don't get it. Look at you and me, buddy. We work hard, we don't smoke, we don't gamble, we don't go down the pub, we don't chase after women and we don't sit in front of the telly all night moaning that there's nothing on. We have a hobby that's given us decades of fun, helped us make hundreds of friends all over the world and we don't do a drop of harm to anybody. What's sad about that?'

I said, 'I know, but don't you think sometimes we should do something that is actually, you know, a bit more grown up?'

'Like what? Fishing, golf, Scientology?'

I thought about it for a while. On his wargame table TK had set up a 20mm Jacobite '45 Rebellion army he'd been wanting to show me for ages. If you lowered your head slightly you could look along the Jacobite line as if you were the same height as a 20mm British officer – the young James Wolfe, perhaps – facing them at Culloden. The sun coming through the window glinted on the claymores of the highlanders. Behind them, Charles Edward Stuart was mounted on a cantering grey horse; his cheeks had been dabbed with a rubicund mix of Humbrol flesh and British scarlet and he was waving his bonnet in the air, urging action.

I thought about the day earlier in the year when some friends had come to visit with their two sons, the eldest of whom, Robbie, was ten. 'Robbie's mad keen on painting *Lord of the Rings* figures,' his mother said. 'I told him you liked painting figures. Would you show him some? I know he'd enjoy looking at them. He's a bit down in the dumps because he didn't do very well in his SATs. Would you mind?'

Robbie was thrilled by the figures. 'Coooo-ul!' he said as I showed him the French Imperial Guard Light Cavalry Brigade. 'Oh, mint!' as I pulled out a drawer filled with Dacian warriors. 'What are those things they're holding?'

'They're falxes, a two-handed cutting weapon like a large sickle. They were so lethal that when the Romans invaded Dacia, the Emperor Trajan fitted the front ranks of the Legions with special armour that covered the sword arm.'

'Wow! So if they didn't have the extra armour those things would just, like, chop their hand right off?' he asked with the hilarious relish of a child confronted with something gruesome.

'Mm, well, yeah. I mean, you know,' I said. I didn't want to sound like I was endorsing brutality. 'That would be a possibility, definitely.'

'Brilliant!' Robbie said. 'This is so totally fantastic.'

Later, when we had lunch, Robbie's mum asked him if he'd enjoyed looking at the soldiers. He nodded enthusiastically. 'When I grow up I'm going to be like Harry and spend all the money I earn on toy soldiers,' he said.

'Well, I don't think Harry actually spends *all* his money on toy soldiers,' his mum said, with a smile at me.

'No,' I said. 'No, obviously not, that would be folly.'

'Well, most of my money, then,' Robbie said.

I thought about Robbie and his duff SATs and about

Arthur on his trudge into work, swept across London Bridge in the grey tide on a dreary winter's morning, his mind filled with the glossy, brightly coloured deeds of the little men. Every man needs a place to go, Montaigne had said, and, for better or worse, this was mine.

'Thirty Years War?' I said to TK. 'Is there any Swedish cavalry?'

'There is,' TK said, 'but we'll have to dice for the cuirassiers.'

Acknowledgements

There is a scene in the film *Ghost World* that I can't recall without feelings of pain and admiration. In it Thora Birch persuades a sassy-looking woman at a music club to go and sit with obsessive record collector Seymour, played by Steve Buscemi. 'So, you like blues?' the woman asks with a grin. 'Well . . .' Buscemi says and launches straight into a spiel about how the guy that was just playing wasn't strictly blues, which is based on a rigid twelve-bar template, but more ragtime . . . And all the time he's talking he has this queasy look on his face. Because Seymour is intelligent and self-aware and he knows he shouldn't be saying this stuff to this person in this place and at this time, but he just can't help it. He is a man compelled.

For a lot of the time while I have been writing this book, I have worn an expression much like Seymour's in that scene in the club. This book is about toy soldiers and the men who collect and fight battles with them. And I am one of them. And I know, because, like Seymour, I am not a fool – well, not in this respect anyway – that this is not a cosy subject, not one, at any rate, that can be passed off as zanily eccentric or wacky yet loveable. It is not crazy golf or heavy metal. It is by no means non-League football. It is not even steam trains. And so I know that even while you are nodding and saying, 'Really? Is that so? How fascinating,' many of you will be gradually edging towards the exit.

I have known this fact for three decades and lived with it. I have rarely mentioned toy soldiers to anyone outside a select circle of cognoscenti who live a separate existence from the rest of my friends. I have done this so successfully and for so long that for many years I lived under the impression that I was two people: the man who is writing this book and the man this book is about. I now realise that is not true. We are one and the same, an unseemly mutation of Aristotle's golden mean.

However expert at pretence he becomes, a man can only keep it up for so long. It is time to stop skulking in the shadows, hiding *Military Modelling* magazine in a desk drawer and pretending the jar full of paintbrushes on the shelf are left over from a brief flirtation with painting watercolours, or that the 30mm Piedmontese infantry on that bookcase are something I've had since childhood, even though I bought them in a shop in Tuscany in 1987. It is time to stop living this double life. It is time to unleash the geek.

For his aid in picking the locks of this padded cell I am deeply indebted to my publisher Richard Beswick, my agent David Miller for his enthusiasm, not only for the idea but also for the pictures of the 25mm Achmaenid Persians I sent him to prove I wasn't making it all up, and the late Peter Rushforth, whose kind words on the pages I showed him convinced me, at least momentarily, that I hadn't gone totally insane.

Much information in these pages about the history of toy soldiers came from John G. Garratt's books *Model Soldiers – A Collector's Guide* and *Model Soldiers for the Connoisseur; Figurines et Soldats de Plomb* by Marcel Baldet; *Collecting Toy Soldiers* by Jean Nicollier; and *Zinnfiguren Einst und Jetzt* by Erwin Ottman. Those wanting to know more about Captain Siborne, his great model of Waterloo and the trouble it caused should pick up a copy of *Wellington's Smallest Victory*, Peter Hofschroer's excellent account of the affair.

I would also like to thank Uwe Wild, who not only borrowed Karl Floericke's massively obscure early wargame book

Strategie und Taktik des Spieles mit Bleisoldaten from the Bavarian State Library but then photocopied and posted it to me with an exact and amusing précis of its contents; Richard Black whose expertise with a computer and dogged pursuit of old figure designers have helped make our website Vintage20Mil the definitive cyberzone for middle-aged blokes who want to read long lists of obscure, out-of-production $1/72$ scale figures when they really should be getting on with something important; Margot Dunne for her stories about re-enacting, Airfix and Sven Hassel; all members of the Old School Wargames Group, with particular mention to Henry Hyde and Steve Gill of Battlegames and John Preece who brought Lieutenant John Cooke to my attention; and finally, everybody I have faced across a wargames table or traded figures with over the past thirty-five years: Peter, Malcolm, Michael, Richard, Matt, Nick, Neil, Roy, William, Clive, Clive, Clive, John, Henry, Roy, Bjorn, James, Alistair, Stuart, Carlo, Geoff, Roger, John and several dozen blokes named Dave.